STORM
IN THE
MOUNTAINS

A CASE STUDY OF CENSORSHIP, CONFLICT, AND CONSCIOUSNESS

James Moffett

Southern Illinois University Press
Carbondale and Edwardsville

Library of Congress Cataloging-in-Publication Data

Moffett, James.
  Storm in the mountains.

  Bibliography: p.
  Includes index.
  1. Textbooks—West Virginia—Kanawha County—
Censorship—Case Studies. I. Title.
LB3045.7.M64   1988   379.1'56   87-20614
ISBN 0-8093-1424-X

Grateful acknowledgement of permission to reprint is extended for the following: From "My Dungeon Shook: Letter to My Nephew," excerpt from *The Fire Next Time* by James Baldwin. Copyright © 1962, 1963 by James Baldwin. Reprinted by permission of Doubleday & Company, Inc. Also from *The Fire Next Time* by James Baldwin, reprinted by permission of Michael Joseph Ltd. • From Conley, T. R. (1976) "Scream Silently: One View of the Kanawha County Textbook Controversy," *Journal of Research and Development in Education*, Vol. 9(3), 93–101. • From "Journey of the Magi" from *Collected Poems 1909–1962* by T. S. Eliot, reprinted by permission of Faber and Faber Ltd. Also from "Journey of the Magi" in *Collected Poems 1909–1962* by T. S. Eliot, copyright 1936 by Harcourt Brace Jovanovich, Inc.; copyright © 1963, 1964 by T. S. Eliot. Reprinted by permission of the publisher. • From the record album *Textbook War—Hills of West Virginia*, by permission of the Rev. Avis Hill. • "Snake" copyright © 1955 by Theodore Roethke from *The Collected Poems of Theodore Roethke*. Reprinted by permission of Doubleday & Company, Inc. Also reprinted by permission of Faber and Faber Ltd. from *The Collected Poems of Theodore Roethke*. • "The Gray Squirrel" by Humbert Wolfe, from *Kensington Gardens* (London: Ernest Benn Ltd., 1924), by permission of Ann Wolfe. • From "A Dance for Ma Rainey" by Al Young, from *The New Black Poetry*, ed. Clarence Major, 1969, by permission of International Publishers Co., Inc., New York.

The paper used in this publication meets the minimum requirements
of American National Standard for Information Sciences
—Permanence of Paper for Printed Library Materials, ANSI Z39.48-1984.

To my wife Janet for the many ways in which she
participated in the creation of this book

Contents

viii   Contents

Preface

Burning books is not a serious form of censorship today. When Alexandria's libraries were set afire by both pagans and Christians, it was serious indeed. Many irreplaceable volumes vanished of which we can only imagine the loss on the basis of the books that do survive from antiquity. But since the printing press and the copying machine, the burning of books has become merely symbolic. What is the equivalent today of the Alexandrian devastations occurs daily as worthy manuscripts are winnowed out for rejection in the selection process of the publishing world by the tight constraints of profit-only marketing.

Few publishers read manuscripts anymore that they have not received from agents or authors already known. Since agents screen for the big sellers they narrow drastically what reaches publishers. There most editors today are told what to accept by the marketing staff, who get their notion of a good book from their field salespeople and the sales figures themselves. Three large bookstore chains are rapidly driving out independent booksellers and establishing categories and patterns for success that publishers feel obliged to fit. Tax laws no longer exempt publishers' inventories, so that most editors tend to reject manuscripts that they think will not pay big the first season out but only pay their way over the long haul.

All of these factors combine to restrict enormously what the public will be allowed to read. Censorship in the United States today comes not from a government suppressing ideas but from a corporate industry making money. The most fanatic censors could not wreak damage of this magnitude. Burned books have at least seen the light of day, and other copies can be found elsewhere. But we will never know what worthy books are not published, no more than we will ever know what the books destroyed in Alexandria had to say.

The constraints on the publication of textbooks exceed by far those just described for general trade books. The stakes are much higher, because textbooks are usually produced in series and in hardcover, most often entail huge outlays of capital for development, and must conform to local school adoption requirements that make for a lose-all or win-all game. The content of textbooks has been very limited ever since 1974, when the most tumultuous and significant schoolbook controversy ever to occur in North America broke out in Kanawha County, West Virginia. The book you are holding is a case study of that dispute and its import.

As director of one of the programs condemned by some there, I wanted very much to speak out about the issues but felt that my remarks might be taken as the vinegar of sour grapes. Actually, my reactions were very complex and included many other feelings and thoughts besides just hurt and anger. After ruminating them for a good decade, I decided to set forth my views of what happened and explain how this case may illuminate phenomena bigger today than then.

One good thing about the dispute was that rural Appalachia had spoken its mind too, for about the first time, and thus joined in the democratic process at last. A goodly part of this book is given over to what the people there had to say, either in the form of transcripts of interviews I did with some of them or of objections others of them wrote about specific selections in the disputed books.

Recounting the story and hearing out the protesters help raise issues that I see not only as more urgent today than in 1974 but as concerning society at large. The rise of the New Right brought to the surface underlying relationships between politics and religion often ignored in our secular age. In analyzing these from psychological and spiritual perspectives as well as educational, I try to point out dangerous traits and trends and so cannot claim to avoid making some judgments. I can only hope that these will be taken as efforts, however imperfect, to find a healing way.

I have broken two rules of liberals. I do not patronize poor, ill educated, or disenfranchised people by exempting them from the same critical examination I feel free to direct toward the rest of society, however much I might champion the same minority or disadvantaged group in the forums of that society. The case at hand has made me realize that our old garden-variety liberals have never fully faced up to the painful dilemma that the people they take under their wing may be the most likely to violate their liberal principles, precisely because cultures of poverty, ignorance, and rejection more readily generate bigotry, racism, and violence. It's easier to behave well if you're well off (though some who are don't).

In *Death at an Early Age* Jonathan Kozol rightly disclosed the appalling mistreatment of black children in the public schools of inner-city Boston. But the villains in that case were the same working-class Irish descendants of immigrants that, in another context, liberals would be defending. These Irish were themselves discriminated against by the

Protestant English, who got to America first and who had been persecuting the Irish so badly in the old country that they left it to come here. In fact, each ethnic wave to the big cities of this country has tended to abuse the next. Oppressors are made up largely of the oppressed, the bitter fact is, for the same reason that the great majority of criminals come from the disadvantaged or destitute pockets of society.

The majority who opposed the books in Kanawha County were mountaineer fundamentalists who have seldom received any attention but ridicule and who have been as grossly exploited as any group in our society. No region of the United States has been so plundered and taken over by outsiders. Miners die because companies cut corners on the expense of safety measures. But the mountaineer's proud code disdains welfare. The book protesters put me in a bind. What do you do when those you would stand up for denounce you as the enemy and act in ways you can't approve? I have done the Appalachian fundamentalists the honor of not patronizing them, for after all we do not exempt those we regard as equals. I have also honored what they had to say by considering all of their objections as thoughtfully as I know how.

In fact, I have taken most seriously what was for them the heart of their outcry—their religious beliefs. This is how I came to break another rule of the liberal tradition. In an understandable reaction to superstition, bigotry, and church corruption of the past, intellectual and academic circles usually avoid treating religion seriously except as an object of study. Certainly it is a professional risk to admit that one might really believe such stuff, a breach of taste at the least. But I feel closest to the book protesters in their insistence on a spiritual framework and in their repudiation of materialism.

To avoid misunderstanding about this, however, let me draw a distinction between spirituality and religion. However divinely inspired in origin, any religion partakes of a certain civilization, functions through human institutions, and is therefore partial, culturally biased. Otherwise there would be no wars between religions or religious countries. Spirituality, on the other hand, is the essential impulse behind all religions before they become incarnated in cultures. It is a perception of other dimensions behind the manifested and of oneness behind the plurality of things. From this perspective arise ways of being and behaving that we call spiritual.

Readers need not believe this themselves to appreciate perhaps that my believing it makes it possible for me to treat the protesters' religiosity as more than poppycock and to play on their theme in ways that may make this case study more interesting than it might have been if I merely scoffed at or ignored what, in their eyes, was the basis of all their objections. Textbooks, schools, and indeed the society itself do suffer terribly for want of a spiritual framework, it is true. Although such a framework cannot come into being the way the book banners tried — and continue to try — it would be best for all if a way *were* found, in keeping with the universalist spirituality of the founding fathers themselves.

Acknowledgments

I am very grateful to the following people for reading the manuscript of this book and offering valuable commentary and suggestions: Edmund J. Farrell of the University of Texas at Austin, Edward B. Jenkinson of Indiana University, Shirley Brice Heath of Stanford University, Courtney Cazden of Harvard University, Sheridan Blau of the University of California at Santa Barbara, and Arthur Egendorf of the President's Commission on Mental Health.

I am most indebted to my wife Janet, not only for unquantifiable discussion of the book during various stages but for much direct assistance in shortening and revising the final draft.

PART 1
THE DRAMA

Prologue
West—By God—Virginia

West Virginia is a unique state that has had identity problems ever since it seceded from the Secession during the Civil War. Because of the mountains it has remained perhaps more of a pocket culture than any other state in the Union, blocked off from the sources and graces of the seaboard and taught to develop self-reliance and self-concentration. Few of the Virginians living on the west side of the Alleghenies could identify with slaveholders and the plantation mentality of the bottomlands. Walled off at the start anyway, they have always looked more to God than to any other central government. Bumper stickers there echo the folk boast, "West—by God—Virginia," and license plates proclaim with the same bravado, "Almost Heaven." Such slogans harmonize with the ubiquitous "Jesus Saves" emblazoned on highway boulders and billboards. I've thought a lot about this state since 1950, when I met a West Virginian whom I married the following year. Visiting her relatives there over the years with our own children, I had had a long time to get to know and to treasure this state before my work involved me there in a totally new and unforeseen way.

In May of 1973 the state supervisor of language arts invited me on behalf of the West Virginia Department of Education to make a day-long presentation the following December in the capital, Charleston. "As far as subject matter is concerned, we can discuss that later. However we are interested in your books with Houghton Mifflin Co."[1] This portion of the letter of invitation referred to a language arts and reading series for elementary and secondary school, called *Interaction*, that I had directed as senior author/editor and that had just been released that year. As an author of two college textbooks used in methods courses for teachers, I had become accustomed for some years before to invitations from school districts, colleges, and sometimes state departments of education to consult or give workshops or talks. But the circumstances of this invitation seemed to aim at asking me to explain not merely my philosophy and practices for teaching language, as I had set them forth in the methods textbooks, but also the new *Interaction* program itself. "There is a good

3

deal of interest in our state concerning your new program, since it fits the philosophy of our State Comprehensive Language Arts Program," said a follow-up letter that October.

Then in November someone in the state Department of Education telephoned me to say that the meeting had been canceled because of the "energy crisis." This had to be an invented reason, but I couldn't even guess at the real one — not until the following year. In September 1974, I was recognizing *Interaction* books held before television cameras on the evening news and reading quotations from them in newspapers and magazines.

Interaction was a work of love. Though the largest program of school materials ever done till then, as the president of Houghton Mifflin stated at its press debut in San Francisco, it began as personal vision and remained remarkably close to its original ideals throughout all the horrors and rigors of corporate production. As much as anything, this is a tribute to the rare moral caliber of the thirty co-authors, whom the publisher allowed me to choose with a free hand unusual in such ventures. *Interaction* co-authors were mostly classroom teachers successfully going about their business, ones I had identified from previous years of developing curriculum in schools as a consultant. I knew they understood from their own experience how I was trying to reform language teaching and believed in it because they had already been working along the same lines. Some were creative specialists in singing or acting or storytelling, folklore or children's literature or visual media. They shared a devotion to youth and growth that far overshadowed any personal ambition.

This team pitched in without knowing what profit, if any, they would make, because the program was unique and risky. As compilers of anthologies, we bought rights to reprint or record selections with little regard for the costs being charged against our royalty accounts. From our familiarity with standard stuff we knew we could have ensured success and fortune by doing the program very differently, to fit commercial bandwagons, and often our increasingly jittery publisher pushed us hard to compromise with conventions we had repudiated at the outset.

Over and over co-authors subordinated personal wishes and feelings to the good of the program. Many had not known each other before I suddenly threw them together, but they collaborated readily, and *Interaction* soon became a very strong and warm family as well as a program. I don't want to think of how often I wasted their work by changing the concept of certain materials or by juggling assignments among co-authors, but they forgave this because they knew they had to if I were to stick to the principles of the program and to orchestrate the mind-boggling complexity of a set of learning materials comprising two film series, dozens of card and board games, 800 activity cards, hundreds of recorded selections, and other materials besides the 172 paperback books of reading matter that came eventually to be banned, as well as adopted, in West Virginia.

Interaction was a calculated risk, and the irony of its issuing from a publisher known for conservatism was not lost on those in the profession, who gaped attentively. Two factors emboldened the publisher to produce a major program that only a few independent teachers had ever tried out. First, my stock was high at the time, and the company bought into me. The methods books for teachers, which it had also published, were not only selling well in college education courses for teacher training but were earning a good school following that seemed to augur well for the embodying of these ideas in materials for youngsters as well. Second, when we signed contracts for the program in June 1970, the country was still riding the crest of progressive energy that had wrought so many changes in the 1960s and seemed to mandate further innovations in schooling.

Through *Interaction* we co-authors aimed to make really feasible the kind of humane individualizing often talked about but seldom done because conventional classroom management and textbooks based on the teacher as master of ceremonies make it impossible. Small working parties of students need to be doing different things at the same time, according to the needs and the capacities and the previous experiences of the individuals. I called the program "student-centered" to indicate this emphasis while avoiding the term "individualization," which had been fraudulently preempted for programmed learning, which is really isolated and mechanistic learning. In England a comparable approach to ours bore the name of the "open classroom," but the term became garbled and misapplied in the United States, and, furthermore, we had based *Interaction* on native experience not on imported notions. Parallel to the British teachers who had worked out a solid methodology for doing what still looked risky and radical here, we were trying to spearhead a movement that, aided by materials designed especially for the job, could eventually establish the practicality of letting individuals take different pathways to the same general goals.

The program was conspicuous for its unusually rich array of diverse subjects, media, and methods. The point of this multiplicity was to ensure that any learner of any background, level of development, temperament, or interest could find plenty of ways to engage with and develop language. For this reason also, speaking, listening, reading, and writing were integrated with each other and with the other arts and media to create a holistic interplay of warm-ups and follow-ups and lead-ins and carry-overs. The methodology alone of placing self-directing students into small-group interaction would have been enough of a risk to run.

On top of this, however, the paperback anthologies, the illustrations, and the recordings reflected the diversity of situations, values, tastes, dialects, and so on that this country discovered within itself during the sixties. We took a strong stand for pluralism and multicultural expression that went far beyond wooing of minorities; we found that a feeling for folklore, a savoring of different styles, a respect for the whole human range made us want to set forth like a feast the varieties of reading matter. Many books were original or rare as school texts — brain teasers and codes, rebuses and jumprope jingles, tongue twisters, transcripts of public events, chronicles and memoir, reportage and research — besides all the usual and manifold forms of modern and folk literature. The formats of the paperback books were as various as the contents — like trade books in a bookstore rather than textbooks — different trim sizes, lengths, illustration styles, and type styles. All this heady stuff stopped in their tracks children and adults alike. How often people said to us, "I wish they'd had books like this when *I* was going to school." But *Interaction* has long since dwindled out of print — while those forces that crystallized against it in mountain-bound West Virginia have gathered strength from coast to coast.

Besides being the state capital, Charleston is the urban center of Kanawha County, which contains as foil for this relatively affluent, sophisticated gem some of the most primitive rural society in America. Miners and other workers and farmers live in hollows focused on tiny fundamentalist churches of 40 to 50 members — pockets within the larger pocket culture of the state itself. Interstates connect Charleston in all four directions, and it lies at the confluence of the Elk and Kanawha rivers, the Kanawha flowing as a major tributary into the Ohio toward the northwest. The terrain flattens enough around the junction to allow a large city to cohere and to provide some beautiful river real estate, but it was necessary to lop off a mountaintop to fit in a jet airport. Flying into there epitomizes the city's situation. One moment you see only mountains, then, curving a little more, you are startled to view a large city down there centered on the splendid gold dome of a classic federal-style capitol facing the Kanawha River. How did *that* get here? Then you start estimating the length of that artificial mesa bearing a runway that begins in midair and ends in midair. You imagine Charleston was airlifted in the same way you are being plunked down in here.

Many places that figure in our story lie outside of Charleston, which had a population then of 70,000 out of the county's 230,000. If you drive west toward Huntington on I-64 you pass through, on the other shore of the Kanawha River, one of the nation's biggest forests of smokestacks and complexes of chemical plants and refineries — South Charleston — an amazing panorama that goes on for miles, disappearing intermittently only to resume at Nitro, the second biggest town in the county, of which it marks the northwestern edge. This stretch of interstate and valley between Nitro and South Charleston, including Dunbar and St. Albans, looks much like many similar outlying industrial districts anywhere else in the United States, not pretty but not squalid. But the country is not far away. Break out of South Charleston southwesterly on two-lane Route 214 and you find typical Upper Valley settlements of a hundred families or less living in modest but well-kept houses set attractively in the hollows or along the creases of the verdant hills. The town of Alum Creek is sequestered back in here, named like many hamlets in the county for one of the little tributaries draining the hills into the king of the county, the Kanawha. Part rural, part industrial, the Upper Valley represents a kind of mean between Charleston and the Lower Kanawha Valley. Most of the leaders and the action in the county drama were generated in the Upper because it stands culturally somewhere between the extremes of the city itself and the pure country life that characterizes the Lower Valley.

Significantly perhaps, I-64 does not continue from the Upper Valley along the Lower but skips over the latter and the equally backwoods Fayette County. Although the same U.S. Route 60 that I-64 parallels from Huntington to Charleston continues southeast along the Kanawha all the way into Virginia, this interstate does not start again until 60 approaches the gracious resort area of White Sulphur Springs, nearly out of the state. So you go out of Charleston into the Lower Valley on this two-lane highway that mimics every curve in the Kanawha River as it hugs the east bank, pass through Belle and Cedar Grove, and enter a part of your nation skipped over indeed.

In the fall of 1978 my wife and I included this stretch in a camper tour we made of the Indian mound culture in West Virginia and Ohio. A few days before, we had left my wife's home town, Fairmont, which like many Appalachian towns has never significantly got over being a depressed area. It's a poignant place. The slopes pitch steeply into the chemically bright green Monongahela River, which cuts the town in two, and the outlines of buildings fighting the angle seem sketched in with coal itself. My wife went to school with a lot of children from the edge of town and the nearby hollows, for Fairmont and the country have never been so starkly separated as in Charleston, the bigger city. She was the daughter of the principal of her high school. Her mother was a first-grade teacher, and what my wife hadn't experienced about the area directly from classmates she could easily hear in the stories her parents had to tell, many about the poor country families they dealt with. Some children out in the hollows are abandoned to the back yard all day and never talked to, so hard is life for the parents; the ghetto is by comparison a rich environment for learning. Fairmont had made the national media in the sixties for the very controversial firing of a liberal president of Fairmont State, which stocks regional schools with teachers. When during their retirement my parents-in-law tried to run a Headstart program in a rural area they encountered so much squabbling and opposition from a jealous community that they had to give up. Country locals fight over outside money like dogs over a bone. But even my wife was not prepared for the rude feeling of Lower Kanawha Valley, the state of the people there, the heavy vibrations.

That skipped-over part of the Kanawha Valley has the blunted and grotesque aspect of the southeastern corner of Georgia that James Dickey described in *Deliverance*. The contrast he builds during the men's drive from Atlanta to the wild river matches remarkably the change you feel driving out of Charleston into southern Kanawha County. (I once met in Atlanta a language arts supervisor whose son, a Harvard anthropologist, was doing a project in that Appalachian corner of Georgia just as if it were a foreign country instead of his home state.) Most human life — mines, little stores, cottages, highway, railroad — crowd between the Kanawha River and the mountains, which are really wild except for settlements along the occasional ravine road. Several hundred yards up the precipitous woods is another world. This place does more than touch me; I feel a rawness, a danger, a suffering.

Nipping across the river at one point to state Route 61, we met, on a similar narrow strip on the other bank, a sad young woman working the counter of a ravine joint who told us of daring with friends to search for a black panther reported to haunt a spot above the highway where we were headed. We weren't so eager to plunge into the rattlesnake-infested wilderness harboring our scatter of mysterious Indian stone works that we couldn't be distracted by tales of ghostly black panthers. She and friends found instead a large, fresh grave, heard strange noises, and felt a sudden physical cold wave sweep over them along with such a feeling of evil that they ran pell-mell back down the mountainside.

Some men she queried for us said the Indian ruins did indeed lie above this hamlet, just as we had read, but that the old mine road led in only partway and that we would have a hard time indeed ever finding the stones hiking blindly around in that dense, snakey brush. For further information they sent us to a post office a few miles away.

This representative of the United States government turned out to be part of an abandoned, side-tracked railroad car with a hatch on the side. You peer into this unpainted, dim interior and see, sure enough, some postal cubbyholes. You face a spent, tubercular-looking "postmistress" resembling the subject of an old homestead photo depicting early hard times and then become aware that an American flag is flying over her outpost, so grimed into the overlying gray of the landscape that you hadn't recognized it.

And this whole county — Charleston, Upper Valley, Lower Valley — is a single school district! In its mixture of identities it is a model of the explosive potentialities within America.

1

Storm in the Mountains

At the time I was to have talked to language arts personnel in Charleston, the Kanawha County District was laboring through the process of selecting $450,000 worth of textbooks in English and reading. A West Virginia State Board of Education resolution had directed districts to select only those school materials "which accurately portray minority and ethnic group contributions to American growth and culture and which depict and illustrate the inter-cultural character of our pluralistic society."[1] In pursuance of this directive, the state superintendent of schools wrote a memo to textbook publishers and county superintendents saying publishers' programs at all grades will need to make clear "that the United States is a multi-ethnic nation"; represent the viewpoints and values of ethnic groups regarding "the formulation of American institutions (e.g., family, church, schools, courts, etc.)"; portray "the dynamic nature of American society (past and present)"; and "assist students in examining their own self-image."[2] Basal textbooks for elementary schools have to be chosen from a state-approved list, but districts are free to adopt supplementary books and materials for secondary school without state approval. West Virginia is one of about two dozen states that have state adoption, which means that local school districts must choose their books from a state-approved list if they want the state to pay for them.

West Virginia law requires that only professional educators may comprise the textbook committees that make recommendations to the boards. It makes no provision for citizen advice. The English Language Arts Textbook Committee in Kanawha County comprised four classroom teachers and one principal. They were assisted by one subcommittee of twelve junior and senior high teachers and another of eight elementary teachers and principals. In 1965 Kanawha County formed an eleven-member Curriculum Advisory Council that included both lay and school people. The members appointed included none from the rural Appalachian culture.

In 1973 some lay members of the council had, for the first time, begun

11

to challenge curricular decisions made by the administration. In the same year the Kanawha County School Board substituted for the council two advisory bodies, one of laity and one of educators. Although members of the lay group were now chosen so as to represent major elements of the county community, they could not vote but merely made recommendations to the group of educators, who officially proposed curricular recommendations to the board, and some of whom sat on both committees.

Through the lay group, theoretically, citizens could have made known to the administration their views on current or proposed textbooks, but this one means of input had not become a reality by the time of the 1974 adoptions because too few educators applied for the professional advisory committee to permit either to be organized. In other words, the previous means of citizen consultation on textbooks had been removed after Kenneth Underwood became Superintendent in 1971 and not replaced. Those miners, fundamentalists, and industrial workers who had long felt ignored by their government suspected later that the board deliberately held back from implementing its own plan for advisory bodies in order to prevent them from expressing disapproval of the new selection of textbooks.

Although selection proceedings went on through the winter without a murmur of protest, there was good reason to think that some factions would contest some of the books once they should become acquainted with them. During the decade preceding these adoptions over fifty schools had been closed in Kanawha County to adjust to declining population and to facilitate school improvements. The consolidation of small local schools into larger, more remote, mixed facilities amounted to one more disruption of rural folk culture, increasingly invaded and derided by city people with very different styles and values. The administration did not carry out this long-range but sensitive operation in consultation with those most affected, who merely muttered pending a more provocative event.

The dormant tension between Appalachian and cosmopolitan, conservative and liberal, first broke out in a contest over a program in sex education that foreshadowed with noteworthy precision the furor to come. In 1969 the county's School Health Education Study had prepared, under a grant from the United States Office of Education, a program of health and family living that included sex education and had been unanimously approved by the Curriculum Advisory Council and the Board of Education, this council being the original one comprised of eleven lay and school people but of no rural representation. The announcement of this program afforded the sharp incident and the focused issue necessary to catalyze resentment.

Alice Moore, the wife of a fundamentalist minister in St. Albans, took the leadership of an opposition force that anathematized the SHES program as anti-Christian and anti-American, claiming it indoctrinated an atheistic and relativistic view of morality. "God's law is absolute,"[3] said Alice Moore, and went on in the 1970 school board election to defeat an incumbent, Carl Tully, who charged that the coalition of well-organized parent groups received support from the John Birch Society and was really seeking political strength so it could take over the school board and dictate textbooks and curriculum.

The National Education Association asserted that she utilized the "spurious support of MOTOREDE," "Movement to Restore Decency," an anti-sex education organization affillated with the John Birch Society. A MOTOREDE publication circulated in Kanawha County at the time declared, 'It is no accident that Communists and others long associated with this conspiracy are among the staunchest advocates of the growing menace of school courses on sex.' "[4]

After the election the whole health and family program was quietly rewritten and sex education eliminated. Alice Moore became a conservative heroine, and the lines of conflict were clearly drawn. Should schools reinforce traditionalism inculcated by parents or teach what is not taught at home? Which parents? Each side accused the other of trying to impose its values on others' children. Thus they posed the dilemma of a single curriculum serving a plural community.

Curiously, however, when the Language Arts Textbook Committee made its recommendations to the board on March 12, 1974, for the adoption of 325 titles, neither citizenry nor media took the slightest notice. Alice Moore did not attend this meeting. By the next meeting, on April 11, the board was legally bound to authorize adoptions of books for the following school year. During the month between these two meetings, the proposed materials were displayed for board members in a special room of the district building and for the public in the Kanawha County Library. No board member and but few citizens came.

On April 11 the board ratified the adoption of the proposed books, the major series of which were D. C. Heath & Company's *Communicating* (grades 1-6) and *Dynamics of Language* (7-12), Scott, Foresman & Company's *America Reads* (7-12) and *Galaxy* (7-12), and Silver Burdett Company's *Contemporary English* (7-12) — all of which were "basic" adoptions — McDougal, Littell & Company's *Language of Man* (7-12) and *Man* (7-12), and Houghton Mifflin Company's *Interaction* (K-12) — all of which were "supplemental" adoptions. Alice Moore objected that the review time had been too short and wrung from the board the concession that sections of the books could be deleted if later found objectionable. The effect of this was to delay *purchase* of the books pending scrutiny.

At home she sampled some of the books, was appalled, and asked for copies of all the books to be sent to her. It may be true, as another protest leader asserted, that in actually perusing recommended texts Alice Moore broke a board tradition. "Historically, the Board had left the selection of new textbooks to the professional educators and refrained from examining the books so as to avoid pressure from book salesmen, parents, or teachers."[5] At any rate, she then telephoned Mel and Norma Gabler in Texas and asked for their reviews of the books. Famous for their effective textbook protests since the early sixties, the Gablers air-mailed to her their bills of particulars throughout the following summer as they prepared them to present to the Texas Education Agency during adoption procedures in the fall for many of the same series. Mrs. Moore was referred to the Gablers by a textbook review organization in New Rochelle, New York, called America's Future.

Elections for two seats on the board distracted the public from the adoption issue until after May 14, when Matthew Kinsolving was reelected and a new member elected, Douglas Stump. Dark horse Stump moved up fast and turned out to be the top vote-getter. "It was generally felt that Stump's overwhelming support resulted from adverse public response to Kanwaha County Schools' administration,"[6] which he had charged with inaccessibility and indifference to constituents. Several months later an outside team of investigators was to corroborate Stump's criticism.[7]

According to the Gablers' authorized biographer, Mrs. Moore expressed her objections at first only privately, to other board members, but, failing to enlist much support there, approached Superintendent Underwood, who suggested a private meeting with teachers. Mrs. Moore agreed but did say enough to a reporter following up on a leak to make Underwood feel the meeting would then have to be public.[8] Rumbling and grumbling had grown to the point that the board set a meeting for May 23 to let district language arts specialists explain the selection of textbooks. Mrs. Moore's first public denunciations of the books attacked relativism in language usage, an oblique conservative strategy that makes it possible, while upholding proper grammar, to discriminate against minority dialects in literature selections.

Confrontation began in earnest at the heated meeting of May 23, when Mrs. Moore escalated her objections to charges that the books were filthy, trashy, disgusting, one-sidedly in favor of blacks, and unpatriotic. Board member Matthew Kinsolving and some parents rallied behind her. Another meeting was set for June 27th to continue debate and at last vote on purchase. During the interim the debate waged on hotly in the media and local meetings as both sides organized themselves for serious contention. Convinced that the board would side with the administration, Alice Moore took her cause to the public. She went on television and exhibited passages from the books at churches and community centers.

The *Charleston Gazette*, the *Charleston Daily Mail*,[9] and WCHS Television[10] endorsed the textbook adoptions. A series of six editorials aired by WCHS during the first week of June played an extremely important role in bringing the controversy and its issues to the attention of the public. The PTA voted to oppose several of the main series:

> Many of the books are literally full of anti-americanism, anti-religion, and discrimination. Too, these books are woefully lacking in morally uplifting ideas. Many of the statements flout law and order and respect for authority. Several passages are extremely sexually explicit.[11]

The local NAACP and YWCA supported the choice of books along with the West Virginia Human Rights Commission. The latter wrote in a press release:

> There has been criticism of the explicit character of some of the writings dealing with Blacks. A thorough examination of these portions reveal that they represent candid portrayals of the lives of a significant number of Blacks today. We believe this to be a positive rather than a negative attribute as it is essential that the educational system not turn its back on consequential issues but deal with them with honesty and thoroughness.
>
> Traditionally, teaching materials have been monumentally deficient in the area of Black studies. This Commission is excited by the prospect that students will be exposed to voices from the past, from the ghetto and from other important areas of Black experience. . . .[12]

All thirteen students polled once on the streets by the *Charleston Daily Mail* opposed censoring books for junior and senior high. Interestingly, most felt the issue was whether they could read black authors.

The Magic Valley Mother's Club circulated marked copies of the disputed books and a petition to ban from schools materials that "demean, encourage skepticism or foster disbelief in the institutions of the United States of America and in western civilization." The institutions were listed:

> The family unit based on marriage of man and woman.
> Belief in a supernatural being, a power beyond human means or human comprehension.
> Political system set forth in the Constitutions.
> System of free enterprise governed by laws of supply and demand.
> Respect for property of others and for laws.
> History and heritage of the United States as the record of one of the noblest civilizations that has existed.[13]

"Further, since the denial of supernatural forces is in itself a form of religion, the promotion of agnosticism or nihilism must also be unconstitutional."[14]

The Episcopal clergy actively countered objectors both at this and later stages. Churches split between mainline, nationally affiliated denominations and local, unaffiliated, fundamentalist congregations. A coalition of ten ministers from the West Virginia Council of Churches and from Catholic, Jewish, and such Protestant churches as Methodist, Presbyterian, and some Baptist issued a joint statement of support for the textbooks that read in part:

> Any treatment, especially in the schools, of questions like war and peace, racism — black and white — religion and patriotism, is bound to raise disagreements and stir emotional response. We are convinced, however, that these matters must be discussed openly if our students are to be exposed to the great variety of issues that characterize our modern society. We know of no way to stimulate the growth of our youth if we insulate them from the real issues. We feel this program will help our students to think intelligently about their lives and our society.
>
> The material that has been considered, or called, objectionable by reason of its treatment of sexual themes represents a very small portion of the whole program. It does not treat sex sensationally nor for its own sake. Furthermore, it is to be used only for advanced senior high students in rare and selective situations. We reviewed some of the most criticized passages and found them not nearly as bad as portrayed. There will always be disagreement about the use of such material. In our judgment the material at issue is not at all harmful, especially given the limited use it will know.[15]

To counter this show of strength, another coalition of ministers organized by one Baptist pastor endorsed a statement that while there was "much good" in the textbooks, "there is also much that is immoral and indecent and thus, we object to their being used in our school system."[16] In a similar reaction seven members of the Dunbar Ministerial Association went on record saying that the books "contain materials offensive to religion, morals, patriotism, and common decency."[17]

Over thirty rural folk churches helped to represent the opposition at the June 27th meeting, which took place before an audience of more than 1,000 overflowing into hallways and outdoors into the rain. Protesters presented the petition of the Magic Valley Mother's Club, now containing over 12,000 signatures repudiating the books. After nearly three hours of stormy testimony, the board voted three to two to purchase all of the books with the conciliatory exception of eight from *Interaction*'s offering for senior high (level 4). Two motions were passed to include parents henceforth on textbook selection committees.

Charlestonians heaved a sigh of relief that the controversy was over, but during the summer the new Christian-American Parents set up letter-writing campaigns, paid for newspaper advertisements, held a rally at the Municipal Auditorium, picketed a company owned by a board member, and demonstrated before the governor's mansion. Another new antibook group called Concerned Citizens picketed the Board of Education, which displayed the books and held low-keyed parent conferences to quietly counter rumors about the content of the books. Concerned Citizens sponsored a Labor Day protest rally at Campbell's Creek, where the Reverend Marvin Horan called on the crowd of 8,000 to boycott schools when they opened the next day. By then the initial protest against particular selections or passages had generalized to the point of reducing the diversity of 325 titles by six publishers to "the books."

In the longest and by far the most thoroughly researched account of the controversy, to which I am much indebted, Catherine Candor-Chandler writes:

> During the late summer rallies new fliers, containing purported excerpts from the textbooks, had been circulated in the community by protest groups. These fliers contained selections not only from the eight books that were deleted from the approved purchase list at the June 27 Board meeting but also excerpts from other books, such as Kate Millet's *Sexual Politics*, that were never a part of the language arts adoption. For example one part of the flier contained a page from a book identified as *Facts About Sex for Today's Youth* dealing with sexual intercourse. This selection showed a picture of the male sex organ and defined several "street words" for vagina with the admonition that although these words are not polite, they are sometimes used and there is no need to be embarrassed by not knowing what they mean. Another part of the flier contained a pictorial demonstration of how to use a rubber.
>
> These fliers, containing blatantly sexual material that had nothing to do with the language arts textbooks adopted in Kanawha County, served to fuel the flames of the controversy. The shock in the community was tremendous and rumors about the content of textbooks were abundant.[18]

From then on "the books" became for many people "the dirty books," including for some people who never examined them or even saw them but took the word of others whose values they knew to be their own. Parents had a chance to look at the books during the first week of school as a still confident administration sent them home with the students to squelch rumors. When, however, some parents didn't find the passages they had seen in the protest fliers, they accused the administration of deceiving them by holding back on the offending books!

Only when schools opened September 3rd did the dispute erupt with enough force to draw the national media, which tracked the turns of its events almost daily through the fall. From such magazines as *The New Yorker* and *U.S. News & World Report* to regional papers and specialized education journals, the press acknowledged in feature articles, periodic summaries, and editorials the national significance of such a controversy over school books. It was then that I saw on television offending passages from anthologies I had last scrutinized while editing selections for them with my colleagues.

Boycotts, strikes, and pickets became the main ways of trying to force the board to get the books out of the schools. During the first week of September parents kept an average of 9,000 of the district's 45,000 students out of schools, mostly in the Upper Valley, where absenteeism in some schools went to 80 percent and 90 percent. Unwilling to cross pickets set up by parents, 3,500 miners, representing all the mines in Kanawha County, also stayed home despite orders from UMW officials to remain at work. Sympathy strikes closed down mines in backwoods Boone and Fayette counties to the south. Roving groups of protesters numbering up to 1,000 picketed mines, schools, school bus garages, industry, and trucking companies. Stormy emotions erupted in violence where some picketing employed barricades. On September 10 Charleston's city bus drivers also honored protesters' picket lines, thus closing down service to about 11,000 people.

The disruption worked. Following much illegal demonstrating outside the Department of Education building and much negotiation within, the board announced on September 11th that it had withdrawn the textbooks from the schools while they underwent a thirty-day review by eighteen citizens, three selected by each of the board members including member-elect Douglas Stump, a vacillating figure claimed at times by both sides who was appointed chairman of the committee. After signing the agreement on behalf of Concerned Citizens, the Rev. Marvin Horan promptly repudiated it that night at a large ball-park rally when the crowd showed it wished to press on by boycott and pickets for permanent removal of all books and dismissal of Superintendent Underwood and three members of the board who voted the wrong way. Another crowd had jeered earlier when Alice Moore told them that the agreement was more than she thought could be accomplished and was "the best we can expect."[19]

A few days later two other fundamentalist ministers took over from the Rev. Horan, who was not only reported to be exhausted but had also changed his mind back again to acceptance of the agreement. Horan was later to reenter the fray and ultimately to be sentenced to three years in prison for conspiracy to blow up two elementary schools. Those who relieved him for now continued to play major roles in opposing the adoptions—the Rev. Ezra Graley of Nitro and the Rev. Avis Hill of Alum Creek. Both were sentenced to thirty days in jail for defying a court injunction, and Graley received another sixty days for contempt of court. Along with others they cheerfully underwent more than once the martyrdom of arrest. The Rev. Charles Quigley, the fourth fundamentalist minister to join the protest leaders, shocked the county community by saying, "I am asking Christian people to pray that God will kill the giants [the three board members who voted for the books] who have mocked and made fun of dumb fundamentalists."[20]

As one high school student said of the book-banners during a walkout the students mounted to protest the removal of the books, "They're shooting people because they don't want people to see violence in books."[21] Ironically, the protesters ran the gamut of insurrectionist behavior that they hated in war protesters and radicals, including even charges of police brutality and biased judicial proceedings.

Violence escalated during the second week of school, and the number of wildcat mine strikers reached 8 to 10,000 over several counties. Two men were wounded by gunfire at picket points and another was badly beaten. Both shooting victims were truckers of neither warring faction. One was shot from a cruising car after trying to cross pickets to work, the other by a probook man who thought he was being attacked by picketers and immediately turned himself in to police. A CBS television crew was roughed up at one place, and car windows were smashed at others. Threats were leveled at the superintendent, members of the board, and parents still trying to send their children to school. Despite arrests for blocking public places and circuit court injunctions against barricading and certain demonstrating, law enforcement became ineffectual, and severe disorder loomed ahead. Along with other Kanawha County officials, Democratic Sheriff G. Kemp Melton repeatedly tried during all of September and October to persuade Republican Governor Arch Moore to send in state troopers, but whenever the governor replied it was only to claim that the state should not intervene in local political rows. "A man could get himself in a box," Sheriff Melton quoted him as saying.[22]

By September 13 the safety of both children and adults seemed so much at risk that Superintendent Underwood ordered all 121 public schools closed for a four-day weekend during which he banned football games and other extracurricular activities and slipped out of town, as did some board members, including Alice Moore herself, who said, "I never dreamed it would come to this."[23] Some schools closed in Boone and Fayette counties, which did not have the disputed books.

One of the language arts consultants for the Kanawha County schools described an especially harrowing aspect of this time in an article in the *Journal of Research and Development in Education*, which devoted an issue in 1976 to "Censorship and the Schools." She makes the point that while some parents were keeping their children out of school to protest the books, others were keeping them out to protect them from the violence of the boycott itself. Fears for the safety of the children turned out to be well warranted, she says, as evidence from the court trials of the book protesters indicted for fire-bombing schools later revealed. She explains:

> A *Charleston Gazette* article of November 5, 1975, concerning the role of Asst. District Attorney Wayne A. Rich, Jr., who served as prosecutor for the persons involved in the school bombings of October, 1974, states: "A few extremists among the churchmen who wanted 'godless' textbooks removed from schools became so fanatical they discussed bombing carloads of children whose parents were driving them to school in defiance of a boycott called by book protesters." Further, in reference to the convictions ultimately obtained in the school bombing cases, Rich stated that one of the convicted bombers testified that he and others had discussed ways to stop "people that was sending their kids to school, letting them learn out of books when they knew they was wrong." [One of] the ways mentioned, Rich said, was to "place a blasting cap in the gas tank of a car and hook the wires to the brake lights or to the signal lights; when the brake was applied or the signal on, . . . it would blow the gas tank up on the car."[24]

She captures the general atmosphere:

> Quickly the cry became "GET THE BOOKS OUT!"—not one book, not one set of books, not one offensive passage—but all 325, including a handwriting program which has been used in our school system for more than 25 years, a re-adoption of literature books which has been used without objection for the preceding five years, and many of the world's most respected literary works, including Plato's *Republic*, Melville's *Moby Dick*, and Milton's *Paradise Lost* and *Paradise Regained*. Even *The Good Earth*, the Pulitzer Prize novel by Pearl Buck, West Virginia's most renowned author, could not withstand the onslaught.[25]

"An English teacher at George Washington High [in Charleston] said that educators and administrators had been repeatedly threatened. 'We are living in the climate of a Nazi world.' "[26]

The Textbook Review Committee began its deliberations, after appointments were made September 24, in an atmosphere not only determined by continued rallies, pickets, boycotts, felonious damaging of school buildings, and other sporadic violence but also by some new factors that included the organization of a probook group called Kanawha County Coalition for Quality Education; a determination by State Superintendent of Education Daniel Taylor that it was probably illegal for a school board to withdraw books it had already adopted; and the announcement of early resignations, because of the controversy, by the president of the School Board, Albert Anson, Jr., who opposed removal of the books, and Superintendent Underwood. The Textbook Review Committee itself introduced a new factor. Six of the eighteen members and an alternate split off and met separately after the first meeting, when a preliminary vote on some of the books convinced them that the selection of the committee had been unfairly biased in favor of the books.

During the period when the Textbook Review Committee was deliberating, the Business and Professional People's Alliance for Better Textbooks began taking an active role under the leadership of its founder and president, Elmer Fike, the owner of a small chemical company who published antibook ads and pamphlets at his own expense and served as liaison with the Heritage Foundation, a conservative think tank. Since 1968 Elmer Fike has been publishing a booklet called *Elmer's Tune* containing right-wing editorial columns first appearing in local newspapers and occasionally in other periodicals. For him the textbook controversy was only one more issue among others, a favorite theme being such governmental regulation of business as environmental controls. The alliance, he wrote in a two-page newspaper ad, "was formed to give those parents opposed to violence and demonstrations a voice in the controversy. This group has issued releases and provided speakers to public groups to give a better image to the protest movement."[27]

On the other side, the Kanawha County Association of Classroom Teachers voted to oppose any recommendation the Textbook Review Committee might make that would undo the original adoption and passed a resolution denouncing the removal of the textbooks during the review period and upbraiding the School Board for abdicating its legal responsibilities in the face of public pressure.

During the period of review an elementary school at Cabin Creek was dynamited and one at Campbell's Creek fire-bombed, both while empty. Other schools were the targets of gunfire, fire bombs, and diverse vandalization. A school janitor was assaulted. Rocks were thrown at the homes of parents defying the school boycott and at school buses, which were frequently damaged. Two school buses were fired on by shotgunners as their drivers returned from their rounds, and at one point most of the fleet of buses for Upper Kanawha County was put out of operation. On October 7, seventeen dissenters were arrested in St. Albans for blocking the garage to prevent children from being bused to school.

For his safety Superintendent Underwood lived secretly for a while at the home of a School Board employee, who told me also that the sheriff's department kept him under constant surveillance during that period. Judge John Goad, who had delivered adverse decisions in the cases of protest leaders, was guarded at home and sometimes escorted out of court. On the other hand, the car of a jailed protester was set afire and destroyed, and according to James Hefley, Alice Moore was threatened by phone and by the firing of shots before her house, and guards watched over her at home and accompanied her when away.[28]

In early November, shortly before the board was to make a final decision on the Textbook Review Committee's recommendations, a package of about fifteen sticks of dynamite was set off under the gas meter of the School Board building, presumably to intimidate the decision-making. After delaying the climactic meeting another week, the board finally met on November 8th at noon in the main arena of the Charleston Civic Center amid fears of violence and strong security measures. The Non-Christian American Parents, recently formed to show that others than fundamentalists denounced the books, had held an all-night vigil at the Civic Center, led by its spokesman, Ed Miller, who later became head of the West Virginia Klavern of the Ku Klux Klan. He vowed no violence from his group. Actually, so wary of the charged setting were all parties that fewer than 100 showed up.

The board heard further testimony from the majority and minority factions of the Textbook Review Committee, who had already made their separate reports, the one recommending return of virtually all of the books and the other rejection of virtually all of the books. Next the board passed unanimously two resolutions protecting students from the imposition of books or indoctrination objectionable to their families for moral or religious reasons. Provisions were made for parents to indicate on a form list sent home which books they did not want their children to read. Then by a vote of four against Mrs. Moore the board authorized the return of all the basic and supplemental books to the classroom except the basic series for grades 1–6, *Communicating*, and the senior high portion (level 4) of *Interaction*, which were consigned to school libraries. This vote compromised the recommendations of the majority report of the Textbook Review Committee, which had favored the return of *Communicating* along with the others.

Shortly after this long-awaited and controversial decision was made, the UMW contract expired without a settlement, adding to the volatile mood in areas where people were already disgruntled by the compromise decision. Most observers believe that the miners went on their illegal strike in the first place partly to reduce stockpiles of coal while contract talks were under way in Washington between the UMW and coal company officials. As other news analysts pointed out, however, miners habitually respond to a wide range of provocations by striking, the one weapon they have to wield in a world over which they feel they have little control. " The common man don't know what to do except what he's done, and that's to go home and sit down,' Marvin Horan told the school superintendent."[29] In any case, the strike played a major role in the book revolt, and Alice Moore openly exhorted miners at times to continue while antibook parents prolonged the school boycott.

Protesters in fact redoubled at this time the efforts to boycott and began organizing private Christian schools. The board mobilized for prosecution of truants under the compulsory attendance law. The Kanawha County Coalition for Quality Education threatened to sue the board for not placing *Communicating* back in the classroom. Violence and mob pressure resumed in the form of shooting at buses and schools, fire-bombing the car of a boycott breaker, bomb threats to officials, and a telephone campaign threatening parents if they sent their children to school. One mayor of a displeased town managed to have Superintendent Underwood and two board members arrested for contributing to the delinquency of minors.

At last the West Virginia State Police committed itself to enforcing law regarding the controversy, influenced somewhat perhaps by an incident of shooting at two of its own patrol cars as they escorted a school bus. School authorities regarded this definite state intervention as a turning point in the turmoil, because the governor's previous reluctance to act had undoubtedly encouraged the dangerous and illegal measures with which some partisans had championed their cause.

No doubt to pacify those resentful of their decision, the board passed on November 21 a resolution that board president Albert Anson, Jr., now resigned, called "a straight jacket on dissident opinion."[30] It set guidelines for textbook selection in the future. The biographer of the Gablers wrote, "With Mrs. Moore forcing a point-by-point vote, [the new policy] spelled out guidelines similar to those requirements which the Gablers had sent."[31]

> Textbooks must not intrude into the privacy of students' homes by asking personal questions about interfeelings [sic] or behavior of themselves or parents . . . must recognize the sanctity of the home and emphasize its importance as the basic unit of American society . . . must not contain offensive language . . . must teach the true history and heritage of the United States . . . shall teach that traditional rules of grammar are a worthwhile subject for academic pursuit and are essential for effective communication . . . shall encourage loyalty to the United States . . . and emphasize the responsibilities of citizenship and the obligation to redress grievances through legal processes . . . must not encourage sedition or revolution against our government or teach or imply that an alien form of government is superior.[32]

According to interpretation, these guidelines could be innocuous business-as-usual or a grave violation of the American heritage of freedom.

The NEA asserted that "if given the interpretation obviously meant by their proponent, [the guidelines] would not only bar the disputed books from Kanawha County classrooms, but would proscribe the use of any language arts textbooks, including the *McGuffey's Readers. . . ."*[33]

On December 1st, 2,000 antibook people led by the Rev. Avis Hill marched through crowds of Christmas shoppers in Charleston waving flags and bearing placards proclaiming "Trash is for burning," "Wish we had more people like Sweet Alice," and "No peaceful co-existence with satanic Communism."[34] Though subsiding, trouble was not over. At a televised board meeting on December 12, Superintendent Underwood, Assistant Superintendent Robert Kittle, and members of the board were assaulted by protesters, including several women, one of whom was identified and later arrested. Some residents of the Upper Kanawha Valley put machinery in motion to secede from Kanawha County. Demonstrations, boycott efforts, and rallies continued to occur until April of 1975, when the diehard leader, the Rev. Marvin Horan, was tried and sentenced to three years in prison for conspiracy to bomb schools.

On December 27, 1974, the West Virginia Board of Education included in their legislative program recommendations that lay people be included in textbook selection committees and that state adoption be instituted for secondary school textbooks. Operating under these new guidelines, a Kanawha County screening committee of fifteen lay members and five teachers rejected on February 10, 1975, parts of all four of the elementary social studies series under consideration for adoption. Since this left little choice to the Textbook Selection Committee of educators, who alone by state law could actually vote on adoption, the first effort to implement community screening raised issues of fairness and legality. These were later resolved by the superintendent of the West Virginia Department of Education, who ruled that the statutory selection committee of five educators should not be restricted to considering books screened by the laity nor be bound to follow their recommendations. In March the board approved a social studies series four to one over Mrs. Moore's objection.

United States District Judge K. K. Hall dismissed a suit challenging the constitutionality of the language arts textbook adoption on grounds that it violated the First Amendment guarantee of religious rights: "These rights are guaranteed by the First Amendment, but the Amendment does not guarantee that nothing about religion will be taught in the schools nor that nothing offensive to any religion will be taught in the schools."[35]

In April of 1975, the board established an alternative school for "the mastery of basic skills, adherence to strict codes of discipline and dress, fulfillment of the obligations of citizenship and acceptance of the responsibility for the preservation of high patriotic ideals."[36] The project was abandoned because of too few applications.

Shortly after school began the following fall, the board restored to the classrooms even *Communicating*, the basal elementary series that it had dropped in November and that had aroused the most resistance. Not a rustle of objection.

2

The Reverberating Network

The protesters lost the battle and won the war. Education professor George Hillocks, Jr., called the Kanawha County dispute "the most prolonged, intense, and violent textbook protest this county has ever witnessed."[1] The fact that nothing like it has occurred since gives a good indication of how effective it was: no publisher has dared offer to schools any textbooks of a comparable range of subjects and ideas and points of view to those the protesters vilified and crippled on the market. Theoretically returned to the Kanawha County schools, they may as well not have been. In many other ways the bitter controversy closed up its own school system as much as it did textbook editorial offices. Let's look at the effects of the dispute, starting locally and moving outward.

Of the immediate aftermath Candor-Chandler gives this picture.

With threats of violence and lawsuits hanging over their heads for using certain materials with some students or failing to use the same materials with other students, teachers were understandably frustrated. The trust relationship between teachers, students and parents was replaced by an atmosphere of apprehension and doubt. A student noted, "In my school we are two armed camps—the teachers against the community. Teachers are afraid to teach. . . ."

Just how far the doubt and uncertainty regarding acceptable classroom subjects extended is illustrated in one principal's comments to *Washington Star-News* reporter John Mathews, "A teacher came to me the other day and asked, 'What do you think? Can we defend teaching this in class?' She was talking about a unit in biology on the sexual reproduction of mollusks."

Although the conflict created by the textbooks ended, controversy remains over what should be in the curriculum and what should be the concern of the school. A great deal of frustration and confusion remains over what is or is not acceptable in the classroom. Many teachers no longer feel comfortable to use their professional judgment in the selection of instructional materials. "They distrust the Central Office staff, the Board of Education and the community. They are afraid for their safety, peace of mind and even their jobs," commented Gene Douglas, Principal of George Washington High School.

A number of teachers and principals, especially in those areas where the textbook protest was most active, either resigned or requested transfers to other positions. For example, one school in the Upper Kanawha Valley, Cedar Grove Community School, that was closed by protesting parents, lost six teachers and the principal prior to the 1975–76 school year. It was generally agreed by the press, school officials and the public that the effects of the textbook controversy would be felt by the Kanawha County School system for years to come.[2]

After visiting the county system a couple of years after the row Hillocks reported this in *School Review*, August 1978:

> Children whose parents granted permission must use the controversial books only in the library, not in the classroom where other children might overhear discussions of them. Or teachers must make other special provision for use of the books. The result is that many do not use them at all. Many of the texts sit in the board of education warehouse. One elementary principal told me that she will not order the books. Her school was in a major hotbed of the protest. She does not wish to disrupt the school program again. . . .
> Some teachers are looking for ways out of education, many others are angry at the vilification to which they feel they have been subjected, and many say they will never feel the same about teaching again.[3]

When I visited the county eight years after the controversy, in June of 1982, people at the School Board offices told me that school morale was still bad. As one sign, the activities of the local affiliate of the National Council of Teachers of English had fallen into depression. A language arts coordinator there said to me, "It [the dispute] did irreparable damage. The teachers were afraid to teach anything. I have no doubt they are still gun-shy about many issues. If you teach noun and verb and parts of speech in the traditional way and have them fill in blanks — that's a good safe way to do it."[4] A young teacher who had not been employed in the Kanawha district at the time of the dispute told me in 1982 that she had found the atmosphere so charged and repressive that in English she dared to teach only very prudently and so she stuck close to her grammar lessons. Even these blew apart, however, when she got to the topic of gender. "My parents don't want me to be taught about sex," some students asserted, and she did indeed hear from their parents.

Kanawha County, as board people there dismally related to me in 1982, was the only school district in the United States to have adopted the creationism textbook program produced in Anaheim, California (Robert Dornan's congressional district) based on the "creation science" that in 1982 an Arkansas judge ruled was not science when he invalidated a state ordinance passed at the behest of a fundamentalist movement, and that the United States Supreme Court itself repudiated in 1987. Although West Virginia has, since 1974, made a law of the multicultural adoption requirement that was only a resolution then, the Kanawha incident has so intimidated publishers that adoption committees will look in vain to find a program truly fulfilling that requirement. The adoption guidelines that Kanawha County passed while in the grips of the fracas (see chapter 1) were essentially drawn from the Gablers' censorship service. In reality these county guidelines and the state multicultural requirement contradict each other.

The controversial textbooks that brought on this state of affairs were never reordered, and the copies originally purchased languished on shelves for the most part, an object of revulsion even to those who believed in them. Adoptions are changed or renewed every five years for each subject, and other books have come in from the chastened publishers, who have carefully retrenched on noncanonical writers and subjects and have dusted off and refurbished their once discarded grammar series of the forties. The programs they put into Kanawha County all suffered severe losses as word spread over the censorship network to other states.

A textbook series represents millions of dollars in investment, and only a few large corporations in the trade can ante up that kind of capital. They will do virtually anything to protect those outlays and make them pay off. Educational philosophy does not play even a bit part in this financial theater. School superintendents and school boards fear offending their constituencies and bringing on themselves what their counterparts suffered in Kanawha. Why risk your job when other textbooks will serve as well, to all appearances?

An elementary English series up for adoption in Texas at the time of the Kanawha controversy and rated near the top right up to the last moment was suddenly dropped, despite its being considerably more innocuous than the West Virginia books. The publisher felt that the failure to get listed owed entirely to effects from Kanawha County. If no textbook showdowns have occurred since 1974 of comparable magnitude and intensity, it is because that one so cowed publishers that no successor could occur. Of the Kanawha County dispute a schoolteacher who was one of the authors of *Communicating* wrote: "Somehow minority opinion has been allowed to effectively dictate in the selection of textbooks, and even, I suggest, in determining the philosophy and content of the curriculum."[5]

But smaller struggles continued, and in 1982 alone the Public Broadcasting System aired two programs dealing with censorship in schools — a portion of the "MacNeil/Lehrer Report," devoted to Texas adoptions and the influence of the Gablers (represented by Mel), and "Books Under Fire" in the "Crisis to Crisis" series. Emboldened by textbook successes and the increasingly regressive atmosphere of the later 1970s, conservatives of the eighties focused on banning regular trade books from school and town libraries, a trend that has grown dramatically up to this writing, in 1987. But the two biggest cases of schoolbook conflict in North America occurred in the year immediately following the Kanawha County case.

The first began on November 7, 1975, when two school board members in the Island Trees Union Free School District in New York decided to see what they could find in a high school library.

> Armed with a list of "objectionable books" that they had received at a conservative political conference two months earlier, they searched the card catalog for volumes they would later label "mentally dangerous." They found nine, many of which deal with the experiences of Jews, blacks, and Hispanics.[6]

Some of the authors were Bernard Malamud, Kurt Vonnegut, Richard Wright, Langston Hughes, and Eldridge Cleaver, who, along with J. D. Salinger, Canadian novelist Margaret Laurence, and a couple of dozen other writers show up with totally predictable regularity in censorship cases, not because they are worse violators of the objectors' values but because they got firmly established early in the network.

When the Island Trees Board of Education removed the books from the libraries and the curriculum, Steven Pico and four other students filed suit against the district on the basis of First Amendment rights. Courts avoided dealing with the issue as long as possible, and even after a United States Circuit Court of Appeals finally ordered the case to trial in 1981 and it reached the Supreme Court, it never received a decisive ruling on constitutionality, because the Court split down the middle. *Pico vs. Island Trees Board* did, however, push litigation over school book banning farther than it ever had ever gone before. In doing so it revealed just how profound is the dilemma about individual rights and local governmental authority.

There began also in 1975 what may be Canada's most significant school book controversy, still being waged as of 1987. The Peterborough County Board in Ontario removed from schools Daniel Keyes' *Flowers for Algernon* because some parents had complained of its "gutter language" and "immoral passages." An article by two Canadian educators in 1985 makes clear that "Prior to 1975 in Peterborough County selection issues were resolved without publicity," but "the situation changed dramatically in 1975. . . ." This change was set up, however, by the removal of two books "immediately prior to 1975,"[7] that is, during the period of the Kanawha County upheaval, which received a tremendous amount of publicity not only through regular news coverage but in special talk shows and feature articles.

The repercussion was typical. Educators "felt that the situation would lead to self-censorship, or what Kenneth Donelson has called 'the chill factor'—the pre-selection and removal of books by teachers and librarians in anticipation of complaints."[8] Subsequently, in fact, two high school principals did remove two novels on their own because they felt sure parents would object to them. Periodically, the community conflict flares up again as some other books become at issue. (Incidentally, an organization called Renaissance Canada plays the same role in censorship there as the Moral Majority does in the United States.)

As a program only a year old, *Interaction* was being considered for adoption in many places at about the time the Kanawha fracas got publicity. This provided a fine cause for the national censorship network. A city that Houghton Mifflin salespeople considered a sure thing — Modesto, California — voted against adoption essentially because of an editorial appearing the day before in the *Modesto Bee* asking whether the citizens really wanted their children to read the immoral books that were thrown out of Charleston, West Virginia.

For several previous years the enlightened and dedicated language arts supervisors and coordinators of the Modesto Unified School District had been casting about for good ways to educate a student population comprising up to 50 percent, in some schools, children of migrant farm workers, mostly Chicano. Though the agricultural towns of California's San Joaquin Valley can be among the most conservative in the nation, the special difficulties of schooling in this district, where half the students may turn over between the start and close of a school year, had caused district curriculum leaders to reach out for innovation, having long ago discovered that traditional approaches were hopeless. These leaders were trying to get *Interaction* into their schools because it afforded the flexible methods and authentic materials that they felt could work where so much else had failed. (As late as 1980 the East Harlem district adopted *Interaction* for the same reasons.) They said after *Interaction* was voted down that the letter in the *Bee* made teachers anxious and was the main cause of the program's being defeated despite their own support.

We recall that the language arts specialists in both the West Virginia State Department of Education and Kanawha County had strongly favored *Interaction* but were overruled by public opinion. Fine! Schools should represent the will of the people, not of school administrators, as I have written in my books to educators. But the public is plural. The opinion that won out in Charleston and Modesto was of only one faction. Whether that faction was a minority or a majority makes no difference if school contradicts home. The "rule of the majority" does not hold when personal values and child-rearing are at stake. That in fact is a point about which the Kanawha protesters were certainly correct. Which means that when they win, others suffer a loss as great as the one they fear.

An extremely well organized campaign, replete with ringers from out of state, pulled off a similar feat on the eve of state adoption in Arizona, which till then had also been regarded as sure to adopt *Interaction* if for no other reason than that its neighbors, California and New Mexico, had already done so, and generally that southwestern bloc votes the same way (and includes, let's note, some of the most conservative citizenry in the nation). *Interaction* had been adopted by California the same year as the Kanawha row, by the largest vote ever accorded a textbook program there. But aside from the example of such an influential state, Arizona seemed very likely to adopt *Interaction* for some of the same curricular reasons that Modesto educators wanted it, since Arizona, too, has many migrant workers and students for whom English is a second language. While in San Antonio in '74 to deliver a lecture to a professional reading association I talked with company field consultants, who said that despite the unconventionality of *Interaction*, New Mexico teachers seemed to know instinctively what to do with the program and were happy with it.

What happened at the textbook hearings in Tucson is recounted in a letter from someone who was there.

> The Reading Reform Foundation, which was (and may still be) power-housed by one woman whose name I can't seem to dredge up from the memory bank, had a very good and direct pipeline to all of the Kanawha Co. activities and people. Many of the things which surfaced in newspapers around the country resurfaced in Arizona as part of the anti-nonphonics programs which had been submitted in the state adoption. On the day of the textbook hearings, the RRF people sat on one side of the room and "others" sat on the opposite side. RRF people also wore buttons with two unfurled American flags on the front and a statement around the edge which said something like "Concerned Citizens of Kanawha Co." These people (many of them simply parents and laity outside of the educational world) wanted only one program on the state list: *Open Court*, ostensibly because of its strong synthetic phonics program. Within their arguments, however, they got into all sorts of values judgments that went beyond their ridiculous declarations of "Phonics cured my daughter's asthma!" and "God believes in the beauty of phonics," etc., etc., etc. Truly, statements like these were actually made.[9]

(As a method, phonics tends to isolate and drill on the sounds of English as they are rendered by the spellings rather than to teach these "phonograph-emic" relations through actual texts, where meaning resides.) "These were educated people," this correspondent added, "who were fraught with lack of reason based on some inward sense of righteousness."

During the first weeks of the Kanawha outbreak the Tucson *Arizona Daily Star*, on September 26, 1974, had said in an editorial called "Militant Ignorance":

> There is reason to believe that what the militant miners in Kanawha County perceive to be against Americanism and Christianity merely is critical of their brand of white supremacy.
>
> The Kanawha County crusade for decency really is no better than an appeal to violent emotion and a plea for continued, blind ignorance. If the protesters succeed they will ensure another generation of stupidity.

A typical polarization occurred in Anchorage, Alaska, another town on the censorship circuits, with a direct line in fact to Kanawha County protesters. In April of 1975, while the Kanawha dispute dragged on, I was invited jointly by the University of Alaska and the Anchorage School District to do, as a regular paid consultant, a three-day credit course for teachers specifically on *Interaction*. This means that language arts specialists and education professors were trying to familiarize teachers with it in order to help bring it into the schools. They seemed totally unaware that the program they were enthusiastically advocating was at that moment being blacklisted by some of their constituents.

In January 1975, the Houghton Mifflin vice-president in charge of school textbooks wrote me, regarding the sales figures on *Interaction* for 1974:

> The West Virginia controversy and the general mood of the nation, coupled with the difficult economic conditions, have taken a toll and will probably continue to do so in 1975. We have had orders cancelled and sales returned primarily on the basis of the Kanawha County publicity. Much of that is balanced, however, by the continuing enthusiasm of those who have been using the total program.[11]

Actually, sales for 1975 increased over 1974 and made this third year the peak year of *Interaction*'s career. Nevertheless, in 1976, the company started phasing out portions of the materials and quit supporting *Interaction* generally. This means that it stopped advertising and other promoting such as workshops or significant booth displays and decided to let the program die on the vine except to the extent it might sell itself. When the home executive office takes this stand, the sales forces in the field tend to drop a program also and not to make further efforts with it in their school visits and their own promotion.

I was told by Houghton Mifflin that it follows a formula requiring a program of *Interaction*'s magnitude to gross, at that time, over $3,000,000 a year after the third year or be dropped. Since *Interaction* earned somewhat less than this in 1975, it failed by the formula despite great favor in the profession. In other words, the company dropped it after its best year because that year was not good enough. Of course such negative assumptions become self-fulfilling prophecies so that sales do in fact go down, as happened with *Interaction* the following year, 1976.

Many factors account for why *Interaction* did not go over in a big way (one of them being, I believe, this rigid corporation formula itself). Co-authors and I had always understood that its many innovations, most having little to do with reading content, might seriously limit the program's penetration into schools. But the Kanawha County uproar played a significant part in defeating our effort to reform the teaching of school's main subject.

It hurt us a great deal not only by lowering sales for the crucial third year enshrined in the formula but also by generally making company executives fear for the company's reputation and hence entire line of textbooks. For both personal and legal reasons they would of course never admit to sacrificing one program for the others, but company people have told me that sales representatives of all textbook publishers routinely bad-mouth their competitors to schools and therefore make certain when they go before selection committees or school principals to carry the glad tidings that so-and-so's books have been condemned as immoral. They know this will strike terror into the hearts of anyone holding public office or bound by the job to cope with the community.

The book dispute hurt us most not by influencing school people directly but by influencing company sales people. After the flurry of publicity settled, not many educators remembered which publishers and programs had been embroiled, *but in such cases the sales representatives never forget.* They remain traumatized and drop the offending program like a hot coal. A large textbook publisher offers programs that compete among themselves within each major market, that is, within each major school subject. It may make little difference to a salesperson *which* program he sells so long as he or she sells *one.*

The chief risk was put to me very forcefully by a salesman who said he didn't want to be associated with either *Interaction* or my name because when he went to a school to sell his line of other Houghton Mifflin books — in math, social studies, science, as well as English — he would be branded as representing the company that put out *those* books. The deadliest fear of salespeople is to become *persona non grata* in schools, for whatever reason, because then they simply cannot function. I feel sure that this fear causes them to exaggerate considerably, and to imagine effects far beyond, as I say, the memory of school people, who are focused other ways ordinarily. Still, one can understand that to be tainted with such emotional conflict as was enacted around Charleston could so jeopardize a representative's whole line that even an easily sellable program would not be worth the risk of association. Within six weeks I learned of three representatives under one regional sales office who refused to have anything to do with *Interaction*. This included unwillingness to set up a display of *Interaction* at the request of a conference host where I was the featured speaker and, in another case, not cooperating with a university education center that volunteered to research and promote *Interaction* itself.

So circular is the influence between home-office executives and field salespeople that it is quite possible that the company's decision to quit investing in *Interaction* was substantially influenced by the perception of negative field attitudes. If salespeople turn against a program, it's dead; the home office cannot control them. Then, of course, the home-office decision exerts a second negative effect on the field, and the original trouble amplifies itself as it goes full circle.

All this is not to say that the disturbance in Kanawha County necessarily caused the demise of *Interaction*, but it shows how far, through chain reaction, can reach such an incident of book-banning. All of the other new programs attacked there also lost momentum and were prematurely phased out or rendered innocuous by alterations. And nothing like them has come again.

3

Kanawha County and Orange County

Who, more precisely, were the book protesters? And how are they related to other Americans?

The *Charleston Gazette* conducted a poll of 386 voters the last week of September, asking, "How do you stand in the Kanawha County textbook controversy?" and tabulated 41.2 percent against the books, 31.6 percent undecided or unconcerned, and 27.2 percent for the books.[1] That three-fourths as many were undecided as opposed surely characterizes the situation at that point. Voting polarized predictably between the affluent Charleston hill sections such as Lowden Heights and the stretches of Kanawha Valley above and south of the city, other areas voting in between.

Newspaper polls in December and January got different results for elementary school — 70 percent opposed — than for secondary — 73 percent in favor.[2] So the age of the children determined substantially how much support the protest movement drew from the populace. In the elementary poll the geographical split was familiar. Four of the six schools that approved the books were in Charleston, out of a total of thirty, whereas in Alum Creek (the Rev. Avis Hill's home) only 9 of 378 parents favored the series, a typical vote for some outlying settlements.[3] Superintendent Underwood claimed that misinformation and fear would account for much of the adverse feeling.

It would have been interesting to know how the parents polled after emotion ran high, would have voted before all the brouhaha arose. We note that the earlier poll in September showed about 30 percent fewer opposed than the two later polls did and that most of the 31 percent undecided earlier seemed, two and three months later, to have sided against the books. At any rate, when in November the board sent forms home for parents to indicate the books they did not want their children to use, 65.5 percent of the parents of elementary children rejected *Com-*

municating, the basal 1–6 series, a figure only 5 percent below that of the newspaper's poll of elementary parents.[4]

An analysis of November election results showed that in the clean sweep Democrats made of all twenty-one offices, those candidates who sided with the protesters tended to receive considerably fewer votes. Dr. Charles Bertram, director of research and evaluation for the Appalachian Educational Laboratory, wrote in an internal paper that "the moderately high negative correlation would indicate that the protest movement does not have the support of the voting public that was generally believed by county residents."[5]

An interesting indicator was the behavior of mayors in the county. In September, when the Charleston mayor remained silent, the Upper Kanawha County Mayors Association called for withdrawal of the books and an end to picketing — not a neutral stance. Later they undertook measures to secede from the county in order to found their own school system. The mayor of South Charleston, the seat of massive chemical and refining works, said he hadn't read the books but if what he heard was true he vigorously opposed them. The mayor of Cedar Grove, which is near Cabin Creek in the Lower Valley, had his police chief serve a warrant for the arrest of Superintendent Underwood and members of the board for contributing to the delinquency of minors by making obscene books available within the school system. At one point in the boycott only 9 children of 922 in the Cedar Grove elementary school reported for class.

Attendance figures during the controversy constitute, in fact, another demographic indicator. Although *average* attendance in the county ranged from 70 percent to 90 percent during the periods of boycotting, it fell to 50 percent and often well below that in the creek areas and from South Charleston on through the Upper Kanawha Valley.

The settlements of the most intense feeling and dramatic incident were rural, folk Appalachian, and fundamentalist, but it is clear from all the same indicators that attitudes scaled along a gradient between them ("creekers") and Lowdon Heights ("hillers"), through industrial, blue-collar Nitro and South Charleston on into the poorer urban, white-collar and professional world of Charleston itself. The resistance to the book adoption mobilized a coalition of somewhat disparate bedfellows. Indeed, the social significance of the whole case lies in this resonance across classes and communities.

Elmer Fike, the aforementioned founder/president of the Business and Professional People's Alliance for Better Textbooks, told me that many antibook people "didn't want to become associated with some of the radical elements. There were some hillbilly preachers who took this thing and really made a career out of it."[6] Board member Alice Moore, the

"Sweet Alice" celebrated in song and placard by the ministers' followers, did not, at the time she first challenged the books, know the Rev. Marvin Horan, whose brand of violent activism she deplored but who probably did more than anyone besides herself to make the revolt so effective. She avoided appearing with him at the rallies of his Concerned Citizens, the major local antibook organization, of which he was leader and which put out the flier with the false excerpts. She seemed genuinely shocked by the dangerous and unruly physical means by which those she inflamed enacted her wish. But she too worked for the boycotts and the alternative schools. She encouraged the miners to go on wildcat strikes and said that without their cooperation the other groups would not have been able to mount and sustain such a protest. Indeed, there seems little question that what made the revolt work here whereas similar efforts elsewhere failed, was the tactics of the labor movement, applied by both miners and others who had learned from their struggles.

Like Alice Moore, Fike was not always comfortable with his allies. Publicly he deplored the violence, but he worked with the ministers and even tried to extend legal aid to Horan, the minister convicted of conspiring to fire-bomb schools. And like the ministers, all while repudiating the KKK, he spoke on the same platform with some of its members. Fike did not like the bad odor that these cohorts lent the cause. Hence the wording "Business and Professional People's" part of his organization's title. What is more important, he differs from the reverends in both ideas and motives. He warrants attention because he represents better than Alice Moore what kind of person we may find ranged between the bulk of the American public and those hellfire preachers in the hollows who may at first appear to this public as quaint and very different. He has a degree in chemical engineering, and as an informed, articulate, and skillful debater who also knows how to make money he clearly feels in a different class from the miners, factory hands, and fundamentalist preachers that his beliefs have cast him with.

He did not attempt to conceal his ideological differences with these collaborators. "Evolution does take place," he told me, for example, "there's no question about it. Anyone who says it doesn't just isn't thinking." The fundamentalists, he went on, are wrong to say the world started as described in Genesis. "The only question is whether God is directing it."[7] He carefully distinguished this from "random evolution," which he does not accept. He believes, as most Christians do, that Darwinian evolution is not opposed to religion. This position on a paramount issue for fundamentalists marks the gap between them and someone who, though sharing much of their regional culture, has undergone some scientific training and the conditions of corporate commerce.

The Reverends Avis Hill and Ezra Graley ran their own businesses, like Fike, and their mountaineer's defiance of law and government resembles too his fulminations against Washington, but I felt their conservatism was more social and moral, his more commercial and political. When I raised with Fike the contradiction of his denouncing the textbooks for "Un-Americanism" while constantly lambasting the federal government himself, he said, "Hell, nobody criticizes the government more than I do, but the textbooks weren't criticizing the government from the standpoint of the oppression and the excessive regulation. They were criticizing the free enterprise system." In other words, they weren't criticizing it for *his* reasons! Fike exhibited, I felt, a plain material self-interest not generally characterizing the fundamentalist protesters.

Mountaineers don't like central government because it disrupts their folkways and has never, throughout their history, seriously come to their aid. (The state and federal agencies charged with safety regulation in mines seldom do their job well, as the number of mine disasters shows.) Businessmen don't like it because it regulates and taxes them. Fike wants government to play a role that will increase, not threaten, his profits. The commercial brand of conservatism he represents allies itself with religious conservatism under the rubrics of anti-Communism and free enterprise and in a sincere sharing of other sentiments of chauvinistic mystique, including unavowed racism.

To begin to relate the participants in the Kanawha County dispute to citizens elsewhere, let's look now at some connections that formed between insiders and outsiders. As early as September an outside group had volunteered aid to the book protesters, an anti-sex education organization in Louisiana called The Hard Core Parental Group, claiming followers in all 50 states, which offered to send food, supplies, and cash.

The Heritage Foundation of Washington, D.C., sent into Kanawha County within a month of the opening of school its counsel, James McKenna, as legal aid to protesters who were getting arrested, chiefly for blocking the operation of school activities in defiance of court injunctions. He worked with the four fundamentalist ministers — Horan, Graley, Hill, and Quigley — who organized for October 6th in Charleston a statewide textbook rally that drew several thousand. Outside speakers besides McKenna were Mel and Norma Gabler, the self-appointed textbook evaluators, who run from their home a not-for-profit corporation called Educational Research Analysts in Longview, Texas, and by Robert Dornan of the Citizens for Decency Through Law in Los Angeles. Under this stimulation the local protest leaders began to plan a state campaign.

Dornan took a leave of absence later from CDL to return to Kanawha County and further support the protest movement. Back in California, he subsequently won election to Congress to represent Anaheim in Orange County, the western home of the John Birch Society and the home of a publisher of textbooks on creationism. His behavior seemed to epitomize for some people around the School Board how outsiders sometimes exploited their participation in the dispute.

Here is how the Gablers' biographer described their participation:

> Responding to an urgent West Virginia request, the Gablers flew to Charleston on October 5 for a whirlwind six-day speaking campaign. Both spoke at a city-wide rally to an estimated 8,000 persons the next afternoon (Sunday) in the Charleston ball park. The next day they separated, and were chauffeured up and down the valley, each speaking twice daily to groups of concerned parents.
>
> One morning Norma substituted for Alice Moore in an appearance before a Charleston women's group. . . .[8]

Hefley also mentions that "while the Gablers were in West Virginia they met with the minority members of the [Textbook] Review Committee for several hours."[9] Then proudly, at the beginning of his last chapter of the biography, Hefley writes:

> The Gablers were scarcely noticed by the national news media in West Virginia. Yet, according to leaders of the protest there, their contribution was significant. "They showed us how to document our objection to a bad text by page, paragraph, and column," says Larry Freeman, a minority member of the Textbook Review Committee.[10]

This minority group of the committee, which, as we saw, split off when they felt outnumbered, put together the book of objections that we will sample later on.

By exerting a very powerful influence on textbook adoption in the most profitable state for publishers, Texas, the Mel Gablers have in effect played a considerable role in restricting what gets published for American schools. Key adoptions like California (alone one-tenth of the United States market) and Texas, both of which provide leadership for other states, determine to an alarming degree what the rest of the nation will be offered. But whereas California adopts such a broad listing that little is excluded, Texas adopts only up to five publishers' programs for each school subject, and those chosen stay in for five years. Given these conditions, to fail to get adopted in Texas is tantamount to disaster in most cases, and publishers will stop at little to ensure against failure. (It is an indication of how calculated a gamble *Interaction* was that it was conceived with no regard for the Texas adoptions, which require hard covers. We knew from the outset that our ungraded classroom libraries of paperback books would not pass there.) Texas procedures include public hearings before the state Board of Education at which objectors may criticize the books and publishers defend them. Written objections, "bills of particulars," may be submitted to the State Board and be rebutted by publishers in writing. Although salespeople not specialists in the subjects are not the best people to defend the books, the procedures are on the whole a democratic way of creating a forum before adoption.

The fact that the Gablers have utilized these procedures so effectively and lobbied in other ways so successfully should not be a cause for complaint. Not only are they in their rights, as Alice Moore was also in her utilization of the Gablers in turn, but democracy would be best served if other parents showed as much interest in their children's education. The public must understand that to an alarming degree the rest of the United States lives with the results of negotiations between the Texas Education Agency and the textbook publishers, conducted under pressure from people like the Gablers. Those chapters, selections, passages, and phrases deleted or altered for Texas will almost certainly be absent in offerings to other school systems because changing plates is expensive. Furthermore, having passed in Texas becomes a selling point elsewhere, a proof that a program has been sanitized against conservative complaints.

Only equally strong pressure from other big markets can cause publishers to put out alternative forms of a book or a program. In 1986 California's commissioner of education, William Honig, refused to accept any of the publishers' offerings in science because they all had seriously compromised the presentation of evolution to placate creationists. This stand threw the industry into consternation: it had to choose between losing a lucrative market or creating, at much expense, alternative science books.

CBS' "Sixty Minutes" showed on a program in 1980 how the Gablers screen and blacklist textbooks and quoted the vice-president of a major publisher attesting to the danger a company like his risks in persisting against their disapproval. Editors keep the Gablers' bills of particulars before them as they work. "The Gablers are the two most important people in education," asserted Edward B. Jenkinson, former chair of the National Council of Teachers of English Committee Against Censorship. "In 1978 they shot down 18 of the 28 books up for adoption in Texas."[11]

This background explains why the visit and consultations of the Gablers were of great importance to the Kanawha County protesters. Through the Gablers a spontaneous local revolt became part of a national network long in operation but just fully savoring its power.

In an issue noting this power in 1979, *Parade* linked the Gablers with the other most significant organization to get involved in Kanawha County, the Heritage Foundation, also represented at the October 8 rally:

Another writer and traveling "consumer advocate" for education is Dr. Onalee McGraw, education consultant for The Heritage Foundation. . . . The Gablers and Dr. McGraw keep in touch with hundreds of state and local groups concerned with improving education: Parents Rights, Inc. in St. Louis; Guardians of Education in Maine; and Let's Improve Today's Education in Arizona—to name a few.[12]

Writing on United States House of Representatives stationery, Congressman Phillip Crane of Illinois' Twelfth District sent out form letters on December 2nd, 1974, summarizing the conflict so as to martyrize the jailed protesters. An enclosed flier was headed, "Police Brutality Used to Intimidate Charleston Textbook Protest." While asking for contributions to defray legal fees and other costs of the foundation's work, Crane wrote:

> The Heritage Foundation in Washington is helping the parents of Charleston regain their right to control the education of their children. Through the legal assistance of their lawyer, Heritage has been in Charleston courts defending protesting parents who have gone to jail for their beliefs. . . .
> Heritage has received inquiry from other parts of the country where parents share the same concern as the Charleston protestors. Legal action may be undertaken in those places. . . .
> I sincerely hope you will be able to help Heritage stop forcing pornography and other objectionable subjects into schools all over America.[13]

The copy of the letter that happened to fall to me was addressed to a construction company in Tennessee.

> As a member of the U.S. Congress I would like to know what books are being used in the Nashville area schools, since federal funds go to almost every public school system in the country. A textbook survey is enclosed so you can let me know if you have any information about this.[14]

(Nashville is one of many cities in the Deep South where *Interaction* was used without outcry or outrage. "Several textbooks under protest in the West Virginia 'book banning' have been used in Metro [greater Nashville] schools for several years without complaint, Metro's coordinator of Language Arts said.")[15] The Heritage Foundation developed—and reinforced—strong ties with members of the administration of Ronald Reagan, within two years of whose inauguration, according to the American Library Association, complaints about books in public libraries increased fivefold.

Other outside organizations that became involved in Kanawha County were, on the rightist side, the National Parents Organization, the

John Birch Society, Guardians of Traditional Education, the Ku Klux Klan, and, on the left, the Young Socialist party and the International Workers party. The Rev. Quigley told Catherine Candor-Chandler "that without outsiders he doubted that more than one hundred people from Kanawha County would have been involved in the protest at this point in time."[16] That point in time was November, when these groups came in and when the decision to return the books to classrooms had been made (on the 8th).

At the end of November protesters held in Charleston a national textbook rally at which featured speaker the Rev. Carl McIntire, a fundamentalist, chastized politicians for not coming out on the side of the protesters. In December the Reverends Horan, Hill, and Graley met in Washington with Congressman Roger Zion, R-Indiana, who read into the *Congressional Record* alleged material from the disputed Kanawha County textbooks and introduced a bill permitting citizens to examine any book in a school and to recall school board members.

At the request of the Kanawha County Association of Classroom Teachers, the National Education Association sent into the county in December a blue-ribbon national panel to conduct an inquiry for three days. The NEA is a large and powerful advocate of educators based in Washington, D.C. In its report a few months later this team supported the board's selection of language arts materials but criticized it for knuckling under (by removing the books in September), which makes "censors of parents" and constitutes "an abdication of the board's legal obligation to maintain responsible control of the schools."[17]

The NEA panel recommended that school authorities offer alternative schooling in "traditional teaching methods" and open up channels for a more sensitive communication with its rural constituents. It also advised the state legislature to stave off inroads on teachers' rights to select materials, give legal authority to the Kanawha board's mandate for multicultural content, and pass a bill requiring as a certification standard that the training of teachers include courses in human relations and multiethnic education.[18]

Concerned Citizens of Kanawha County and the Business and Professional People's Alliance for Better Textbooks held in January of 1975 three days of hearings of their own before a local panel. The resulting report was to go to citizens of Kanawha County and to Congress in Washington. Out-of-state speakers came from an Arizona publication, the Arizona legislature, the Heritage Foundation, Parents of New York United, the National Parents League (an Oregon-based organization which assists formation of parent-run schools to avoid corruption of children in public schools), Fordham and George Washington universities, a Maryland parents organization called CURE, and a member of a Maryland board of education, among others.

On January 18, the day after the Rev. Horan and five others were indicted by a federal grand jury for conspiracy to blow up two elementary schools and other School Board property

nearly two hundred protesters gathered at the State Capitol to welcome the Ku Klux Klan to Charleston. Rev. Horan, free on bail, and Ed Miller, founder of the Non-Christian American Parents group, appeared with Dale Reush, grand dragon of the National Knights of the Ku Klux Klan of Ohio, and James Venable, imperial wizard of the National Knights of the Ku Klux Klan from Stone Mountain, Georgia. Visiting Klansmen, in full dress with robes and hoods, held a brief rally on the steps of the State Capitol before proceeding to an indoor rally at the Charleston Civic Center where the number of spectators more than doubled. Venable told protesters that the "Communist, Socialist, nigger race is going to dominate this nation." Visiting Klansmen pledged support of Kanawha County protesters, including possible legal aid for Rev. Horan and told the Charleston audience to apply for membership in the KKK.[19]

Not only did the local NAACP, the state Human Rights Commission, and the mayor of Charleston denounce the KKK involvement but also Elmer Fike's antibook organization, the Business and Professional People's Alliance for Better Textbooks. In March a contingent of over 70 Kanawha County protesters joined with Boston antibusing forces in a Washington rally to oppose federal intervention in local school districts.

By far, the majority of outsiders contributing to the controversy represented the right wing. Among the five factors beyond the control of the School Board that fueled the conflict, Candor-Chandler counts outside intervention. In a press release of February 6, 1975, the NEA said that its panel

concluded that the protest would not have been as prolonged and intense had it not been "infiltrated by representatives of highly sophisticated, well-organized right-wing extremist groups. . . .

These groups, which have provided legal, organizational, and financial assistance in the textbook conflict, are either directly associated or in apparent close sympathy with the John Birch Society, NEA charged.

The protest would not have been as unyielding and violent had the educational materials in dispute not been multi-ethnic and multi-cultural in content, according to the NEA report.

After reviewing many of the protestors' objections to writings by or about blacks, the NEA panel concluded that the protest is, at least in part, "a reaction to the black presence in America."[20]

To this statement was attached a list that mentions groups I've already referred to.

By "the protest" NEA seems to mean only the turmoil following the opening of school, not the controversy and demonstrations of the preceding spring and summer. In the longer perspective, outside intervention occurred relatively late, as I've indicated, at least overtly enough to make itself known to others than the dissenters. I think a fair assessment of the role of outsiders would not assume they fomented the original outcry but that they eagerly seized on the book dispute to expand a previously existing network of textbook surveillance and to strengthen more general conservative movements.

The involvement of outsiders in the Kanawha County dispute gives some idea of how much the feelings and beliefs enacted there are shared by others across the continent. It would be a serious mistake not to recognize the consonance between the attitudes of some of the poorest, least educated people in America and those of some of the wealthiest and best educated, because this psychological kinship spanning socioeconomic differences lays the basis for an alignment of forces that often determines United States policy and hence that may help decide the planetary future. It welds religion with economics and politics; that is, it confuses spiritual with material motives.

The relationship between Elmer Fike and his fundamentalist allies parallels a relationship between Orange County in California and Kanawha County, dissimilar as the two regions may appear on the surface. Between Los Angeles and San Diego, protected from Pacific fogs by the low coastal hills, thrive in warm hollows and along sunny slopes those grand groves of glossy-leaved oranges and avocados. Magnificent Mediterranean-style homes with red-tile roofs spill purple ice-plants down their cliff yards to the ocean itself. The string of well-to-do beach towns culminating in La Jolla, by San Diego, are playgrounds filled with yachting marinas, seafood restaurants, hibiscus, and fancy boutiques. This stretch of shore and hinterland contains some of the wealthiest and most conservative citizens of the United States (along with the poor Chicanos who work their lands and service their households). The former range from ranch owners to millionaire celebrities to retired admirals. Orange County itself, which contains Robert Dornan's congressional district, a publisher of creationist textbooks, and the western home of the John Birch Society, occupies that portion of the stretch between Long Beach and Camp Pendleton, the Santa Ana Mountains and the sea. It includes, besides the one large city of Santa Ana, San Clemente, where Richard Nixon lived in a beach mansion which he was accused of unlawfully improving at taxpayers' expense; Newport Beach, which drew spotlights during the Watergate proceedings as the home of John and Martha Mitchell; Anaheim, the site of Disneyland; and the famous old mission beach town of San Juan Capistrano, to which the swallows return.

Although it is impossible for me to describe unsatirically the tanned

and gilded life of this area, I have to say that some of the most impressive
people I've met in education circles have been in Orange County. At the
turn of the sixties into the seventies, before *Interaction* came out, I consulted several times in the Newport Beach–Costa Mesa Unified School
District, where secondary school people wanted to work into classrooms
the curriculum I was developing in literature, drama, and writing. Later,
I filmed for *Interaction* some remarkable activities in choral reading and
theater improvisations that teachers had set in motion at Laguna Beach
High. Principals and teachers were intelligent, sophisticated, and tal-
ented like many others from Orange County I have known through the
California Association of Teachers of English or met at various conventions and conferences. The faculty of the English Department of the University of California at Irvine had me there in the early seventies and
later in the eighties to discuss English curriculum and teacher training.
They too were questing, receptive, and flexible. Because of the wealth,
Orange County can attract such teachers. Because of its sophistication it
asks for creative schooling — or did then, at any rate.

But this represents only one side of this very curious county. Its people, like those of Kanawha County, are divided over values. While a
playland like Newport Beach is not a working city like Anaheim, no
more than Charleston is Campbell's Creek, nevertheless conflict does not
all come down to gross socioeconomic or cultural differences. As
Charleston split within itself, so did Anaheim, which was another of
those communities that convulsed itself over school books in the wake of
the Kanawha County revolt.

> Part of the 33,000-student Union High School district in Anaheim, Cal. —
> the largest west of the Mississippi — voted to secede and form its own school
> district after the Union school board banned sex and drug education and a
> course on women's liberation. The board eliminated flexible scheduling;
> required seniors to take a course called "Free Enterprise," which reportedly
> includes attacks on government interference in society and excludes discus-
> sions of unions; banned from high school reading lists all of Shakespeare's
> works except *Hamlet* and *Romeo and Juliet*; banned all of Charles Dickens'
> works except *Oliver Twist*; and found all but one of Mark Twain's works
> "unsuitable."[21]

So here is another large school district pulled apart by its divergent
factions. And it is not even the whole county but just one urban area of
it. How finely can one analyze conflict into social differences before the
differences become merely individual differences within the same class,
before outer conflict becomes inner, and we are faced with personal
ambivalence. My impression is that many parents in these conflicted districts, like many elsewhere, really want creative schooling that will

expand the consciousness of their children but yet fear losing the minds of their children to the minds they will meet in books. A little learning *is* a dangerous thing.

For various and sometimes amusing reasons my name has wound up on mailing lists for fervid organizations located in Orange County. While on sabbatical leave in 1961 from Phillips Exeter Academy in New Hampshire, my wife and I rented for the year a house in the San Francisco Bay area from an eccentric right-wing dowager who still had a locked closet full of hoarded sugar from World War II. (Such instances restore the meaning of "conservative.") While cruising the world she subscribed us, without our knowledge, to *The Cross and the Flag*, put out by the once infamous Gerald L. K. Smith, a rabid hatemonger from the Deep South who had found a home in Orange County. This magazine, which called even Dwight Eisenhower a Communist, spat into our home each month an astonishing poison against blacks, Jews, and Catholics — explicit and unabashed diatribes.

Over a decade later, after I was residing in California and lobbying vigorously with other teachers against the installation in the state school system of Planning, Programming, and Budgeting Systems, I began receiving literature from conservative organizations in Orange County and elsewhere in Southern California. Since Washington was railroading PPBS into states, the movement became identified as a familiar cause — the undue intervention of federal government into local affairs. I have more than once decried a tendency to employ federal funding to standardize and mechanize the curriculum across the nation. By denouncing PPBS with colleagues before the California Department of Education I had become a conservative hero! (It's perhaps germane to mention that the largest audience to which I ever spoke about PPBS — or any other subject, I'm afraid — was in the Anaheim Convention Center, where the Southern California Council of Teachers of English had sponsored a special conference to halt this federal invasion.) My reward for coinciding with a conservative view — and this happens naturally from time to time because I don't try to line up either right or left — was to be pelted by literature advocating patriotic chauvinism, militarism, federal deregulation of business, free enterprise, anti-Communism, and other noneducational planks in the familiar platform. Then purely as an author in English education I received newsletters and newspapers from phonics foundations, who always attack the "look-say" method (as Elmer Fike does) in a simplistic, evangelical crusade that exults in its own partisanship.

Predictably, these organizations center in Orange County or the Phoenix area of Arizona. These are places, like San Diego and certain other localities in the Southwest, where for a long time people have been retiring, many wealthy but many not. Orange County I see as a handy symbol for these rightist sites. Age and wealth partly account for why these become conservative strongholds, but the Southwest also has strong traditions from settler days of a hacienda aristocracy among big ranchers that dislikes drifters and foreigners, resists sharing its land, and prides itself on lineage. This blood-and-soil mentality differs not greatly from Appalachian heritage. Neither in turn differs, except perhaps in intensity and concentration, from similar traditions elsewhere in America — Yankee in New England, Antebellum in the Deep South, or Old World immigrant in the Midwest. The resonance between elements of Orange County and elements of Kanawha County tells us clearly that mountaineers are not freaks.

The affinity between these two otherwise disparate counties seems less remarkable when one considers how many Americans share opinions with the book dissenters. Of 1,518 adults polled by George Gallup Jr.'s organization in 300 areas of the United States during the early 1980s, 44 percent accepted as true the statement that, "God created man pretty much in his present form at one time within the last ten thousand years," which is a creationist credo. One-fourth of these people had graduated from college.[22]

Dimensions of Tolerance, a study conducted during the late 1970s by political scientist Herbert McClosky of the University of California at Berkeley and scholar Alida Brill of the Russell Sage Foundation, revealed that less than 40 percent of the American public consistently supports such civil liberties as free speech, free assembly, and due process of law. Sampling not only the general public but also judges and lawyers, community leaders, government officials, and police, the researchers found that even fewer Americans tolerate assertion of civil liberties by unpopular groups such as minorities and homosexuals.[23]

Perhaps the strongest single indicator of how much many other Americans agree with the West Virginia book protesters is the extraordinary popularity of Ronald Reagan, who was not only supported by some of the same organizations that aided them but whose platform, virtually plank by plank, coincides with their views and values. Though launched into politics by Southern California millionaires, Reagan gradually won over people of all classes, even those hurt by his economic policies, as the republic reacted to postwar changes and drifted into the retrenchments of anxiety.

But, shifts in the public psyche aside, we all think too narrowly, are overattached to the things of our little world, to our own blood and soil, in an age when even our everyday fixation of ideas and customary loyalties may cost us the world itself. Anybody whose understanding is incomplete is partial, and whoever is partial is avoiding knowing something, is censoring. So let us listen more closely to what book banners say. They more nearly harp the thought of mainstream America than first appears. They utter that part of everyone that forms the only conspiracy that can ever hurt us.

Ballad of Kanawha County
Mary Rose (alias)

(*Textbook War—Hills of West Virginia*, a record album by Pastor Avis Hill and company.)

Chorus: Sweet Alice, Little Avis, Graley, Quigley, Horan,
           What are you doin' in them mountains stirrin' up a storm?
           Don't you know you're rousin' people 'round the U.S.A.,
           Tellin' folks right from wrong and God-fearin' ways?

Our bridges fell in, the dams gave way, and they strip-mined our
           beautiful hills.
We turned our cheek when the bridges blew up, but they even blew our
           stills.

Chorus

Yes, we turned our cheeks seventy times seven, we did not resist
Till they came for the souls of our precious ones, and now we're gonna
           resist.
Now they come for our kids with the dirty books and their one-world
           plan,
But they got a surprise from us mountain folk, because now the Lord
           said stand.
Well, first to come were the miners from the deep dark bowels of the
           earth.
They know what it is to trust in the Lord for their every breath.

Chorus

Next to come was the NEA, the textbook leaders of our land.
They said our religion was due to the hills; we needed help and more
           plans.
Well, we always thought our help came from God, Jesus, and the Holy
           Spirit too.
As for professional help, we've had it for years without believing in the
           ACLU.

Chorus

One nasty cold night at a School Board meetin' the superintendent was
           there.
They pulled out a plug, excitement broke out, fists flying everywhere.
One board member hid under a table, and the superintendent went
           down.

Then an angry mountain mama mashed his face. Would you believe that
    super left town?

Chorus

On February 22nd of *The Daily World* out spoke the Communists:
"You're racist," they said, "and know nothing too, and you're backed by
    big business.
The books are fine, they mean a decent education, a break for academic
    freedom."
But what they *really* mean is, "Read the books, kids, and we'll soon have
    your nation."

Chorus

Now Supreme Court judges we never voted for way over there in
    Washington,
Some folks said they committed treason for the shape our nation's in.
You can't pray in school, you can kill a baby, you can bus the kids for
    hours on end.
It's OK to fight an undeclared war and find out that men aren't men.

Chorus

Now listen, America, you might give in to the Supreme Court mess,
But we're standing for God, children, and country, liberty, and
    happiness.
So if you're a believer, not just a pretender, for the Lord Jesus Christ,
Throw out the dirty books, stand up for the Lord and your child's eternal
    life.

Chorus

PART 2
VOICES FROM
THE FRAY

4

Father, Make Them One

Exactly eight years after the textbooks were formally adopted I interviewed in Charleston three protest leaders and a member of the school district's central staff. I was mainly concerned to hear what protesters said in their own words, but for perspective I wanted the view of at least one person on the other side and of a different cast of mind.

To the three antitextbook people—the Rev. Ezra Graley, Elmer Fike, and the Rev. Avis Hill—I gave my real name and purpose. I did not volunteer to say that I was one of the textbook coauthors, but I was prepared to say so if they asked. Graley did in fact ask, when I said I was in education, "You didn't put out any of them dirty books we had here, did you?" I said I did produce some of the books, but they weren't dirty. He didn't seem inclined to pursue that, and so we both just dropped it for good.

Hill, Graley, and Fike have all been on CBS's "Sixty Minutes" and the "Phil Donahue Show" as well as other talk shows and have given countless interviews to newspeople including the BBC and other foreign media. They were veterans by the time I got to them and readily made themselves available.

Alice Moore had moved away by the time I visited there, and the Rev. Marvin Horan, who had long since finished his prison sentence, told me he did not have time for an interview. I think their views are well represented by the remarks of their cohorts. Another important figure had moved away, James Lewis, the rector of St. John's Episcopal Church in Charleston, whose articulate and persistent opposition to the protesters generated a pastoral duel. All three of the protesters I interviewed talked about him with anything but indifference. He clearly had got under their skin. Surely, the fact that a Christian minister could support such books, not to mention other causes they regarded as equally unsavory, accounts for much of their intense and somewhat puzzled feeling about him. His words deserve sampling. In a feature article that ran in many newspapers around the country he wrote:

> Steeped in the belief that there is only one way to salvation, these Christians also maintain that there is only one way to education. Unhappy with a

language-arts program which develops verbal skills by utilizing role-playing and open-end discussion, the opposition demands a rigid system of education by mechanical learning. To them, education is not a process of drawing a student out, but of pouring facts in.

The antitextbook people of Kanawha County are confused and angry about everything from marijuana to Watergate. Feeling helpless and left out, they are looking for a scapegoat. They are eager to exorcise all that is evil and foul, cleanse or burn all that is strange and foreign. In this religious war, spiced with overtones of race and class, the books are an accessible target.

For people who are fearful of the fire of hell and ready for a fire which cleanses and purifies, the clean white pages of the now-famous books make good fuel. What they forget is that the smoke from such a blaze will linger for a long time in this valley. The pollutants of nearby chemical plants, which hover over the Kanawha River, may do harmful things to the body, but the fumes of burning books are capable of destroying a man's soul, the very soul the people want so desperately and passionately to save.[1]

I visited Ezra Graley in his home just off Dupont Lane outside the town of Nitro. (The names tell their own story!) This is a pleasant backwater, a lane's end on the Kanawha facing St. Albans on the opposite shore. These two towns in the Upper Valley played a big role in the controversy. Graley runs his roofing business out of his home with the aid of two strapping sons. His machines and vehicles line the lane leading to his house, which is a cut above the neighbors' frame cottages—a larger, newer, and more substantial brick house opening out in back onto a spacious lawn spreading down to the Kanawha. It's quiet around here except for the occasional crowing of a rooster.

A burly man in his mid-fifties then, the Rev. Graley was the pastor of the Summit Ridge Church of God, a part-time pastor like virtually all of the unaffiliated fundamentalist preachers of that area. He was easy to talk with, and we were both comfortable. He spoke quietly and deliberately in the semi-Southern accent of Appalachia. I have quoted him at length in order to capture as much as possible the personality and the movements of mind of this very representative personage.

GRALEY: We had a lot of people come in that we didn't invite in like the KKK and the NAACP. They come in. When we started off it was just a couple ministers, or three ministers trying to get good textbooks in our schools, and it growed and growed and finally it went nationwide and probably news of it, I know, went worldwide, but it grew into a big thing and then some of the more radical groups got into it, see. A lot of them didn't pretend to be Christians, but they was interested in their school, their children's education, and there's none of us in West Virginia, and still I don't know of *anybody*, that really thinks them four-letter words and all that cussing belongs in a classroom, or in textbooks. . . . They haven't give them any education. It's taught them anti-everything. Just about everything in the textbooks was *anti* — anti-authority, government, parents, or any kind of authority. So we was against that 100 percent, and still are.

MOFFETT: You felt free in your struggle, though, to resist authority too didn't you, in the sense that you didn't accept the decision of the School Board and you did break some injunctions and so on. I'm not saying it was wrong, I'm saying you felt that there are times when you're right in challenging authority.

GRALEY: Oh yes, there's times that you're right. You know, a lot of people say that it says in the Bible, "Obey the laws of your land," but I never found that in the Bible and I'm a minister of twenty-five years. I've never found where it said, "Obey the laws of your land," because in the old Bible, Moses he defied the king, and Daniel defied the king's decree, and the Hebrew children did, and then you come on down into the New Testament, Paul, when they tried to get him not to speak, that it was against their law, he said, "What's better — for me to mind God or man?" And I think that we are to obey laws as long as them laws don't conflict with our worship of God or try to do away with our God.

MOFFETT: I think there are a lot of people who would accept that principle of obeying a spiritual law over a human law. The problem comes that equally sincere people have different notions of spiritual law, and then you get into conflict. This is what concerns me.

GRALEY: Yeah now, I think though it's people more or less don't know what the Bible says. They're good Christian people, seem like, but they said, "Well we'll do ours a-praying, we'll pray about ours, we'll pray about our problems and let *God* work them out." Well I'm sure Joshua prayed about his problem, but he had to march around Jericho seven times, you know, and Gideon prayed about his problems, but he also went then. . . .

MOFFETT: Well, Christians can agree that the Bible is an inspired work of God, but they go to it and they come back with different things. I can see it's partly maybe because people are at different stages of their development.

GRALEY: I think it's just a lack of understanding really, cause I know a lot of things that I stood for or against back when I first started out for God, I have studied more deeply in the Bible and I've changed my mind on a lot of things, you know, that I would have died for back then.

MOFFETT: A lot of people have said this, that the reason that they do Bible study year after year is the Bible deepens in meaning as they mature and as they study and they grow, but what it means is that people are going to interpret it differently at different times. It seems to me the practical problem is what do we do about this? Is there something we should learn from the book controversy about how to get along with people who interpret the Bible differently?

GRALEY: I really believe that if everybody that's truly been borned again—like Jesus said, "You must be borned again"—I believe if they're truly borned again, I think they'll see the word of God just about the same, because I don't think that it was written to cause divisions; it was written to—and Jesus prayed in his prayer, "Father, make them one, even as you and I are one." And I think these people don't want to see it, or don't see it in a holy light, is just people who don't want to live a good life, just wants to play around the banks, you know. [Laughs.]

MOFFETT: You're saying then that if the interpretation is different that they're not being really serious?

GRALEY: I don't believe that they're really serious if their interpretation —now, I know some of these people up here that was against us and fought, stood up against us, they went along and blessed homosexuals and everything else. He said he didn't marry them, but he blessed their relationship. [The Episcopalian minister, the Rev. James Lewis.]

MOFFETT: Were there, say, a number of people who opposed you who were just ordinary Christians?

GRALEY: Yes, now the Methodists, you know, they belong to the World Council of Churches and they go along with a lot of this stuff, and some of the Presbyterians, but even in our own church I had a lot of conflict there. People thought I had no business out there, standing up for what I felt was definitely right and others thought it was right.

MOFFETT: Well, that's a different thing, whether to be activist or stay out of it. I mean a different interpretation, understanding. How did you account for the fact that there were other sincere Christians who didn't feel the same about the books? Did that bother you?

GRALEY: No, no, at that time, you see, the news media gave it on the liberal side, we feel, and they made us—they tried to make us look as though we was people that didn't believe in education, to start with, we was book burners. But you turn it right around and the same news media didn't say a word and tell the public about them burning truck loads of Bibles that they confiscated in our schools, took them out to the incinerator and burned them.

MOFFETT: Who did that?

GRALEY: The Board of Education gathered them up and took them out there. Alice Moore found some of the books—some of the Bibles, partially burnt, where they was there when they dumped them in the incinerator. All right, now who—.

MOFFETT: Where did they get the Bibles? They weren't supposed to be *in* the schools, were they?

GRALEY: Oh yes, they was Bibles in schools till Madalyn O'Hair got the Supreme Court to rule against prayer and Bible reading in schools.

MOFFETT: Were there other ways in which you felt some of the real stories that you know of the controversy did not come out through the press?

GRALEY: This was the main thing. Now, good Christian people, they had been taught all their life that they was not to defy the law in any way. They was to obey the law regardless of what the law said, and it wasn't just people out in the country. I heard a minister, one of the prominentest ministers we've got in the U.S. today, and the best man I know of that's against all this stuff and doing more for our country I feel than anybody, is Jerry Falwell, but I heard him make a remark one time that somebody called this Betty Ford a slut (laughs), and he said anybody that was a Christian should never talk about a dignitary or something like that. Well . . . the verse of Scripture come to me right then that Jesus when Herod, Kind Herod, sent and told him to get out of town, he said, "You go tell that old fox I do curse today and tomorrow this city and then I'll leave." But he called Herod a fox, Jesus did, and so people today — it's just a teaching I guess they had that they was not to defy the law regardless, and I brought out to my church at that same time — the Supreme Court sent word down to West Virginia University that the doctors out there would abort upon demand or lose their license, and they said they would not abort even if it meant losing their license. So these doctors defied the Supreme Court, which was the highest court of the land, see? And I asked my church, I said, "Now was they right by saying, 'We're not going to murder them little innocent unborn babies?' Or would they have been right to have went ahead because the Supreme Court told them to and abort them babies?" Of course they agreed they was right by not doing it.

MOFFETT: Some of the objections to the textbooks were that they were part of a Communist conspiracy or plot. Do you believe that?

GRALEY: Yes, I thought it was a Communist conspiracy.

MOFFETT: Can you say any more about that?

GRALEY: Not really, because Eldridge Cleaver wrote a lot of it, a lot of those books, and where was he at? He was in a Communist country, see, at that time. Sure, I felt it was to destroy the family, the morals and the family, and I still believe that that's what it's all about, and our television programs is geared right up with the textbooks.

MOFFETT: Who do you feel was behind that kind of a plan, through the textbooks?

GRALEY: Well, to pinpoint the thing, I don't know. I couldn't — cause you'd go to the U.S. Congress and senators and they'd let on like it's local, and you come to the local officials and they'd say, "Well, we have nothing to do with it, it's got to go back up—it's federally funded," and all that. You go back up to the federal and they just pass the buck around. Some of them maybe innocently didn't even know what was in the books, and probably didn't bother with finding out.

MOFFETT: Well, the publishers themselves, as you know, are big capitalist corporations. That's kind of a funny thing too, the idea they might be part of a Communist conspiracy. Those are not Mom-and-Pop operations. Do you think they've somehow been made unwitting tools?

GRALEY: Yeah, but maybe they had—maybe Eldridge Cleaver and Malcolm X and all them people had raised so much cain, maybe they had enough power or influence over the federal government that they would threaten these publishing companies with federal fund withdrawal if they didn't print their books or something, I don't know.

MOFFETT: You feel the federal government may have—?

GRALEY: I feel the federal government had the most to do in it, cause at that time our Congress and Senate, I think got full of—if not Communists, socialist people, you know, if there's any difference in that word. (Laughs)

MOFFETT: Wouldn't it bother you though if there were remarks made in the textbooks that blamed our federal government?

GRALEY: No, not the government that was in at that time, no sir, not when we couldn't even fight a war over there against the Communists and when they allow Jane Fonda to go over there and run free in North Vietnam against our troops. To me this was an act of treason and she pulled no bones about what she is.

MOFFETT: Well, if we say it's OK to criticize the government sometimes but not other times, maybe depending on which administration is in, that would really lead to a mess, wouldn't it?

GRALEY: You know right from wrong, and I know right from wrong, and we was all taught right from wrong, and now there is no right and wrong. It's do whatever turns you on, you know, there is no positives or absolutes now. . . .

* * *

MOFFETT: Do you see a difference between whether the author of the book is saying something, or whether a *character* in one of the stories is saying something? Do you feel a difference there?

GRALEY: No, I don't feel that them curse words and four-letter words has any place in the vocabulary, in our school system period. Now if they want to downgrade theirself or degrade or demoralize theirself enough to put it in the college books that'd be all right maybe, cause they're adults. I don't think they should do it with the taxpayers' money, at all.

MOFFETT: Looking at the objections to the selections themselves — and I've been through that book that was put out by the splinter group of the Textbook Review Committee — not even half of those objections were based on the language. There were a lot of different things they objected to. Did you feel that the language was the most serious?

GRALEY: No sir, I felt the anti-family, anti-authority was the main thing because — children, who do they obey now? Nobody. They always say, "Do your thing. Do whatever turns you on." Regardless of what anybody says about it. So they're doing it now.

MOFFETT: I know some of the high school kids, I guess, in Charleston, were quoted as saying — some of them got mad because the books were taken out — that people objected to violence in the books but didn't object to violence in real life, referring to some of the barricades and the blocking and the fire-bombing and so on. In other words, they seemed to be influenced by what I think all kids are influenced by — what adults do, maybe more than what adults say, or what they read in a book.

GRALEY: Probably their parents that stood up for those books, regardless if they was Communist or socialists or what, or some kind of religious group. I feel that them children, if they were borned and raised that way, you know good and well they're going to go along with what Mom and Dad say is, about 90 percent of the time. Sure, my boys, if I told them the governor wasn't any good, then you ask them do they think he is, and they'd say, "No, I don't like him." And you'd ask them why: "Well, Dad said he wasn't no good," see?

MOFFETT: I think what you're saying is true, that the family influence is very powerful. In other words, how strong are books compared to the real people that you grow up among?

GRALEY: I think in school the influence of the textbook is far greater than the influence of the home.

MOFFETT: Really?

GRALEY: Yes sir, because they have them children six or seven hours a day drilling this into them. A parent — if a father works he comes in tired and he may spend 15 or 20 minutes with his child and in devotion or just sitting down telling them the facts of life, and he may not spend any time, but the schools got them every day there. And what I can't understand — now they said, "Well, why fight them in school? You got it on television, you've got these X-rated movies." All right, you've got to be eighteen to go to X-rated movies, and after you become eighteen there's no one that's going to get you by the arm and force you to go, or make you go to a movie, to see a X-rated movie. All right on TV, if it's on there and I'm a parent here and I want my kid to watch it, that's all right, watch it. But when the compulsory school attendance law *makes* them children come, sit in a classroom under this teaching and all these bad words and indoctrination going on in the classroom — they're forced to do that. So there's a lot of difference in school textbooks and the movies here at the theaters or what they show on television. . . .

MOFFETT: Have you talked with some parents on the other side of the fence who say they *do* want books in there that have, let's say, black stories that have some street language, because they want their kids to know how those people live?

GRALEY: About 90 percent of the people I've talked to that was absolutely against us doing the textbook protest, and even stood up with the other people, the other side, now say, "Boy, we see that you all was right. If we had it to do over we'd be right out there with you."

MOFFETT: You mean if it happened over again there wouldn't be any resistance?

GRALEY: There wouldn't be any resistance, they'd be on our side, yes. Very few have I found — because now we see the fruits of that, our children, you can't even — it's dangerous for a mother or any women, or anybody practically, to be out on the streets. You don't —

MOFFETT: That was true before the books came up, wasn't it?

GRALEY: Oh, no, no we didn't lock up our doors. There wasn't a door locked here until that book protest started — never, never did. You could come to my house and walked in any time you wanted to.

MOFFETT: Do you believe all these negative things like increase in crime and so on are due to the schools?

GRALEY: Yes, definitely so. I believe that crime — because they taught them crime right in them books, yes. And I believe that the crime increase — and you know they'll say, "Well, let's give them — let's appropriate more money for recreation and it'll be a different story." You can stand in one spot up here and count about five baseball fields right here in the Institute. They've got tennis courts, they've got racquet ball courts, they've got everything in the world that's recreation, and crimes keeps increasing. See, you can't —

MOFFETT: I work a lot with teachers around the country, and I know there are good teachers and there are bad teachers and all sorts because it's a huge profession. What I get from them sometimes — they get tremendously frustrated a lot and say, "Well, parents are always blaming us. For everything that goes wrong in life they blame the school." So this is a situation where we're in danger of everybody blaming everybody else. There are a lot of things going on that people don't like in this world, and *nobody* likes the increase in crime, but —

GRALEY: Well, if we'll get back to teaching and allow the parents to whip the children. They've hollered "child abuse," if you spank the child. It's a funny thing though. If a Christian spanks their child it's child abuse. But if it's these liberals out here drinking all night, come in and cut their child up, they wouldn't much ever be said about that, but you heard all across the country where they confiscate children from parents that tried to bring them up and spank them a little bit once in a while, and I think until we get back to the issue of corporal punishment in schools, and if the parents come and interfere with the teacher, unless the teacher is absolutely picking on that child, you know, and it's evident that they are, but I think if a child needs spanking the teacher ought to be at liberty to spank them. . . . and these little children, I've heard them, no better'n five years old tell their parents they was not going to do something, or just rip out a big oath. All right, then they go to school and the teacher whips that child or spanks it, and then here comes the parents down on the teacher. Back when *you* was in school, if you got a whipping, if you needed it you got it, didn't you? And usually if you went home and told your parents that you got a whipping at school you got another one there at the house.

MOFFETT: Do you feel that most of the problems we're dealing with today come from the school one way or another?

GRALEY: No, I think that parents — but well, it could. I believe that it all stemmed from the school system, or most all of it, because over the period of years these people would go on to college, you know, and maybe when all them riots and everything going on in college, on the college campuses, now these are the parents. See, they did all this, they was corrupted there in the college, in schools, after they got away from the teaching of Mom and Dad, and I believe that now there's a great swinging back, cause you take these same people that when we was in that book protest would defy us to the very bottom, now they see and say, "Well, I know I wasn't brought up that way, but I got away from that." And now these are the people that had been corrupted back in the sixties and around there in the school systems, and now they have their children and they go by Dr. Spock's doctrine that use child psychology see instead of — of whipping the child. . . .

* * *

MOFFETT: Do you think we're in danger of becoming a fascist state?

GRALEY: Yes, I do. Yes. Unless we get good leaders that will bring this thing back. We had a welfare state, and practically one man working kept one that wouldn't work, and we was getting where generations, you know, come up on welfare and that just handed on down to the next gen-

eration. I'm so happy now that I believe if we get it back off where if a
man is able he should work, regardless.

MOFFETT: Are you happy with most of the things that Reagan has done
now?

GRALEY: I'm *very* happy with him. Yes. Yes sir, I'm very happy that he
is standing up and saying, "Boys, we have had this disarmament so long
and Russia didn't go along with SALT I or II either, didn't do anything
they agreed to do, and just kept building their defense, and offense too,
offensive weapons," and yeah, I'm glad that he is man enough to say this
thing has gone far enough, and we're going to cut out a lot of these welfare people, and we're going to make people work that's able to work,
and I'm 100 percent for just about everything he's done. And I'm a Democrat and raised in a Democrat family, and here been all my life, strong
Democrats. I belong to the labor unions. I belong to 128 Carpenters'
Union.

MOFFETT: Do you believe teachers should belong to a union?

GRALEY: No. No, I definitely don't. I don't think anybody that is paid
by taxpayers' money should belong to the union, because — we see what
happens: they shut down the schools and the city garbage and all this.
No, I don't think they should. Any private enterprise that can raise a
product or something, in order to pay a higher wage, then that's a different story, but every time they strike and get all these raises — I think
teachers are paid very adequate for no more work than they do. No more
hours than they put in, and I've went to classrooms before and be in there
half an hour and never see a teacher, and the kids be throwing erasers
and paper wads and books across the classroom. . . . But it's nothing but
a madhouse in all the public school classrooms that I've been in, and
that's why I'm for getting the school system completely out of the federal
and the county and state's hands, get it back into the church's, and then if
a Methodist wants to teach his kids some little doctrine or whatever, let
him do it, if —

MOFFETT: So you'd be in favor of going to private schools?

GRALEY: I'm in favor of the Christian schools, yes sir.

MOFFETT: Where would the poor people get the money?

GRALEY: Well, the poor people that you talk about being poor will
drink up and smoke up a whole lot more than it will take for their children to go to a private school.

MOFFETT: The rich won't have to give up smoking and drinking.

GRALEY: Well sure, the poor men always has it rougher than the rich, it
don't matter whether their kids're in school or not. He don't set T-bones
on his table every day; he may have to have beans and potatoes, and the
rich man get a T-bone or whatever he wants to or just eat out at a nice
restaurant. Sure that's always been.

MOFFETT: But I mean if you go to private schools it would tend to discriminate against the poor although certainly not intended to do that.

GRALEY: I think that what we need is a voucher system where we can — that the portion of our tax — it's not fair to the Catholic, it's not fair to the Jewish people, to have to pay their tax to the public schools when they have to finance their own private schools.

MOFFETT: This is a time when federal money has been cut back severely. To run a voucher system wouldn't you have to have a lot of federal money?

GRALEY: No, you could do that with the county portion of your tax. I should be able to pay my tax to the school of my choice . . . the percentage that goes for education — now they're forcing me, you see, to pay for this garbage in these books, they *force* me to do it. They'd sell my home if I don't pay my property taxes.

MOFFETT: The thing is, other parents are furious too, because their kids are forced to go to a school they don't like, and they're forced to pay money for an education they don't like. They don't agree with you, but they *feel* the same way you do for the same reasons. They feel —

GRALEY: These people though that's kicking against the Christian schools, where are they forced to go to a school against their will? They love these public schools.

MOFFETT: No, many of them don't. They're very unhappy, you're not the only ones unhappy. This is what I mean. It's very hard to satisfy the public because they want different —

GRALEY: I never knew of anybody in this book protest that was *for* those books that wasn't wealthy people. They could have sent their children to any private school they wanted to. I never seen a poor man out there —

MOFFETT: Did you feel the textbook controversy was a conflict between the rich and the poor, mostly?

GRALEY: No, I wouldn't think so. I think it was a conflict between the — well, I believe it was all a Communist conspiracy, myself. Still do. And I'll always believe it. That they was behind all that. Sure, they had people that said Rev. so and so, you know, in front of their name, but when that same Rev. goes down here and says he's going to lead the May Day Parade with the Communist party, what do you think that fellow is?

MOFFETT: Why did a lot of parents like the books? Does that mean they were all Communists too?

GRALEY: I think that was parents that was either Communists or some of these parents that had growed up in the sixties when they was burning the colleges and all this and was brainwashed. I think our news media was very very far to the left, and I still think so.

MOFFETT: Some of the textbooks were adopted in the state of New

Mexico, which is a pretty conservative state, and in Oregon, and were adopted in a lot of cities like Baton Rouge, Louisiana, places—

GRALEY: Baton Rouge wanted me to come there and speak against them, see. The only thing is, I found this to be true all over America where I went: they *do not* bring the textbooks in until they get the board of education stacked. They get the deck stacked against the public, and I feel that they're Communists infiltrates to the top and gets in, and they spent millions of dollars, you know. If Castro thought he could get a governor in West Virginia, a Communist government, him and Brezhnev would definitely spend *millions* of dollars to get him in this office. . . .

* * *

MOFFETT: Did you feel that some selections were downright porno-graphic?

GRALEY: Yes, very much so.

MOFFETT: Can you remember any of them?

GRALEY: That *Souls on Ice*, it was probably a library book, but it was very filthy and pornographic.

MOFFETT: Pornographic means that the whole purpose of it is just to arouse people sexually.

GRALEY: Yes, well, one of the 11th-grade English books, I think, was telling about this little red-headed chick that made so much a night as a prostitute. I think that was advocating prostitution, the way it read. [See chapter 8.]

MOFFETT: You mean, if something bad like that is mentioned it means you're advocating it?

GRALEY: No, but they don't never come on around and tell the bad part of it, see.

MOFFETT: I mean if your newspaper or magazine has a feature article on, let's say, prostitution, do you assume they're advocating it?

GRALEY: If they brag on that little gal and how much she made, yes. . . .

* * *

MOFFETT: What's the main experience when you're born again? Do you feel you were born again?

GRALEY: Yes, sir. I think it's a definite feeling, that you feel the weight of the whole sins of the world is lifted off of you, whereas you had a heavy heart burdened down with sin, and now you feel that them sins is all been pardoned and you're—they're gone and you're just free—just seem like you could fly through the air almost. It's an experience that anybody'd have to experience theirself.

MOFFETT: How did it happen for you? If you feel like saying.

GRALEY: Yes. Well, I went to an altar when the minister gave the invitation for those who wanted to accept Christ to come forth. And I prayed, but I didn't feel like I was really borned again or converted. My sins I didn't feel like had got a complete job, and then I come home after the church service and prayed, and probably two o'clock in the morning it seemed like the whole weight of the world lifted off of me. The burden of sin was gone, and so then we walked in newness of light. You just get a whole new outlook on life. Now probably before I'd got saved or borned again — the experience — I may have went out there and said, "Boy I want them books," cause I — but there's a lot of difference in religion and salvation. . . .

MOFFETT: Would you accept the principle that the language of the Bible differs from place to place? Some of it is to be taken more literally than other parts of it?

GRALEY: I think that when Christ ever spoke of a grain of wheat abiding by itself he went on to explain too that when we die, as long as we're in ourself, then we abide alone, but when we are dead to self, then we bring forth fruit.

MOFFETT: Right, so it's a symbolic interpretation?

GRALEY: Yes, but he didn't leave us in the dark on anything.

MOFFETT: He did it often because the disciples were a little puzzled and they pressed him for meaning.

GRALEY: These was ignorant and unlearnt men too, you must remember that. He knew they understood fish, the fishermen, and he understood that some of them knew about a sheep, and if one sheep was lost they'd go out and find him, search for him.

MOFFETT: Wouldn't it be reasonable to think that some of the rest of the Bible was also written in popular language that people could understand? In a symbolic way?

GRALEY: But I don't think that changes the interpretation, the meaning, regardless of it's a parable or not. I think the word of God never contradicts itself, and I don't see why we'd have so many different interpretations of it.

MOFFETT: I'm sure it doesn't contradict itself. It's just that people get different understandings, because they're at different stages of growth, and each one feels *he's* right because for *him* at that *moment* —

GRALEY: Well at that *moment* he *is* right, see.

MOFFETT: But somebody else who's at another stage, he's sure *he's* right, so they go at loggerheads about it.

GRALEY: That's why your child if he's — my boys, they's a lot of times —

they're good workers but they run across things every day or two—
they're right in everything they're doing, usually, on a building or something, and then they come and ask me, "Well, Dad what do we do about
this?" and when I explain it to them—maybe when I first start talking to
them, they say, "No, that ain't the right way, we don't do it that way," or
won't do it, but then they finally see it that way and do it. And then from
then on they're up another step. I think you've got to grow in this thing.
When a child's born he has to crawl before he walks.

MOFFETT: Can you imagine that there'll be another stage for *you* where
you'll feel differently than you do now?

GRALEY: I hope there's a stage that I'll be a lot closer to God than I am
now, and I feel very close to Him today, but I always want to reach a
more—you have a desire to be more perfect each day because I don't
think anybody is perfect, but every day we want to strive to be more perfect. And I don't think anybody will obtain that absolute perfection until
this old mortal puts on immortality.

MOFFETT: We've got to keep growing all the time we're here.

GRALEY: But you do have to keep growing, yes, cause there's no stop-
ping place. You're either going forward or backwards, I think. But then
Christ said that some of 'em would bring forth 30, some 60, and some
100, see, and he gives a talent to everybody as their ability. He's not
going to give me a job out here like he's give to Jerry Falwell or Billy
Graham or something because my ability just won't let me do that, and
God's not going to give me something beyond my ability. So maybe I'll
be the one that in all my lifetime won't bring over 30, in His eyes, 30
bushels in my whole lifetime, where up here's another one that can bring
forth 60 and some even 100.

MOFFETT: If we encounter people in this life who *are* more spiritually
developed, they might look crazy to us.

GRALEY: Yeah.

MOFFETT: So it's hard to imagine—isn't it?—how we might be quarreling
with people who are actually more developed than we are, but it would be
hard to know it, wouldn't it? Because we haven't reached that stage yet. I
think children have this problem—don't they? They haven't been there yet
so they can't understand sometimes where we got something.

GRALEY: All right, you take Joshua, the foolish thing in the world to that
king and all would have been for a man to stood up against that city and
go against the wall of the city and not have anything but a bull horn in his
hand. See, that was crazy, to go up against them with nothing but a ram's
horn, to blow on. Yeah, I think—but you see, Joshua got crazy enough to
do that. To most people and to his men that probably—when he said,
"Boys let's go up here and all we're going to take is a ram's horn," and—

MOFFETT: He knew something they didn't know.

GRALEY: You see? To them the man's crazy.

MOFFETT: That's exactly what I mean.

GRALEY: And just like the little Naaman to go down and dip in the Jordan, seven times, see? They thought he was crazy, and *he* thought it was crazy. But finally old Elisha, that had to run from the king and everything else, he's the one that told him to go down there and dip in Jordan seven times. Well, that was the craziest thing ever was. That old man was out of his mind telling him to go down there and dip in Jordan. But it worked. Naaman's men finally convinced him that that was the only way he was going to ever get well, or he had nothing to lose, by going. "Go try."

MOFFETT: This is something that we maybe have to always keep in mind: it's difficult recognizing higher spiritual levels of development. They may look *criminal* to us.

GRALEY: But just in the past month I have seen sugar diabetes healed, through anointing and laying on of hands. Now, this is in my church, this is not somewhere else that I've read about this. These people actually stand up and testify that they've been back to their doctor and that their doctor said that their sugar was normal, back to just right. . . .

MOFFETT: Do you do the laying on of hands yourself?

GRALEY: Oh yes, yes, and of course the church gathers up there. We all — everybody that wants to, and we agree in prayer, because the Bible says, "Where two or more agree touching any one thing it shall be done," see, and we believe that and so we anoint with oil and pray the prayer of faith. "And the prayer of faith will save the sick and the Lord raise them up," James says. . . .

*　*　*

MOFFETT: Is there anything else that you want to add, anything I didn't ask you? Do you want to ask me something?

GRALEY: No, I think we're on our way to recovery. I really believe it. I believe our book protest broke the whole — if not the whole nation, and part of the world. Because I understand that during that time, that in Paris, France, the headlines of their paper one morning, when they put me in jail up here, was, "Thank God there's still men that'll stand for what's right." We just kept yielding to Communism and these radicals out here hollering around until the silent majority, I thought, had to get up on their feet while we still had a foot to stand on, or be overthrown by Communism.

I gave him several opportunities to end the interview, but each time we started in again. When I referred to the chronic conflicts between Israel and the Palestinians as a holy war, he said this was not so, for the Israelis were merely defending their country and opposing the Communist PLO. But when I said the Jews had felt in founding Israel that they were fulfilling a Biblical prophecy, he laughed and said, "Can we doubt that when they fought that seven-day war and whipped them in seven days, outnumbered 100 soldiers to one? That sounds like David and Goliath, don't it?"

A torrential summer rain and crashing thunder had been upstaging our conversation. We hovered near the doorway opening on the fine lawn rolling down to the Kanawha River. He had told me earlier, when I praised his grounds, that some townspeople had objected to his filling his edge of the river with scraps from his roofing business. When the authorities tried to stop him, he said, "I told them this ain't Moscow but America — I can do what I want." He gestured to the banks, green now and dotted with young trees.

Somehow, at this last moment, we got onto matters of race. He said he had talked with the local NAACP and they hadn't agreed with him. He said he didn't approve of the racism of the KKK and disowned the connection while admitting that he agreed with "90 percent of their ideas." When I asked if he believed in intermarriage, he said, "Each to his own kind." Moses married an Egyptian, a black, he said, but look what happened: she died of leprosy. Clearly, this was not meant to be. The rain had stopped, and I was preparing to leave. He indicated the lawn with a sweep of his arm. "Birds all peck seeds together, all mixed up, but each mates only its own kind."

5

Free Enterprise

Elmer Fike's company is in Nitro proper, which is a long string of chemical companies on one side of a highway and a string of housing on the other side. Lost amid a patchwork of these chemical yards is Fike's small company, barely marked by a dusty, unadorned cement-block building. Around the doorway of Fike's office on the second floor are plastered bumper stickers reading "Feed Jane Fonda to the Whales" and "If saccharin is outlawed, only outlaws will own cancerous cats," in keeping with his reputation for resisting the regulations of the Environmental Protection Agency. He had quickly made room for an interview at the end of the same day I called him. He has done countless interviews on the book controversy and readily hands out copies of *Elmer's Tune* and his many other writings. He would have been in his mid-fifties during the book imbroglio. He sounds tired and mechanical until some question stirs him to new thought, and he does indeed think. We did the interview in his office, and from time to time he took telephone calls, the last one from his wife, who was holding supper for him.

FIKE: Ever since the federal government's been in [education], the achievement has gone downhill, and I think it's primarily *because* of the involvement of the federal government.

MOFFETT: Do you think now that they're getting out of it that it will get better?

FIKE: They're not getting out of it, yet. I hope they will.

MOFFETT: They're cutting down on funds.

FIKE: They're not cutting down very much. They're not cutting near — I think they'll improve, sure. I think if the schools got back to more local control they'd be better. They might be more diverse schools, at different places, but — It's pretty terrible. Some guy from ACLU was being interviewed on National Public Radio and he was talking about the prayer-in-school amendment, and he said with the coercive influence of the educational system today he didn't think it was possible to have a strictly voluntary prayer. I turn that around and say, "If the environment of school is that coercive today, can we have a diversity of educational approach that's really essential to preserve a democracy?" Have we got a system that's so coercive that everybody's following the same party line that's dictated out of Washington? If we are, we're in one hell of a shape. And I think we *are* in a hell of a shape.

MOFFETT: Does that mean that Washington is putting over a radical line in the schools?

FIKE: I don't think Congress is doing it deliberately, but Congress of course in their legislation to support education deliberately set it up so that they would not have any influence on it. So what this means is that the Department of Education has just got a blank check to do whatever they want to do, and that's what they're doing. They've had some really stupid programs that they've promoted and pushed, and one of the worst ones of course was MACOS. . . . [*Man: A Course of Study*, was a popular target for book banners because of its "humanism." The federal government did fund development of MACOS and other reformative textbook series of the 1960s, as in physics, biology, and mathematics, thus lending substance to charges of curricular influence from Washington.]

MOFFETT: Some of the main objections to the books seem to be that they criticized the government's authority.

FIKE: Well, it was just typical left-wing lying. You don't have to read the textbooks. If you've read anything that the radicals have been putting out in the last few years, that was what was in the textbooks. They were questioning everything, and the books put an awful lot of emphasis on the radicals of today, whereas there's very little information about the historical and the traditional heroes of our country. For instance, they had a book in there that had interviews with Charles Manson [an interview with Charles Manson appeared in *Interaction's Transcripts 1* for advanced senior high school] but they didn't have things in there like *The Man Without a Country* and the typically patriotic things, you know, the story of — and one other thing that I got criticized for a great deal was, we ran across a place in there — well, the committee had just been going through the books and pulling out four-letter words and curse words and things like this, you know. So they came across the classical expression of Admiral Farragut, which said, "Damn the torpedoes. Full speed ahead!" So they noted that down along with all the other damns and hells and swear words and stuff. Well, a lot of the papers picked this up and said we were complaining because there wasn't any patriotism in there — the books didn't talk about our heroes — and here was a case where we objected when they *did* put one of the heroes in. So I got the passage and read it, and actually the way they treated the quotation of Admiral Farragut they took it out of context, and they were making fun of that quotation. They were saying, "We can't afford to talk like that any more. It would get us in real trouble today if we were to say, 'Damn the torpedoes and full speed ahead.' " And so they were actually making a caricature of one of our heroes.

MOFFETT: Do you feel that *all* people who criticize the government are radical?

FIKE: The textbooks were not especially *criticizing* the government. They were holding up—they were criticizing the free enterprise system. That's really what they were doing. And in fact Stein, an editorial writer for the *Wall Street Journal*, wrote and said that a lot of people were complaining about the textbooks here in West Virginia, and he read some of the books, and he agreed there was basis for criticism, but we weren't criticizing for the right things. What he said was that they were a total attack on the free enterprise, capitalistic system, which they were. That's what they should be criticizing about the textbooks. So I wrote him a letter and said, "Sure, I agree with you, and I've said that many, many times, but the news media won't report that kind of criticism. They try to make us look like a bunch of rednecks."

MOFFETT: Does this mean that some kinds of criticism of the government are all right but not other kinds?

FIKE: I'm not worried about criticism of the government. It wasn't so much criticism of the government. It was portraying the Communist governments and the totalitarian governments and the socialist governments in a very favorable light as opposed to a very critical attitude about the old free enterprise system and the freedom that we have. . . .

MOFFETT: Do you feel there's a conspiracy?

FIKE: Well, I don't know that it's a conspiracy so much, but the whole publishing industry and the whole Eastern media is so left-oriented, so liberal-oriented, that—I don't think it's a conspiracy; I think those people just got there and control the situation, and that's just the way they think. I don't call that a conspiracy. . . . The publishing business to some extent is just out of touch. They don't see anything wrong with what I see as really bad.

Here's what they did. I think they made a mistake. Back in the late sixties, when all the riots and stuff got started, everybody became socially concerned, you know. So a lot of these publishers went around —it takes eight or ten years from inception to completion—and they were concerned about all these riots and race riots and war demonstrations and everything, so they went around and talked to people: "What should the textbook offer to make it more responsive to the needs of the people?" Well, everybody they talked to said we ought to, you know, talk more about race relations, we ought to talk more about minority groups and all of this kind of stuff. So they believed all that, and they started to write the books based on the problems of the inner city and all that kind of stuff. Well, you know, sure, the inner city's got those kind of problems, but why in the hell do we have to indoctrinate our children out here in semirural communities with the problems of the inner city? . . .

* * *

The textbook supporters . . . were the country club set. There's a term came up that I had never heard before. They claim it's used in West Virginia a lot — the "hillers" and the "creekers." The hillers are the people that belong to the country club and live up on top of the hill — the rich people, so to speak — and the creekers are the people who live up in the hollows. I live with the creekers, but theoretically I should be a hiller because I have a college education, and I own a company, and I have the prestige and the social graces, theoretically, that entitle me to be a hiller, but I'm a creeker at heart, I guess. But that was kind of the conflict it was.

MOFFETT: That sounds like it was the rich versus the poor.

FIKE: Oh, it was to a very large extent. At least that was — now let me go back and say that there were a hell of a lot of people of the better educated and upper social status who sympathized with us but they didn't want to do it publicly. . . .

MOFFETT: I understand that the Heritage Foundation contributed to your side.

FIKE: I've contributed to the Heritage Foundation all through the years. I was one of the first to contribute to the Heritage Foundation, and I know what they were doing. They didn't put any money into this *locally*. They got involved in the whole educational system nationwide as a result of this, and they've written a lot of publications promoting traditional, basic education. But they never put much money in down here.

MOFFETT: Maybe they did it mostly through legal support.

FIKE: They didn't even do much of that. That was grossly exaggerated. The textbook supporters tried to make it *sound* as if there were a lot of people coming in here giving support. I suspect *I've* spent as much money on one of the women by the name of Fay McGraw, who kept her children out of school, and they brought truancy action against her twice. The first time, I got it thrown out of the JP court. The next time, they won in the JP court, and we got it thrown out at the circuit court level because they hadn't done their homework. They didn't have the necessary legal work done properly. I think if we had gone to a jury we could have probably beat them. But I paid for that out of my own pocket. . . .

* * *

MOFFETT: Did you feel it was fair that the Rev. Marvin Horan served time for fire-bombing schools?

FIKE: No, I really don't. I feel that guy was railroaded. I really think he was railroaded. I think what happened was that he probably, at some meeting—he was a very emotional kind of guy, and he was pretty upset about this thing, and he probably at some meeting said, "By Golly, we ought to burn the schools down, blow them up" or something. I don't question but what he *said* that, you know. The only thing that tied him to it was that a gas can that belonged to him was somehow involved in the commission of the crime. *Very* tenuous thing, and he had very poor legal representation. In fact, I got my lawyer to get into the thing to try to help him out, and his lawyer was so inept that he didn't even have the witnesses lined up; he was just a terrible case . . . and my lawyer went down to the courthouse to try to get ahold of their lawyer to try to bring up some points that proved the defense, and the case was already over! The case only lasted just a few *hours*. You know, a case like that—look how long—look how long they go with Hinkley, God knows! . . .

* * *

MOFFETT: What do you feel the real conflict was about? Was it just the textbooks?

FIKE: It wasn't just the textbooks. They brought it to a head and made clear what the so-called progressives in the educational system were trying to do. The traditionalists objected for the following reasons—and I'm reading from "The Textbook Dispute Updated": [For the sake of completeness, more is included than he read. This is one of his own editorials.

The traditionalists perceive education as a process of teaching the child the basic knowledge and skills. Since some indoctrination is inevitable, it should promote the accepted social attitudes and morals of the society in which the child lives. The job of the schools is considered to be the transmission of the tradition of the parents to the children in order to preserve society. Books and supplementary material should be chosen to promote that end. While other cultures and governmental systems should be considered, the American system should always be the yardstick by which others are measured.

The progressives claim to object to any indoctrination because it gives too much power to the agency that determines the thrust of the indoctrination and because it does not teach the child how to examine ideas critically. They would prefer that the child be allowed to examine all philosophies with a minimum of guidance. Thus, the child develops the ability to choose what is best and will not, as a mature adult, be easily misled or indoctrinated by demagogues who offer simple solutions. The philosophy is most easily summed up by the statement, "Teach the child how to think, not what to think." The progressives also prefer a minimum of discipline and greater freedom for the student to decide what or how he will study.

Traditionalists object to the progressive philosophy of education for the following reasons:

1. Basic skills are slighted. Instead, the available time is used to explore all sides of every issue.

2. Most children need discipline. Without it they end up wasting time and learning little. Declining test scores bear witness to this fact.

3. It is difficult to arrive at new truths without a solid basis in fact. New ideas are usually only slight extensions or variations of known facts. A sound knowledge of facts — what to think — is essential training for how to think.

4. Students are not mature enough to debate moral values in an objective way. Without the necessary understanding of the complexities of real life situations, the student is apt to oversimplify and attempt judgments beyond his ability. Those who do not become pompous simply become confused by the smorgasbord of ideas they are indiscriminately fed.

5. Some selection of materials must be made, and what is selected results in a form of indoctrination even though the progressives claim otherwise. The complete lack of material supporting traditional patriotic values supports this contention. Although the progressives claim that the material does not indoctrinate, it is written in such a way that it subtly attacks traditional ideas. While the material supposedly only asks questions, the questions are asked in such a way that the desired answers are elicited from the children, and the teachers' manuals often give the answers the teacher is supposed to get and states clearly what attitudes the teacher should strive to instill.

6. It appears that the progressives (at least the radical element that appears to be in control) do not approve of the American system as it now stands and consider education of children a means to affect [sic] the dramatic change they consider desirable. The traditionalists consider that the legitimate goal of education is to preserve the society. Necessary changes should be determined and made by elected representatives through the legislative process or by consensus of the adult community. A complete change of direction should not be the prerogative of the educators.[1]

MOFFETT: Were there real difference in values that are never going to be reconciled?

FIKE: Well certainly — tremendous differences in values. And it comes to the question where you wonder if we've got such a diverse society if a public school system is a viable way to go. This country survived for a hundred and twenty years without a public school system. You know, we've been almost as long without a public school system as we've been *with* one.

MOFFETT: How would you pay for private schools?

FIKE: My lord, if you didn't have your taxes to pay for public schools,

you could sure afford to pay for private schools. Private schools are tremendously cheaper than public schools — they've gotten totally out of
hand.

MOFFETT: Are you thinking of a voucher system or of just cutting the
taxes?

FIKE: Aw hell, just cutting the taxes. I see some merit in a voucher system, but I prefer tax credits or tax-deductible expenses. I prefer not to
give vouchers simply because if the government is giving you the money
they are exercising control. And I'd just as soon they didn't *have* any control. The control is where the money is.

MOFFETT: Are poor people going to be able to afford this?

FIKE: Listen, let me tell you about this Fay McGraw —

MOFFETT: They don't have much tax money to *save.*

FIKE: Let me tell you about this Fay McGraw. Let me tell you about
this Fay McGraw. [Laughs.] She and her husband worked as janitors,
and they had a total income of about less than $12,000 a year, and they
put their two kids through private school, because they would not send
their kids to public school. I'm not worried about the poor people finding
the money. It's the rich people who can't find the money — they're so deep
in hock to buying things they don't need and don't want.

MOFFETT: But what I was thinking is that if we count on a tax cut it will
be harder on the poor because they don't pay that many taxes in the first
place.

FIKE: Fay McGraw got the money to send her kids to private school.

MOFFETT: How did they do it?

FIKE: Well, they did without. And their kids got out and scrounged
and saved, and — I did her income tax for her one year, and her report-
able income was something less than $6000, and she had a daughter in a
private college, in East Valeria. They raised their own food, they made
their own clothes, they did everything. But they felt it was important.
Now, besides that taxable income, I think he was on Social Security at
that time but they had another name for Social Security. But it can be
done if people want to do it. . . .

* * *

The First Amendment says [he looks it up] — I keep it handy
here — "Congress shall make no law respecting the establishment of religion or prohibiting the free exercise thereof." And we clearly are prohibiting the free exercise of religion in the schools today. The freedom of
religion stops at the schoolhouse door. No other activity does. The Constitution protects every other activity in school except the right of religious freedom.

MOFFETT: OK, if we go that way, would we just teach the religions of all the peoples of the world?

FIKE: No, no. No, you don't have to teach it at all. You don't have to teach it. You just ignore it and let the kids do what they want to do about it. Just ignore it. That's what they should do. But they *won't* do that. I don't know if you're familiar with the case we had here in Charleston, Kanawha County—Hunt versus the School Board—that was tried in court. And a bunch of kids that wanted to have a religious club were meeting before school. They were *bus* students, and after the bus ride they had a half hour of free time before classes started, so they started a religious club. The Kanawha County Board of Education said they couldn't do that, took them to court, and it was stopped. Now, that was a purely voluntary religious exercise. And the judge said the School Board was within its rights to prohibit it. In fact, he questioned if they could even allow it if they wanted to. And this has been held in many other cases around the country, so we've gone way beyond. . . .

* * *

MOFFETT: What is your general view of Communism? What does it mean to you?

FIKE: You know, George Ball, the secretary of state, I heard him on an interview. He made two statements about Communism that I thought were totally wrong. One, he said: the ideology of Communism has gone out, it's out of the balloon, it has no real impetus any more. Nobody in the hierarchy really believes in the ideology of Communism any more, so that we're really not dealing with an ideological situation; we're just dealing with power brokers with expansionist tendencies. Well, of course there is some truth in that. The ideology went out of Communism back with Lenin. He gave up the whole concepts of Communism right in the very beginning because they didn't work, and he established totalitarianism. I don't think he made any *pretense* of establishing Communism. He *did* make a pretense—pardon me—he made an enormous pretense of establishing Communism, but he never really established the *philosophy* of Communism. He started with a totally autocratic system right from the beginning where you're told what to do or else. And that's not Communism. You know, it's not a dictatorship of the proletariat at all, like they claim it's going to be. It's a totalitarian form of government not greatly different from what Hitler had. It's an autocracy just the same as all the rest of them except that it's an extreme case of it. But they use the *ideology* of Communism in order to gain supporters, to get people to support their ways, and they're being very effective at that. They're using, as I understand it, somewhere between ten and a hundred times as much money in propaganda as we do in this country.

MOFFETT: Maybe we ought to get a new term. Maybe instead of talking about anti-Communism, we should talk about antifascism or antitotalitarianism.

FIKE: I agree with that. We shouldn't even refer to them as Communists, because they're not Communists.

MOFFETT: I heard on the radio driving into Charleston this morning a minister talking about prophesies in the Bible, and he says that the Soviet Union of today has been prophesied — its military might and its authority over other nations.

FIKE: Yeah, but you know, it's happened time and time again. It's not anything new exactly. It's just that these people are more effective. Their technology is better developed, so they have better control of their people than they ever could in the past. With mass communications indoctrination is easier and better. With computers it's easier to keep track of people and do all sorts of things. So the technology makes them more powerful than in the past. But on the other hand, we're doing absolutely *nothing*, or very little, to combat it. There are a lot of things we could be doing we're not doing, and I think it's a big mistake.

MOFFETT: You mean besides military?

FIKE: Oh yeah, besides military. We could be cutting back on our trade with them, we could put the heat on them in lots of ways, we could — Even our Voice of America is not an effective propaganda tool because — I don't know whether you read about the controversy that's been going on — the Reagan administration put some guy in there to reform it and really start using a hard line toward the Russians, and they threw him out — didn't want to do it, didn't want to *cause* trouble with Russia. Their whole motivation is questionable.

MOFFETT: I think that generally Reagan has started to turn things around and get tougher.

FIKE: Yeah, but he has not done near what he could have done, near as much as he should have done. For instance, there was a resolution up before Congress just a few weeks ago to reestablish the Monroe Doctrine, sort of, and the State Department testified to water it way down, so we're not taking nearly as strong a stand as we could take or, in my opinion, should take.

MOFFETT: You probably read the NEA report on the book controversy.

FIKE: Yeah, I testified. [Shuffles papers on his desk.] Here is the testimony I gave, "Academic Freedom or Censorship," because that's what they claimed their hearing was all about.

MOFFETT: One thing they said was that the objections were strongly racist.

FIKE: That was absolutely ridiculous! The only people who were racist were the blacks. They grab on every issue they can and try to make it look racist. I went to talk to them, and they nearly threw me out because I quoted a black author, and that made them very mad. I went to the NAACP in Charleston and I said "I think you misunderstand us. We are on the same side of this thing as you people." . . .

MOFFETT: They didn't agree with you that you were on the same side?

FIKE: Well, that wasn't it at all. [Chuckles.] They were committed to be against us. . . . I really felt that the whole textbook thing degraded the blacks in many respects, degraded them terribly. There was one tape they had that told the story of a black man and how a bunch of redneck people, down in the South presumably, cooked up a deal that he had got a white girl pregnant, and the thing went out, and it ended up lynching him. That was the whole story. [This was the "The Eye," a short story by J. F. Powers included as both text and tape in *Interaction*'s *Monologue and Dialogue 1* for advanced senior high. Like certain other *Interaction* books for secondary school, this came in two versions, only one of which, the one we called the "mature" version, contained "The Eye." The story is a monologue in the vernacular by one of the rednecks.] And I had a black preacher here from California — I didn't have him here, he came in — and I said, "I'd like for you to hear this tape." Well, it was terrible the way they referred to the blacks all the way through . . . as niggers and, you know, no-goods, and worthless, and all that. You know, the old stereotype of the redneck of the South and how they treated the blacks. And I said, "I want you to hear this tape and see what you think of it." He almost cried. He was a grown man. He just thought it was horrible. So I said, "I'll tell you what let's do. Let's take it up to the guy who's head of Human Rights, a black man, state Human Rights Commission, and let *him* hear this tape." So we played that tape for him and said, "What do you think about that? Do you think that ought to be in schools?" He said, "Yes, I think it ought to be in there because it shows how the black [Fike corrects himself.] — the white — people used to treat the blacks."

MOFFETT: He said "used to"?

FIKE: Well, I suppose — I don't remember. But it's sort of the attitude of the white people toward the black. [He changes to a ringing, pompous tone.] "It ought to be in there to make the white people ashamed of what they've done." I played this tape for my daughter, who's a schoolteacher in one of the rural counties of West Virginia, and I said, "What do you think about it?" and she didn't think it was a very good tape. I told her what the fellow from the Human Rights Commission said, and she said, "Well, the students *might* think that, but it would more *likely* reinforce their ideas, and they'd say, 'By God, he got what he shoulda got.' " She said it would *reinforce* the kids; it wouldn't make them feel *ashamed.*

MOFFETT: Can you imagine a way whereby they might have discussed the story and made sure they didn't take it the wrong way?

FIKE: Oh, theoretically you can do that, but, you know, who's gonna do it? Who's gonna do it? I think there are some people who would have heard that story and it would reinforce them and there wouldn't have been anything you could have said that would have made it any better. But what got me was, why would they object to *Black Sambo* and *Huckleberry Finn* and accept that sort of story? It didn't make any sense to me at all.

MOFFETT: No matter what offends you, in a way you're the judge since it's all about what offends whom.

FIKE: Well, I took the position — I think it's written in here in one of my essays somewhere — that no one should be the judge except the man himself. If it offends him, take it out. And if it gets to the point where we can't have an educational system, then let's close her down and let everybody have their own. If you can't have an educational system that's free of offense to some groups, then maybe we shouldn't *have* public schools any more. Maybe we ought to go back to the neighborhood schools so the blacks can have their schools and the whites can have theirs and the Jews can have theirs and the Spanish can have theirs instead of trying to put everybody in the same room and then trying to teach everybody everybody else's culture. You know, some people contend that education is passing the culture of the parents on to their children. How can you do that when we have all this busing?

MOFFETT: Well, how can you do it when you have a whole lot of different people in the society who don't *agree* on the culture?

FIKE: If you have the neighborhood schools, in general you end up with similar cultures. You see, by getting into busing and trying integration and everything, then you've destroyed the possibility of *passing* people's culture on to their children. Maybe that's good and maybe that's bad — I don't know.

MOFFETT: What did they say at the NAACP when you were there?

FIKE: Well, I told them a story. Here's the story, just briefly. [Hands me a copy of it.] What I objected to was that many of the books about the black culture made it appear that the blacks didn't have an opportunity in this country. Well, I said I don't think that was a fair presentation anymore. There are plenty of opportunities for blacks. And I started to read to them a passage from George Schuyler, or Skooler or whatever his name is — he's a black author — and now when I mentioned his name, they just — they wouldn't hear of him, that was the end of it, they wouldn't even listen to me anymore.

MOFFETT: Why was that?

FIKE: Well, he's not one of their boys. He's — they don't like him.

MOFFETT: He's local talent?

FIKE: He's local talent. And the passage I wanted to read from Schuyler said, "In spite of the difficulties that still exist, the black still has more opportunity in America than in any other country in the world." And Schuyler points out that the essential ingredient for them to arrive in the social status is *hope*, that they must have a feeling of *hope*. And I thought that made a lot of sense. And I went in there and I told them about how I started out in Florida in the Depression and we were share-croppers, but I never gave up hope. And that was the story. But these textbooks teach the blacks there *is* no hope, and I think that's a terrible mistake. You ought to be teaching young people that there are tremen-dous opportunities, and there's a chance. And I started to read this pas-sage by George Schuyler and — wow!

* * *

MOFFETT: Some people have charged that the books are un-Christian. Do you think that this is true?

FIKE: Well, there were *some*. There's no question that there were *some*. There were stories in the third- and fourth-grade textbooks that referred to the story of Creation and many other stories in the Old Testament as myths. And it would tell a myth that was almost identical to this. Now, you know about the myths. They were trying to indoctrinate the chil-dren that their whole religious heritage was based on myth, and there's no real basis. It is a real offense to destroy young people's faith in a reli-gion by referring to these as myths. They would mix up the myths of the Bible with Indian myths and all those kinds of myths. . . . If they wanted to stay away from religion, that was all right, but they were not staying away from religion. They were *dabbling* in religion and trying to destroy the religious feelings of the people in this community.

MOFFETT: What about Genesis?

FIKE: I don't think there's any contradiction between the story of Gene-sis and the scientific concept of evolution.

MOFFETT: The fundamentalists feel of course that both evolution and Genesis can't be true.

FIKE: Well, you know, the fundamentalists say the world was created in seven 24-hour days, just like it says in Genesis, but there's awfully good evidence, *very* good evidence, that that's not so. There's also irre-futable evidence that evolution took place. Now, to those people who would say that evolution as where we are today is the result of random action without divine direction I would say that it's pretty hard to imag-ine that anything as complicated as a human being came into being by random evolution. . . . [From chemistry he develops the argument that staggering odds are against the random rise of life.] Let me give you another example. My daughter is studying entomology. She's going to get her doctor's degree out at Berkeley, this month, and she is doing *evolutionary studies*. She is working on developing spider mites through evolutionary processes, beneficial spider mites that will eat up the harmful spider mites. And of course she's using evolution, and it's done all the time to evolve various species that will do what we want them to do instead of what we don't. What they do is select the ones that do what you want and breed and modify them, so that we in effect control evolution, create things that have different strains and different tendencies and different resistances. She was in a meeting with a group of scientists, and they were talking about these kinds of problems, and they said, "This insect is *designed* in such a way that it can withstand so-and-so; this plant is *designed* so that it will do this." That's the way scientists talk; they say it's *designed* in order to— And my daughter said, "Did you ever stop to think that we're talking as if somebody really designed all this, as if there was a hand that planned it." Well, there was a big silence; nobody even wanted to discuss that possibility. These people are by and large publicly committed to the idea that it's all the result of random action, but when they're *talking* about it, they talk as though it's all the product of some kind of design. . . .

MOFFETT: I think it's the same here as with "anti-Communism"; maybe we ought to change the terms, and instead of talking about anti-Darwinism or antievolution—

FIKE: We ought to talk about "random evolution" instead of just "evolution."

Mrs. Fike telephoned to remind her husband that it was supper time.

My teen-aged waitress where I had dinner afterward recognized *Elmer's Tune* lying on the table and volunteered to tell me that Fike spoke to her high school about "his ups and downs in business" and that he speaks occasionally at other schools about business and free enterprise.

6

Through a Glass, Darkly

When I told Avis Hill I liked his native-stone fireplace and chimney, he said that his wife and he had built it, as they had other parts of the house, which was one of those modest but comfortable and attractive homes speckled along a stretch of Route 214 that makes up the hamlet of Alum Creek. He had lost, he explained, about $75,000 during the controversy, presumably for legal costs and other support of the cause. This included his plumbing business, and now he has become a full-time minister of the Freedom Gospel Mission in Alum Creek.

The Rev. Hill is younger than Ezra Graley by a good ten years—a small wiry man that I imagine was a scrappy, high-energy hell-raiser as a kid. He vaunts his independence and his lineage from early North Carolinian mountaineers, the sort that takes a stand so tough that invaders bog down and give up. I found him likable. When not merely echoing old points he and others have scored many times, he can be open and honest. Topics he had not thought a lot about before brought out this side. Like this one.

HILL: In the Kanawha County textbook controversy there was a book in the elementary class that, in that book, taught role-playing, and they had a street riot. It was right in the book, and the teacher was to show the kids, and they were going to act out a street riot, OK? Today you sit down to watch television—I've walked in some houses, and there's some programs on TV today, one in particular, it's called "The Hawk." And I go into someone's house and I'm sittin' there and here comes a little fellow, three years old, and he's showing his muscles. And here that little rascal jumped right straight at me, and the parents thought that was funny: "He's a hawk." It works on TV. When Evel Knievel tried to jump the Grand Canyon, the next day the hospitals were full of little kids who tried to jump fences and ravines and things, see? So the role-playing and the little kids — they — they go ahead and show the rioting. They — they — teach to role-play. Well, it'll come back home to you. It'll catch up with you. That's the reason there have to be guards in the schools today.

MOFFETT: Do you think people tend to do the things they read about?

HILL: Monkey see, monkey do. And yes, it works that way. It sure does.

MOFFETT: Of course for the original riots there wasn't any model, at the beginning.

HILL: Well, at that point there was just that oppression and people got fed up. And there was no other place for them to vent their frustrations except in the streets, because they weren't understood, they weren't listened to, they weren't done on, they were talked about, they were third- and fourth-class citizens.

MOFFETT: Do you think people who don't feel that need but who do role-play, say, in school or read about it, are going to have some of the same strong reasons —

HILL: I think psychologically, I think subconsciously, I think —

MOFFETT: Even if they don't have these real circumstances in their life?

HILL: I think that for every action that takes place in a person's life if they would open their mind or allow themselves to be in a position to where that can affect them subconsciously I believe it will plant the seed there, and I believe that somewhere it'll start to break them down. That may be farfetched —

MOFFETT: There's some problem about telling the difference between the real thing and the made-up thing?

HILL: I think most people in life fantasize a lot.

MOFFETT: You think most people do confuse the real-life thing with things in books?

HILL: In fact, we have a group of people that don't know reality. I think we have a problem today with people being able to realize what reality really is. And the TV and actors, it's all so much reality, as we watch it on the screen, and it's one thing to read it with the mind but it's another thing that brings it into a whole new sense in role-playing — when you act it out.

MOFFETT: You're saying it's more powerful than reading is?

HILL: Oh most definitely. I preach the word of God teaches that. He says, "Be ye not just *hearers* of the word, but be you also *doers* of the word." Faith without works is dead. If you read something that's just like going to school. You go to school and you got your degrees, you're out. What good is education, what good is knowledge if you store it in your head and you never put it to use? When it becomes productive it's not while it's stored up here, but it's when you go to putting it together, and actually bringing it about. And that brings it into a whole different realm; role-playing brings it into a whole different realm than just reading it.

MOFFETT: In role-playing you pretend to be somebody else. Do you think that's a bad idea to do that? That they'll forget who they are. You know what I mean, if you —

HILL: I mean, let's look at it from this perspective: how many movie stars do you see that lost their identity from role playing? [Laughs.] You know, they wind up OD'ing on drugs or wind up dead in some motel room because they've lost their identity. Sure, role-playing, it tends to have an impact on peoples' mind. And there came a time in the textbook controversy, to be quite honest with you, I realized I know that as far as the educational structure and as far as mainstream society is concerned, I was looked on as a nobody; I was spoken of as a backwoods fundamentalist Bible-toting, foot-stomping, Bible-thumping preacher. You know. *National Geographic* looked at me as self-ordained, but that didn't bother me, but there came a time when back a few years ago when I was recognized and the press was beating a path to my door, and the Japanese press and BBC and NBC and ABC and CBS, and they knew me by my first name, and they were there and I was on the boob tube at six o'clock every night, and people were calling and the Donahues and this and that, and there came a time in my life — that, you know, just human nature, the old ego starts building, the head will start swelling. That happens with man. Same way in any other thing; all you have to do is pat people on the back and tell them how good they are and lift them up and bolst them up, and, man, you can make them think they're the Queen of England, or they're the King of France.

MOFFETT: So you feel you went through some kind of development from all this yourself?

HILL: Sure I did. Sure I did. I — I — I where I started [Laughs.], when I started I — I — I was on an ego trip for a while. There's no one that gets thrust out like that that can keep from getting an ego trip to a point.

MOFFETT: There's an awful lot of attention.

HILL: Yes, but I'm glad I woke up, you know, I didn't go off the deep end.

MOFFETT: Well, maybe you just learned something from that.

HILL: Oh, I'm sure I learned, yeah, I don't look at life in any other way except every day is a new learning experience. If I don't learn from each day there's something wrong. I'm not going to stand still. Either you go forward or backward —

MOFFETT: That's mainly why we're here.

HILL: Right, so each day is learning and I learned a lot. If I had it to do over again, the basic philosophy that I — is still the same today. I've learned some new techniques; I would do some things differently, but I'm not saying that my ultimate goal wouldn't still be the same.

MOFFETT: Well, I'm not going to try to center on role-playing because we're not here to do that, but I know what their rationale is. Some of them say the way to learn what other people feel is by getting in other people's shoes.

HILL: It is a way to learn. Yes it is.

MOFFETT: Do you feel it's misused? Is that it?

HILL: Yes, abused and misused.

MOFFETT: You mean it wouldn't *necessarily* be a bad way to learn?

HILL: I've used it. I use it in church.

MOFFETT: How do you use it there?

HILL: I use it from the Word, a positive part of the Word. As I said, the Scripture says, "Be ye not just hearers but be ye doers of the word." Now —

MOFFETT: Do you mean in the sense that in your preaching you act out the things you might say — ?

HILL: Well, I believe in divine healing. A lot of churches, a lot of religions don't believe that. I believe that in God's word, in His word he said, "They shall lay hands on the sick, and they shall recover." Well now, I don't believe that I can just talk and it happens. I believe when God's word comes alive is when you put it into effect, and you go to using it. I don't think I have that healing power — don't get me wrong — but what I'm saying is that God's word don't lie, and if it's truth, and I feel it is, then if I carry out the truth then he'll comply. He cannot lie, he has to — carry out what he says he'll do. If he doesn't he's a liar and then what's the point of me serving him? You see what I'm saying? So yes, I encourage when someone is sick I encourage using the Scripture. It says, "Anoint with oil and pray." I anoint with oil and I pray. I *carry out* the word of God. That's role-playing, but it's from a positive standpoint of not hurting, not tearing down but building —

MOFFETT: There's a connection I haven't quite gotten yet — it may be my problem — between your role-playing idea and the word of God. You were saying — ?

HILL: OK. I don't — I don't — I'm not teaching role-playing as something — some fantasy or some playing the part of Jesus, you see. Maybe the role-playing is, you put yourself in the shoes of this particular situation that we've presented here, but it's role-playing to the extent that it is factual, that it'll work, and it does work, and what I'm saying —

MOFFETT: Do you put yourself into another role?

HILL: I put myself into — I'm a Christian, number one, and that's all that's necessary. He said, "These signs shall follow them that believe." I'm a believer. So I'm automatically in that role. The only thing that does not *make* it work is the fact that I don't *do* it. When I *do* it, then God's *obligated* to *honor* his word, because he said, "I cannot lie." That's what the Scripture says, he cannot lie, so if he *said* to do it, we *do* it. And by *doing* it, puts the faith in God we have to work.

MOFFETT: I guess you mean by role-playing, in this case, you mean putting on—putting yourself into a higher role than one ordinarily plays, one that God has sort of set for us?

HILL: [Sigh.] In essence, the—

MOFFETT: A more elevated role than we usually play.

HILL: Yes indeed, yes, because the Christian is weak, because it is there and it has *been* there since Christ's days, but the church has just failed to use it. They have looked over the top of it. They're overlooking. There's so much more there, *in* the word of God *for* the church, but they're failing to put their faith to work and they're failing to *use* what he has given us.

MOFFETT: This makes me think of that whole issue about, you know, interpreting the Scriptures. Do you feel that your approach is the literal interpretation, or do you find yourself varying, sometimes more literal and sometimes more symbolical?

HILL: No, there are symbolical, symbolic passages in the Bible— words, candles, trees, and things—they take on a symbol—

MOFFETT: Revelation—it's pretty hard to take that literally.

HILL: Yes, right, so there are symbols to be used. So when we say "literally" I don't mean literally word per se but I do mean the interpretation of that word without taking away out of the Greek, or the Hebrew, of that interpretation.

MOFFETT: But apparently some ministers feel that some books of the Bible have to be interpreted literally and some not. For example, Genesis, there's a feeling there that that should be interpreted literally but not others. How's a person to know which parts of the Bible to take literally and which not?

HILL: Those things which are literal are just as plain as the nose on your face. They're spoken absolutely, you don't have to read, you don't have to search it out, it's there, it's plain and—

MOFFETT: Well, Christ spoke in parables often—

HILL: Yes, he did, to get his point across.

MOFFETT: When he was speaking to the people.

HILL: Yes, they couldn't understand.

MOFFETT: Right. But those you don't take literally, right? Because He Himself, Christ Himself explains many of those to the disciples. When He speaks of tares, he doesn't mean tares.

HILL: Oh, I see. Yeah, well no, in that, when he speaks of when the good seed was planted and the tares came up, that choked it out. No, I speak to that as Christ meant to them, "To Christians you are the sheep, you are His sheep, you are His followers, and those tares are the world, those who are unsaved that will grow up amongst you." So he said, "Abstain from the presence of evil." So, you don't—because the bird lands in your hair, don't mean you let him grow a nest there, so to speak. That's a parable itself. So not literally — but I *speak* it as literally: yes, this is what Christ told the disciples. This is what he's telling you today.

MOFFETT: Do you try to give any sort of guidelines to your own flock about where to interpret more literally and where not to? This is a big issue, it seems to me, because there's an awful lot of disagreement among Christians about passages in the Bible, and a lot of it has to do with how symbolic it is. And when it is symbolical then people interpret the symbols differently.

HILL: Yes, I know that. I realize that.

MOFFETT: And it seems to me that this creates a lot of differences among very well meaning Christians.

HILL: Well, now you see, I know the interpretation I have will differ with a lot of people, but the interpretation of God's word — I've read different Scriptures and will get different interpretations, and different sermons from the same Scripture.

MOFFETT: And all believe it's the inspired word of God, sincerely.

HILL: Yes, yes, but, as we read in the Bible, it says, "The half has never been told," and we only scratch the surface, and that's what makes the word of God so intriguing, so interesting. That's what makes it still the world's best seller, because there's so much in there that's never been brought out, and it's deep and there's secrets in there.

MOFFETT: People are at different levels of understanding and that is something that you have to realize.

HILL: Yes, sure do.

MOFFETT: You know, like when I was a child I spoke as a child —

HILL: And when I became a man I put away —

MOFFETT: And that whole passage in Corinthians is obviously implying that when you grow up you see differently.

HILL: But you go toward God, you don't go away from him.

MOFFETT: Right, everybody is going toward God, but they're at very different stages.

HILL: Surely, oh yes, right, we call that sanctification in the church we go to.

MOFFETT: Varying degrees of sanctification, right?

HILL: Yes.

MOFFETT: Well, seems to me what this means is people are bound not to understand each other, unless they realize just that, that they're all at different stages of understanding, and they're all going to God but they're talking about it differently. It's too bad to see them conflict about it.

HILL: It is, it is for a fact, it is for a fact, but on the other hand, just to give you an example, the Episcopalian priest who was in the forefront as far as the clergy is concerned was Jim Lewis, who was front and center protextbook. Jim's Episcopalian faith, and many Episcopalians didn't agree with Jim Lewis because I've got their names and addresses, and many of his friends left his church over it. I don't believe the Christians today—the Bible is absolute in Romans about the gays and homosexuals and about "thou shall not kill" and being proabortion, and Jim stood for those things, and Jesus even spoke, he said, "Ye shall know them by their fruits." I don't believe that a Christian can take a life, like a—they can call it a fetus if they want to . . . and try to clear their conscience with it. In all good conscience I could not take two gay women and bring them into my church and bless their marriage. I could not allow the Communist party to have meetings in my church. You see what I'm saying? So there's a deep split between me and Jim Lewis. And Jim once asked me, I was standing in a parade in South Charleston on Armistice Day, last year. The Communists were coming down to disrupt that Armistice Day parade. Our congressman was there. Jim was there holding up his peace signals and signs, and I was there carrying the American flag. And " There's no peaceful co-existence with Communism." You can't co-exist with Communism. They push and push and push. Jim came over to me and said, "Avis, why can't you and I have a dialogue?" I said, "We don't believe the same way. Your standards are different from mine, and as long as your standards are different from mine it's an impossibility for us to have a dialogue." We cannot compromise. I cannot compromise my beliefs. I'll not let down in what I believe, fundamentally. Fundamentally as an American I cannot coexist with Communism. . . . Cause what they're wanting is my freedom, they're not there to bargain.

MOFFETT: Was that the big difference of opinion between you and Lewis?

HILL: A good bit of difference, yes. Well, not particularly Communism, cause I didn't call Jim Lewis Communist, and I'm not calling him a Communist today, you understand? Jim Lewis served in the Marine Corp. I'm not calling Jim Lewis a Communist, and I don't want nobody to ever think that I called him that. However, I'm somewhat upset about how Jim Lewis can do those things. I just can't for the life of me understand him.

MOFFETT: How do you account for a guy like him? Been in the Marines—

HILL: [Sigh.] Somebody somewhere has turned him sour.

MOFFETT: Does he seem sour about this country? I don't know him, you see.

HILL: Well, you see, that's what I can't understand. He *talks* that he's not, but he *shows* that he is.

MOFFETT: Shows it by—?

HILL: By allowing these forces, who are anti-American, to come into his presence.

MOFFETT: Anti-American? Are they Communists?

HILL: Yes, they're Communists, and I think it's anti-Christian to want to kill a baby. . . . He may not think so, but I think it is, because I believe when God said in the Ten Commandments "Thou shall not kill," he meant it. . . . I believe that God would allow me to kill if the Communists were overpowering America and he meant to protect my family. . . . But I don't believe that God meant for us to kill babies, for us to kill children. . . . I believe government is creating, is sanctioning murder today, in abortion. And I believe that because of that, I believe America is going to pay for that. I believe doctors and nurses and hospitals and institutions are going to pay for that.

MOFFETT: What do you think about the soldiers who killed all those civilians in Vietnam?

HILL: Well, yes we did.

MOFFETT: You know, once we got over there and got the war going and all.

HILL: Sure. Right.

MOFFETT: A lot of guys feel guilty about that—

HILL: Sure they feel guilty.

MOFFETT: And many have cracked up.

HILL: And it would surely upset me, it would surely upset me to kill, but you've got to realize something. We weren't the aggressors.

MOFFETT: Were you in Vietnam?

HILL: No, I wasn't, but I have a lot of friends that were. We weren't the aggressors. We were defending the people, who wanted to be free, and Vietnam was invaded, by the—atheistic society of Communist China, North Vietnam, and we were defending freedom. . . .

* * *

MOFFETT: How did you become a leader?

HILL: Just happened. A week before school started I had been in a twelve-week tent revival in St. Albans, and we'd seen hundreds of souls come to the Lord and make decisions. I had people out of the church kept coming to me all summer long. The books were on display all summer, being showed different places, and the Sunday before school started— Labor Day on Monday, school was to start on Tuesday—at the St. Albans roadside park, some of the people had been coming to tent meetings said, "Rev. Hill, please come over to the roadside park Sunday." Said "Whether you look at the books or not, we'd like for you to give the invocation, and the benediction." They'd been after me so long finally I gave in. . . . I didn't have time all summer. And even though the group had been meeting, and they'd had the big meeting up at the warehouse and had been on the radio, and Jim Lewis had been on the radio, I'd stayed completely away from it, didn't want to get involved. Went up there that Sunday just to offer the invocation and benediction. . . . and when I got there they had the books there on display, and they started bringing me books and showing me passages, and I began to leaf through them.

And that spring before school was out my daughter was going to Ann Bailey Elementary School, and the teacher gave my daughter — she was a fifth grader — a book on evolution, how we evolved through the monkey thing, and told my daughter to read that book and bring it back and give a report on it to the school. My daughter brought it home and I was — at that time I wasn't even going to church — but I had that strong Christian background, upbringing. She turned to me — and my daughter had gone away to church camp that summer before, and she'd made a decision to serve the Lord, and she'd always been taught in creation and she'd always been taught that evolution was just a theory of Darwin — she came to me and she said, "Daddy," she said, "My teacher told me that I had to give a report on this book," and said, "I don't believe in it and I don't want to give it. But she told me that if I didn't give the report on this book she'd fail me." I said, "Honey, you tell that teacher" — and at that time, it was before I was in church and I used some well chosen adjectives to go along with it — I said, "You tell that teacher that you don't have to give that report, that your daddy said you didn't have to give that report on that book." She went back to school the next day and she went to stand up in class. The teacher said, "Paula, will you stand up and give your report now?" She said, "Mrs. So-and-So" — whose name I'll not use — "I'll not give that report, and I'll not read that book in class." She said, "I have a book I *will* read," and she opened her Bible — and I did not coach her because it didn't bother me that much at that time — she opened her Bible, and she began in Genesis 1, "In the beginning God — " and the teacher failed her.

And then I went up there on that Sunday afternoon, and I saw that garbage, that trash, that four-letter words, and if I had've spoken when I was going to school, if I'd have got caught writing on the bathroom *wall* when I went to school, the principal would have tanned my hide and probably expelled me, and now there they were in plain view that did not need to be in the school books, in the textbooks, and there they were being brought out in the education concept saying, "OK, here it is, society approves it and it's alright, now let's do it." And that upset me. My daugher was failed because *she* believed in creation and was being *forced* to read about evolution and give a report on it. She received an F, and now I read it in the textbooks.

And today I . . . drive by the schools and I see quart wine bottles and I see beer bottles and I see students drinking and I see them smoking their dope, and that wouldn't have existed in 1961, not in West Virginia, not in this county that I graduated from. When I went to school in 1961 our school was twenty years old and it looked like it was a new one on the inside. You didn't see students leaning against the walls with their feet on the wall, dirtying and defacing the school with initials and names all over it.

MOFFETT: Do you feel it's all the fault of the school?

HILL: I feel it's all the fault because the discipline's broken down, and the kids were just as mean then as they are now. [He goes into a long speech here blaming schools for crime and other ills.]

As I was leaving, he gave me a copy of a record album that he and his family and friends had made, titled *Textbook War—Hills of West Virginia*. In large red letters, the word "war" leaps out of the front cover, which bears also a photo of the Rev. Hill, surrounded by his family, squatting on the steps of the Kanawha County Jail wearing a coonskin cap and holding a long mountaineer's rifle. His wife, two sons, and two daughters are wearing costumes of red, white, and blue. On the back of the cover is a collage of news photos of events of the controversy. The Rev. Hill sings (very well) and a spirited, highly accomplished bluegrass band of fiddle, piano, and banjo play several songs written about the "textbook war." However appalling some of the ideas expressed in the words may strike some of us, it is nigh impossible not to fall in with the rollicking music and exuberant performance. For one reason or another I recommend the album most highly. With the Rev. Hill's permission I include here the lyrics of three of the relevant songs because they may express best of all what the protesters felt they stood for as well as what they fear. Another of the songs appeared at the end of chapter 3.

Kanawha County Surprise
Robert Hoye

Chorus: Kanawha County, gave them a surprise!
They never figured we'd ever uprise.
We were still willing to compromise.
But our little children will never read those lies.

When the police arrested Graley, Horan, and Hill,
They figured prison would soon break their will,
But he will perish who takes up the sword.
You got the law, cops, but we got the Lord.

Chorus

Well, the liberals will come, and they'll stripmine the land.
They'll steal and they'll rob and they'll take what they can.

Liberals will send their children off to Yale.
Miners can go on and go off to jail.

Chorus

Our Lost Heaven
Joy Harmon

(Sung to the tune of John Denver's "Country Road")

Our lost Heaven, West Virginia, dirty textbooks, broken-hearted
        mothers.
Life is rough here, rougher than the sea.
Our rights have all been taken, protesting peacefully.

Chorus: Country road, take me away from home, take me today.
        West Virginia, our lost heaven.
        Country road, take me away.

All my memories gather 'round her,
The way she used to be,
The way I want to remember.
Discontentment hangs across the sky,
Like the morning sunshine,
Makes me want to cry.

Chorus

I hear a voice in the morning as she calls me.
Radio reminds me of my home. I'm astray.
Ridin' down the road I get a feelin'
That I should 'a left home
Yesterday, yesterday.

Chorus

Give God the Glory
Avis Hill

While travelling down life's highway seeking Satan's evil ways,
I wandered in and out of all worldly things today.
I hurt the ones that loved me and caused them all that pain.
But Satan had his holt on me, and I could not refrain.
I thought in desperation. I was no good within.
I felt my friends would be better off
If I would put an end to my wicked ways, deceitful plots and all my
        personal gain.
I'd take my life and end it all so they could live again.
My Christian friends approached me and they told me how to live.

They said I turned my back on God and I had no peace within.
And through these wonderful people, well, I changed my life of sin.
I want to give God the glory for taking me back in.
And I want to tell the world about Jesus and how he saved my soul.
And I want to tell the world about Jesus and how he made me whole.
Yes, I want to give God the glory for saving my soul.
I want to give God the glory for making me whole.
Well, he picked me up, cleansed my heart, and gave me the victory.
Now I want to give God the glory for saving a wretch like me.

7

Race War, Holy War

I read all about the wars over religion — the hatred, bloodshed, and violence — but they did not come home to me until this controversy.

— A Kanawha County high school student testifying before
the inquiry panel of the National Education Association[1]

I talked with a staff member of the Kanawha County School District in a remodeled but still-spired white wooden church facing one side of the small public square upon which the School Board building itself is located. The old church houses the offices that have overflowed from there and forms part of what employees call "the complex." We talked in the one relatively unoccupied room available, a lounge next to which lay a larger room in which the textbooks had been displayed — first for preadoption perusal and later for examination after the controversy began in the fall. She preferred not to be named and is cited as STAFF.

STAFF: Textbooks weren't the issue. No one will ever convince me. The major issue was a political one and had to do with the black-and-white issue. Now, there are people right here in this complex who would deny that, vehemently.

MOFFETT: What else political?

STAFF: Part of it was the desire to set up a different *kind* of school system. The whole movement for a voucher system started in the Anaheim area. I think all those things are a part of it, along with the black-white thing. I think it's a marriage of the conservative forces and the fundamentalist Christians. . . . A lot of the fellows around here were drawn into it and loved the publicity they got because it was the first recognition they had ever had. Most of them uneducated semiliterate. . . . New sports jackets, new patent leather shoes. That may sound like a terrible thing to say, but that's the way I saw it. . . . The whole experience was so traumatic for me. I'm not over it yet and never will be. I thought I might lose my mind, it was so frustrating.

94

MOFFETT: What was the hardest part? You had all these people coming in. [To examine the books after school started.]

STAFF: As a general rule, they weren't too offensive. Most of them were very very nice, and most of them were simply frightened out of their wits. They thought that somebody really was going to corrupt their children. Many could hardly read, but then many — fairly educated people — would come in, read the books, and say, "I can't see a thing wrong. What are they talking about?" So many just didn't want to read the books at all. They just took at face value what they heard. . . . It was really traumatic. In early October of that year the books were all removed from the schools. The superintendent just gave the order, said, "Take up all the books. They're to be taken to the warehouse." We're talking about hundreds of thousands of books. In many schools, the teachers told me, they stood there and cried. The *kids* cried. The students at George Washington High School, one of the city schools, refused to give up their books. They kept them. The books were stacked to the ceiling in our storage facilities. Eventually they were put back into the schools, but many of them were really not used.

MOFFETT: When we were putting *Interaction* together we were trying to implement individualized reading, so we suggested that schools buy only a half dozen copies of each title so they could afford more titles.

STAFF: That's the way they were purchased.

MOFFETT: Of course it never had a chance to operate that way, and we weren't thinking specifically of censorship, but we figured that if it ever did happen that parents objected to some books, you could honestly say that their kid didn't have to read any particular book.

STAFF: That's not the way it worked. They didn't want *anyone's* child to read —

MOFFETT: Did they *say* that?

STAFF: Oh yes. You know, we've always had a policy in this county that if you objected to something, your child didn't have to read it. An alternate selection would be — but that wasn't the way it worked.

* * *

MOFFETT: Was Alice Moore sincere and in good faith?

STAFF: No.

MOFFETT: Or do you feel she was politically ambitious?

STAFF: Not to achieve an office but to achieve an issue.

MOFFETT: Was the issue other than what she said?

STAFF: I think the issue is black and white. There are many people here do not believe that. But I think the greatest shock to me was realizing that the strong prejudice was right below the surface. And I'm not a crusader or anything.

MOFFETT: Because you felt the prejudice crossed lines?

STAFF: Every line, every line.

MOFFETT: You feel it's worse here than in other parts of the country?

STAFF: No, probably, but it's here. And yet when we integrated in '55, when we integrated our West Virginia State College, one of the best black colleges in the country, the integration went very very smoothly. We've never had any outward riots or anything of that kind.

MOFFETT: I didn't mean that as a leading question, but things were more intense here, and I wonder why *here*.

STAFF: I think that was the *major* issue. There were lots of subissues, like the consolidation of schools that had taken place. Many people hated to give up their community schools. It's going to happen again, because of loss of enrollment in our school district. So that has been an issue. Jealousy in some of the rural parts of the community, jealousy against the rich people, the town people, that kind of thing. There were a lot of issues.

MOFFETT: I'm trying to tie all the things together. [She laughs.] The platform seems to be made up of planks that don't necessarily go together in an obvious way.

STAFF: Well, it's difficult *to* connect it.

MOFFETT: Militarism and phonics — what connects them?

STAFF: This great stress on intensive phonics — I was rather amused: one of the elementary supervisors at the time of the controversy was a very very conservative stereotype of the schoolmarm, and one of the things objected to in one of the first-grade books in the *Communicating* series was "Three Billy Goats Gruff." Kids have grown up with "Three Billy Goats Gruff" forever. They supposedly objected to it because the troll was vicious and he looked fierce under the bridge and all that. And the program that Mrs. Moore was advocating is an intensive phonics approach. When it was adopted, this teacher came in the hallway there, and she said, "You wouldn't believe this book." She was leafing through it, and she said, "Here is the troll — and he is stark naked." And this is the book they were wanting. You see, there's no logic at all to their objections. Let me tell you one other thing — talking about those early books — that I thought was really interesting. The board members didn't come in to look at the books.

MOFFETT: Preadoption, you mean?

STAFF: Uh-huh. And during the process we set up the room next door and had it all ready, and only one member came in, one day, and he wasn't coming in to read the books. I think it was a second-level book in the *Communicating* series had a version of "Jack and the Bean Stalk" that people objected to. We all leafed through it and couldn't figure out why they were having such a fit over "Jack and the Bean Stalk." Well, openly, they were saying, "You're teaching children to steal, and you're teaching them to kill." You know, didn't make sense. Anyway, when this board member came in, we asked him. We were in the room next door here. And I'll never forget. He took the book, and he put it down on the table. "It's not what's in the book — it's the *cover*." Well, we hadn't even *thought* of that. It was a collage of several different figures, on the cover, and in the foreground there are two children, and the little girl is carrying a big bouquet of daisies, and the little boy is leaning over like this [Bending forward.] smelling them. And he took his finger and went like this, clockwise, and he said, "*That's* what they're objecting to, in my area," and he circled that little boy and girl. The little boy is black, and the little girl is white. That was so traumatic for me. . . .

*　*　*

Even with the terrible drama of what happened there were some funny things. One of the funniest happened in the room next door here. A young couple came in and wanted to see the elementary books. One of the elementary consultants was helping them, and all at once she noticed that they just looked very angry, threw down the book, and started to leave. So she went back to see what was wrong. And they had found the adjective "onomatopoeic" and they thought it was a dirty word. . . . [Both laugh.]

*　*　*

I remember there was a selection in the *Man* series from *Babi Yar*, and they [the minority members of the Textbook Review Committee] objected to that vehemently. Of course that's part of the approach they have, that the Jewish massacre really didn't occur.

MOFFETT: That's right. That's kind of the latest wrinkle, isn't it, that the Holocaust was made up?

STAFF: That it was made up. There are books out on that now. So they objected to that. There was little logic in the *way* they objected. It was almost impossible to *answer* the objections. We tried that. We wrote reams of answers to things that appeared in the daily paper, but who wants to read those answers? They're calm and sensible, and the newspapers didn't even want to print them.

MOFFETT: There wasn't even any field of contest on which to grapple.

STAFF: And how do you reason with a person who has no background in literature? Trying to explain to him the symbolism of something? You can't do it.

MOFFETT: Uh-huh. Symbolism seems to be a problem anyway, doesn't it, because of the tendency toward literal interpretation?

STAFF: Oh yes. Just *literal*, right across.

MOFFETT: Do you have any feeling about that? You know, as an old English teacher I recognize literal interpretation as a problem that a lot of English teachers deal with. A good part of literature is symbolic. Is it an *inability* to think symbolically? Some kind of concrete-mindedness?

STAFF: Well, I think that's a big part of it. Also, I think poor teaching. Much of it is a result of poor teaching. You know, we put so much stress on naming the author and name the characters and describe the characters but not much on anything beyond that.

MOFFETT: In a way, that amounts to saying that the pigeons have come home to roost — that we get such problems from the public because we have *created* them by not teaching better.

STAFF: Well, in a way we have. And yet we have a *good* school system. Through the years it has been recognized as one of the leading ones in the country. But that doesn't mean that we have perfect teachers.

MOFFETT: Well, it's a national problem, isn't it? Getting students beyond being literal-minded, and they vary a lot among themselves.

STAFF: And then — you mentioned the fundamentalist ministers — many of them had quit school at junior high age. And teachers hadn't had a great deal of chance to give them literary experience. . . .

MOFFETT: Did you feel strongly a sense of conspiracy theory among the antibook people? That this was a conspiracy of some liberal establishment?

STAFF: I think that is what they *wanted* people to think.

MOFFETT: You mean you don't feel they necessarily believed that?

STAFF: No. No, I think they would like people to *believe* that, but I don't think they really did. I think they were simply *using* people. And the books were the vehicle for political gain.

MOFFETT: You say by "political" you don't necessarily mean seeking office.

STAFF: No, but to get across their *views*, their ultraconservative *view*.

MOFFETT: That would sort of help explain one thing, wouldn't it? That kind of conservatism doesn't seem to come from any particular kind of social group or social class. Some of the people are very well educated or very wealthy.

STAFF: The money supporting them *has* to be coming from wealthy people. There's too much of it.

By way of supplementing the interview, she gave me a copy of an article that a language arts consultant for the district had written for the *Journal of Research and Development in Education*, which devoted its spring issue of 1976 to "Censorship and the Schools." It is a moving and eloquent account. "And through it all—the frustration, disappointment, confusion—three times I cried."[2] The first time was when word reached her office that bewildered little school children were being harassed and told to go home. The second occasion came after a young teacher with a two-month-old baby told her that her mother-in-law, who had been listening to a neighbor woman denouncing the textbooks, said, "I hate to think that you'll be raising my grandchild!"[3]

She cried a third time on reading an objection written by the Citizens Textbook Review Committee to "The Cherry Tree Carol" from an *Interaction* book of ballads.

> The latter selection had been my own favorite ballad from years past. Traced to 14th-Century Scotland, "The Cherry Tree Carol" has been one of our most popular literary works handed down in the oral tradition in this Appalachian area. Its message of the power of God resounded again and again in the homes of our forefathers. I remembered some 30 years ago when my teaching career began in a rural high school in West Virginia. During our study of folk literature, one quiet, shy girl agreed to sing a simple little ballad she had learned from her grandmother, who in turn had learned it from her mother. That beautiful song was "The Cherry Tree Carol."
>
> But now I read: "*Objection:* The lyrics of this song are subtly sacreligious [sic] and can be construed to cast aspersions on the scriptural account of the virginity of Mary the Mother of Jesus."
>
> I left the office.[4]

During the second month of that stormy school year the author was asked to speak to a minister who kept returning to the Central Office to look at the texts and voice his strenuous disapproval to whomever he could buttonhole. Alarmed by his argument that the books should contain no references to religion at all, she responded that if you removed religious references from the classroom you would have to ban much of the world's great literature such as the works of Dante, Milton, and Tolstoy. Would he really want that? Yes, it would have to go. When she asked him if he would also eliminate history and social science too for the same reason, the reply was again, "Yes, I would." With mounting consternation she asked about art—the Sistine Chapel, the statue of Moses, all the music expressing religious feeling and faith. He had had a religious painting on the wall of his church. "I finally got rid of it!"

"If you remove literature, history, art, music, then what will we have left? As a citizen of this community, I don't feel as you do. I want my children and grandchildren not only to read well, but to be well read; to understand the role of history; to appreciate the vast richness of man through his art and music. Do you have a right to deprive children whose parents do not agree with you—to deprive them of an education?" I said.

"Their souls are more important!"

"But this approach is anarchy, and we live in a democratic society. Would you discard our form of government?"

"That too may have to go. Don't you people know that this is a religious war, that it will be greater than the Civil War?"[5]

After the interview I ate my lunch of peanuts and bananas on a bench in the little square, facing the School Board building. On this spot had occurred numerous demonstrations, eventually made illegal by injunction but continued despite arrests. I visualized the crowds of incensed parents that had milled here at first when the books were up for adoption and then again many times in the months to follow as they monitored the highly charged board meetings. I could see the staff glancing nervously down out of their office windows to check the action during the day, as some had described to me. I remembered photos in the newspapers of young mothers sobbing uncontrollably, like children themselves. All that passion.

PART 3
WHAT'S IN
THE BOOKS

8

Commies and Sex

I was no stranger to some of the attitudes so well voiced in the last chapters. I did not need to go to West Virginia to hear them. My parents were Southern, and I grew up in Jackson, Mississippi, until high school age, when we moved to Toledo, Ohio. So I knew well how many people feel in the Deep South and Middle America. In the sleepy Jackson of the Depression era nearly everyone I knew routinely talked against Jews and Catholics and treated blacks still with a mixture of intimacy and subjugation left over from slave days. Some people were still fighting the Civil War with a chip on the shoulder and a regional chauvinism comparable to that in West Virginia. People of both states have striven by overcompensation to repair the damage to identity entailed by secession and by living as a subculture within a larger general culture — a plight, we note, shared by those other minorities against whom they have often discriminated. Tracing family genealogy has always been a heavy industry in Mississippi and the rest of the Deep South, where one way to recoup status has been to prove blood purity and descent from illustrious forebears.

I was dismayed, hurt, and angry when these book-banners knocked down the program on which I had spent over three years of full-time work and which I had expected to spiritualize some of public education. But I understood these people. Hearing them in the interviews was like listening to voices from the past, not just from my youth but from many visits to West Virginia with my wife and daughters.

My heart is with them. They are right about many things or at least right in a sense, at some level of understanding. They should *not* have had my books crammed down their throats. Avis' daughter should *not* have been forced to do a book report on evolution. A metropolitan school district should *not* have ignored the known feelings and views of part of their constituency in catering to the wishes of the more articulate and affluent. (But I grieve too for the suffering of those school administrators and teachers torn by the forces around them. I know how they feel too.) The curriculum should *not* be a standardized thing forced on all

103

alike. It *is* wrong for opportunistic outsiders to rob and pollute the land and siphon off the profits out of the region. Appalachian folk should *not* be derided and disparaged by people with more money or education than wisdom or compassion. They *should* resist materialism and stand up for the underlying spiritual nature of reality.

I would like Alice and Avis, Elmer and Ezra, and others who think as they do, to know that a person responsible for one of the programs they so abhorred does not at all resemble the enemy they picture and does not regard them as the enemy. I'm a family man, love this country, and believe in the underlying spiritual nature of reality. I think the Soviet Union is totalitarian and the United States has come closer to a spiritual realization of government than any other country on earth. But I think the objectors are dreadfully wrong in some ways that endanger far more than outsiders the very family, country, and religion they think they are upholding. So while letting the objectors speak in their own words I am also going to comment and interpret. Such profound and explosive misunderstanding must be counteracted and defused. If I were to let the objections stand, at face value, I could not fulfill the purpose of this book, which is to illuminate and thereby perhaps help to alter some dire courses of events.

Also, as a creator of the disputed textbooks I am in a unique position to know some things, and I must say what I know. I know exactly how and why *Interaction* came into being. In fact, I am, necessarily, the only person who was so situated as to know at once all the details and the overview of this vast undertaking—to negotiate with the publisher, to read all the thousands of selections that did and did not go into the books, and to work with the two and a half dozen co-authors who compiled the books and the army of company editors who assembled items and ordered art on the publisher's end.

Given an unusually free hand, I decided what books there should be and set the concept of each book. I did this according to categories of literature like fables and sonnets, plays and essays, or of other familiar library classifications—into topical fiction like mystery stories and science fiction, into nonfiction like autobiography and chronicles, or into information such as reportage, research, and how-to-do-it. The neutrality of this derived quite naturally from the intention to represent every kind of reading matter produced by our society and to do so by common types encountered outside of school, as in libraries and bookstores, or by the more unusual categories of the various first-person and third-person viewpoints from which much fiction and nonfiction are written (*Fictional Memoir* or *Letters Real and Imagined*, for example). Some other unusual categories for school books were riddles, brain teasers, maps, captioned photos, comics, advertisements, transcripts, and jumprope jingles, but these too are common types of discourse.

The importance of this breakdown here is that it aims entirely at familiarizing students with the range of available kinds of reading matter and hence rules out books organized by themes or ideas. The ideas that might enter into a given book were totally open, biased only by the nature of the *type* of writing—folk literature or scientific reportage, for example.

Within a single book, my job was to set the balance and representation of different factors such as epoch, ethnic or geographical origin, style, tone, reading difficulty, sex and other personal author traits, topic or theme, and so on. Not all of these can be perfectly balanced within each book, because each type has limitations and each book is too short, but one can achieve balance across the whole classroom library of books, as I believe I did with co-authors' collaboration. Many of their first submissions I rejected and we were constantly juggling selections in a book till it seemed to me to settle down right. I never deliberately biased a book or tried to give it a message. We were aware that many youngsters would be meeting some types or topics for the first time, including definitely the children of so-called liberals and radicals, but such opening of doors partly defines education itself.

As the director of a textbook program denounced as a part of radical or Communists conspiracy, I feel obliged to state publicly that no collusion occurred between the publisher, the authors of *Interaction*, and any political or other ideological organization, nor did any of us aim to put over a particular philosophy. As large corporations, textbook publishers tend toward conservatism, political and otherwise—not perhaps the editors but certainly the executives, who make the big decisions. The NEA put the matter very well:

> To accuse American textbook publishers—one of the most highly competitive participants in the American system of free enterprise—of taking part in a communist plot to overthrow this very system is such a self-contradictory allegation that it defies rational response.[1]

Nor was the federal government involved in any way in the production of *Interaction* or, so far as I know, any of the other language arts programs listed in Kanawha County. The charge of federal influence, which Fike made there and the Gablers in Texas, has a rational basis, however, because the Great Society policy of the sixties did include funding for the development of new curricular approaches designed to offset the Soviet educational lead implied by the launching of Sputnik. The United States government did fund textbook development in math and science, social studies, and even English to the point that when commercial publishers began to bring out these programs special royalty arrangements had to be made in shifting from the public to private sectors. But this trend had died away by the time the programs purchased in Kanawha County were being produced.

In any case, I would never have done a program under federal auspices, and indeed *Interaction* was regarded as being personal in conception to a remarkable degree. I chose my co-authors for their understanding of how children learn and their knowledge of literature, language, and communication, not for any political, economic, or religious view. I take responsibility for whatever similarity they share, and what they share most is a commitment to growth.

What the objectors do detect that seems to them like a conspiracy is precisely this commitment to growth, which conflicts, as we will see, with some parents' wish to keep their children as they made them. If you feel that enlarging your child's repertory of information, ideas, and points of view will alienate your child from you, then you will of course feel also that educators are guilty of brainwashing and psychological kidnapping. To the extent some parents want schools to do little but reinforce their home training and transmit their culture, they must construe our less selective offering as betrayal and alien indoctrination.

Elmer Fike was closer to the truth in rejecting actual conspiracy in favor of the less distorted view that the "Eastern publishing and media establishment" controls textbooks and imposes its values on the books. He felt that "liberals" in power just naturally turn matters their own way, including textbooks. But we have to ask why it is that news-gathering media like TV and the press, or authors of textbooks, or publishing editors generally believe in the open market of ideas and oppose cultural bias.

More broadly, we have to ask why, generally, the better educated people are the more they support a textbook program such as *Interaction.* Why do more teachers support it than parents? It is clear that the supporters in Kanawha County were better educated than the opponents, and this holds true generally all over the country in censorship cases. Academic learning certainly does not guarantee intelligence or wisdom, and some of the most creative and original minds shun it, but if people who have had more of it are wrong about what it requires, then we should just scrap formal education. The significant minority of well educated people who do oppose books like ours tend to be in business, people of a type that Elmer Fike fairly represents.

At any rate, the real explanation, as Fike realized in his own way, is that people committed to learning — teachers — or to fact-finding — the media corps — or to dissemination of learning and information — editors and librarians — naturally favor textbooks that most further growth, information, and learning. These are all relatively well educated people as well. It is in the nature of conservatism to hold back more on growth, information, and learning (to conserve). In other words, what may be felt by some conservatives as a deliberate collaboration to brainwash children — a conspiracy — results logically from the nature of certain professions.

There is one other unfounded and libelous generalization about the textbooks that I must reject out of hand before plunging into the specific objections, which can be commented on individually. Like the charge of conspiracy, the charge of "filthy" and "pornographic," leveled repeatedly at nearly all of the disputed programs, amounted to a blanket accusation that opponents never supported by citing passages from the books because nothing in any of the books even vaguely approached the explicitness about sexual organs or sexual acts, the obscenity of sexual expletives, or the intention to titillate or arouse, to which the term "pornography" is commonly applied in either legal phrasing or common parlance. For this point let's look at the most popular molder of opposition to the books in Kanawha County.

Before the Textbook Review Committee amassed its detailed book of objections, the means for proclaiming the books' abominations were excerpts exhibited on radio and television, in leaflets and fliers. These disseminations typically quoted from the books and embedded the passages in criticism. Since these excerpts aimed to arouse the public to block or rescind adoption, we may suppose that the excerpters chose the most damaging and inflammatory passages. Distributions at rallies and small church meetings were extremely effective as a matter of fact. Catherine Candor-Chandler describes a flier put out during June of 1974, before the books had been formally purchased.

> The protest was escalated by the distribution of an estimated 50,000 fliers addressed to "Concerned Citizens — Be Aware of School Book Controversy." The flier contained twelve excerpts from the proposed books. Of these twelve two were identified by title only, one was identified by title and the author's name with the comment "A black American poet," and one was identified only as having been written by Eldridge Cleaver. The other eight excerpts gave no indication of either the title or the author and in many cases started in the middle of a sentence. Nowhere did the name of the series or the grade level in which the material was to be used in appear.[2]

The fact that the protesters could never find any "filthy" or "pornographic" passages in the books comes across most clearly in ruses resorted to to fill the empty accusation. This ethical violation was pointed out by three very different chroniclers. In chapter 1 I have already quoted Candor-Chandler's account of the dissemination of false excerpts.

Another account issued from George Hillocks, Jr., who did research in Kanawha County on the controversy and mentioned the same flier. An author of one of the other textbook series criticized Hillocks' commentary for being soft toward the protesters,[3] which makes Hillocks' following account of the flier especially credible, although I think Hillocks was merely inclined, like myself, to temper his analysis with sympathy.

> The most egregious distortion was a four-page flyer distributed under Ezra Graley's name as leader of a group calling itself Concerned Parents Protesting Text Books. The first and fourth pages quote extensive passages from the textbooks in question. At the top of the first page the following headline appears: "What Is the Kanawha County Text Book Protest All About? Judge for Yourself." At the bottom of the first page appears the words, "continued on last page." Interleaved between pages one and four are diagrams taken from books entitled *Facts about V.D. for Today's Youth* and *Facts about Sex for Today's Youth* — purportedly for use with seventh to ninth graders. Page two of the flyer presents diagrams of a "rubber" and how to use it. Page three presents a definition of sexual intercourse, along with the "street words" for vagina and diagrams of the "erect" and flaccid penis. The clear intent of the flyer is to suggest that the interleaved pages were in the textbooks. They were not, of course. According to board of education officials, the pages were copied from books in school libraries.[4]

Candor-Chandler noted that this flier was printed as a public service by the American Opinion Bookstore in Reedy, West Virginia. In its list of outsiders supporting the protest, the NEA confirms that the "store's manager has printed excerpts from the disputed textbooks and other handouts for the protesters," and it describes the store as "one of the outlets for the John Birch Society materials."[5]

Our third informant on the practice of substituting excerpts is the member of the Kanawha County Schools staff whom I interviewed. It was from her I first heard of it.

STAFF: So much of it was hearsay. Protest groups printed excerpts not only from the books under adoption, but they printed excerpts we never did find. We hunted and we looked and we never did know where they got them. And some of them were frightening.

MOFFETT: Were some of them not from the textbooks at all?

STAFF: Some of them weren't and some of them were. . . . One of the fundamentalist preachers went to Washington, for example, and took some books and didn't identify what books — I have no idea that he had the books that were adopted in the school system — took them to our senator, Byrd, a leader in the Senate, and said, "Would you want your grandchild to read these?" and he said, "No." Well, that just spread all over the papers. That was our senator condemning our textbooks. And I would be willing to bet that the books were not the adopted books. So it was a maneuver that paid off for them. In Reedy, a little 400-population community in Roane County, which is one of the adjacent counties, there is a man who is an avowed Nazi — there have been several feature stories in our papers about him. He's one of the biggest publishers in the world of anti-Jewish literature, and much of the material that was published and disseminated over the valley and surrounding area, most of those materials were published in his bookstore.

MOFFETT: Is that where the passages came from?

STAFF: I don't know that he created the passages, but he did print all the material. And they stood at the gates of companies like Union Carbide and the Du Pont plant and they handed out these leaflets full of passages from the books, and some, as I say, were not even from the books.[6]

Elmer Fike's Business and Professional People's Alliance for Better Textbooks cited series, book, and page or title with reasonable if not total accuracy when they quoted excerpts in a two-page ad, "What Your Children Will Read . . . ," in the *Charleston Gazette* in mid-November and (revised) the following April. These quotations presumably represented the worst the protesters could come up with regarding vulgar language and sex and other offending material detectable in brief quotations. The ad does not claim that more offensive material was found elsewhere or allude to passages unquotable in a newspaper. The majority of these excerpts take the form of lists of single words or phrases, mostly the same swear words repeated over and over. The reviewers had a field day with *Interaction*'s books of play scripts. Of course, vulgar language in the textbooks occurs almost entirely in direct dialogue, which is to say it is used to mimic actual colloquial conversation.

The samples below were taken from the ad and represent the very worst words used in *Interaction*, and, I feel sure, in the other series too. In reading them please take account, in your reaction, of the effect that lists like this, endlessly repeated around the community had on people by reducing thousands of selections in hundreds of books, written by all sorts of authors on all sorts of subjects, to a few column inches of coarse expressions. This tactic may very well prejudice even people who don't worry about "swear words" in school books, just because such drastic reduction inevitably leaves the impression that the books contained nothing of value. Besides, swearing palls on you very quickly whether you disapprove or not.

Except for a rare hell or a damn perhaps in the more mature selections, elementary school books were not really involved in this issue at all. Vulgar language arises in certain selections in certain books in secondary school — some plays, short stories, or monologues containing the directly quoted speech of certain kinds of characters who use that kind of language, the omission of which would make very difficult the realistic rendering of those characters. These passages were in level #3, ordinary secondary.

Scripts 2
    page 163   "Feel my old bag's tits"
    page 173   "them sons-bitches too ornery"
    page 190   "Goddammit! All this crapping 'round and footsying" . . .
                "Ass!"

Scripts 3
    page 87   "That fat old bitch"
    page 91   "God, he'll fix it." "Hell, no."
    page 92   "Damn thing" "Yes, by God"
    page 99   "Goddam cards"[7]

All the examples from *Scripts 3* are from one play, *Blue Denim*, which deals with teen-age difficulties and centers on an unwanted pregnancy. It tried to help teen-agers consider such issues more maturely. So this play disturbed objectors for its subject matter as well. "Page 99 is reproduced in its entirety," the ad said, "to give you a better idea of the content of this play."

(. . . ERNIE deals him two off the top and taps the deck to indicate he doesn't want any cards. Then, carried away by his own act, continues:) Matter of fact I had occasion last week to help a fella out of a jam.
ARTHUR: What're you talking about?
ERNIE: Clifford Truckston. The guy that lives next door to my aunt. Getting drafted next month and his girl's knocked up.
ARTHUR: (Impressed.) No kidding!
ERNIE: And who's he have to come to, to steer him to a doctor? Me.
ARTHUR: Did he have to? I mean, do *that?*
ERNIE: At first he thought he'd get four other guys to swear she'd put out to *them*, too, but then he decided he'd better do the honorable thing and get her an abortion.
ARTHUR: (Throws in his cards.) I'm out. Deal 'em.
ERNIE: (Picks up the cards. They ante.) Cost him over a hundred, cash! (Shuffles and deals.)
ARTHUR: (A great effort to be nonchalant and keep up his part of the "man of the world" act.) I'm gonna be *really* careful from now on!
ERNIE: A guy's gotta be. (A very short pause.) Did your old man ever take you into the bedroom and give you the old pep-talk? About women and diseases and all?

ARTHUR: No, he never.

ERNIE: Mine did. He really did. Only he waited till I was twelve, for God-sake! All I could do to keep a straight face.

ARTHUR: (Puts down two discards). My dad never told me a thing. Too embarrassed.[8]

Presumably this is one of the "dirty" passages.

Unquoted from elsewhere in the play are these two exchanges, which, had they been included, would certainly cause one to look very differently on the page that was quoted. Janet is the girl friend of Arthur.

JANET: (Crossing Up Left of the couch and above to Center of couch, and watching them with amusement.) You know something? You guys slay me!

ARTHUR: What?

JANET: (Crossing to above the table.) This big act you put on!

ARTHUR: What act?

JANET: (Crossing to above Right of Ernie.) Down here playing poker — drinking beer — swearing every other word![9]

Later, after Janet and Arthur have become more involved and Janet has become pregnant, the two boys return to the subject that before was only a joke.

ERNIE: If it was me, I'd give up this abortion idea. No kidding, Art.

ARTHUR: How can we? I can't just go upstairs and tell 'em! My mom'd start to shake — when she gets upset she starts to breathe funny. And my old man just goes up in smoke! If I was to go up and just tell 'em something like this — the shock might kill 'em even. Besides, Ernie, they trust me, and they're countin' on me.

ERNIE: (Seriously.) Look, I'm not trying to scare hell out of you or any-thing, but — Well — like I said before — it's murder.

ARTHUR: (Sharply.) Don't keep saying that. We didn't mean it to be a baby. (Quietly.) It was just her and me — we didn't think — (Suppressed vehemence.) Besides, it hasn't even got a heart or a name yet. It's not a per-son — just — trouble!

ERNIE: (Strongly.) It's *alive*, isn't it? — listen, Art, these operations are dan-gerous. I mean, the doctors that do it aren't so hot sometimes. That's why they got kicked out of the profession, 'cause they weren't very ethical to start with.[10]

A major purpose of the play was obviously to let teen-agers raise with each other those very points that some adults might raise in regard to swearing and abortion.

I can understand that this swearing should bother certain people, especially if some of it is regarded as "taking the Lord's name in vain," but where is the filthy content and the pornography? Whether coarse street words should never appear in some school books depends of course on one's assumptions; my purpose here is only to show that the protesters misadvertised the books in claiming they contained "four-letter words," since what people usually understand by "four-letter words" are those that did not appear in the books, certainly nowhere in *Interaction* and, so far as I know, not in the other textbooks either. Had they found them, the protesters could certainly have cited the selections. As with all of the worst accusations, one searches vainly *in the textbooks themselves* for the actual evidence.

Long before the Kanawha County incident publishers were terrified of incensing schools. They do their own precensoring and always have, no matter how ridiculous editors may personally feel it is to be shocked by taboo words or by natural functions of the body that the Creator allotted us. To the extent swearing expresses negative emotion I can agree that it is not a good thing, but this avails little if the same negative emotion comes out anyway in more acceptable language and other behavior. The real problem of course is the anger, disgust, hostility, and so on that engender the use of words that provoke others.

Let us hope society will arrive at a stage where our own words no longer hold a power over us beyond our control as if they issued from a supernatural agency. "Fighting words" is a false expression; *people* fight, not words, nor can words "make" us fight. That too is primitive magic thinking. We cannot blame others if we react with anger, shock, dread, or lust to their choice of words. My reactions are my own response and my own responsibility. Words are servants, and, like the Sabbath, are made for man, not man for words.

Since profane or coarse language often fills the speech of people living in dehumanized environments — battlefields, ghettos, assembly lines — the practical effect of banning such speech is to cut off the voices of soldiers, workers, minorities, or others whose plight tells us things we don't want to hear. Witness the banning from some libraries of combat stories of Vietnam, the ruckus in Pennsylvania about Studs Terkel's book of interviews, *Working*, or the incessant objection to black and Hispanic accounts of their experiences, all on grounds of vulgar language.

But let's not forget either that most people who object to swearing do it themselves. Censoring can be a misdirected effort to clean up one's own act. The basic meaning of "vulgar" is "common," from which derives the meaning "coarse," and the fact is that coarseness is common — widespread — and the language of the man in the street is street language. We can ban this language on behalf of raising standards, but we must realize that in keeping these voices out of books we discourage the owners of those voices from reading books or, for that matter, from improving their language.

The most sexual content Fike's crew could come up with for their ad — or that any other group could in any other dissemination of quotations — were the following two passages from *Interaction*. The first excerpt was quoted over and over as an example of, presumably, explicit sex or pornography, and the Rev. Graley referred to it in the interview in chapter 4.

"A True Story"

A tall, red-headed chick. She had been mainly a whore, actually, with very expensive johns, who would pay her a hundred dollars a shot. And she was a very lively chick, who took a lot of pot. Really a remarkable, beautiful, good-hearted, tender girl. I had a special regard for her from years before, because she had really put herself out to straighten me out and here she was like a big, expensive whore.[11]

"A True Story" is a title the Alliance made up. The selection was Jane Kramer's "Allen Ginsberg at Columbia" from *Biography 2*, an account of his undergraduate days in the forties that plays up the dark comedy of the difficulties he and his friends got into. Kramer quotes at length Ginsberg's own recital of events, and it is from this quotation that the offending passage is taken. He mentions the whore briefly while describing how she and other old friends that he thought too much of to throw out began to take over his apartment and, over his protest, fill it with stolen goods. He finally went away himself. The whore figures only in the passage quoted.

Ginsberg comes off as a picturesque character from another era. Other selections in the book, are Winston Churchill's "Henry Plantagenet," Virginia Woolf's "Mary Wollstonecraft," Gaius Suetonius' "Nero," and biographies of Anaïs Nin and Bucky Fuller. Stripping the selection of its real identity and setting certainly leaves the impression that the whore is featured in some sexual story. Actually, it is the familiar story of a kid getting in trouble in college through the company he keeps.

You will not learn from the ad that both of these passages appeared in *Interaction*'s level 4, our most advanced, which was intended for college-bound senior high students. Furthermore, the ad pointedly states that the samples were taken only from those books that the board returned to the classrooms November 8, whereas *Interaction*'s level 4 was *not* returned. This means that two of the eight excerpts displayed in the ad, the two quoted here, were not, as the title claimed, "What Your Children Will Read." Never identified, the fictional diary from which the second excerpt came was "Me and Miss Mandible," a short story by Donald Barthelme.

Fictional Diaries

13 September

Miss Mandible wants to make love to me but she hesitates because I am officially a child; I am, according to the records, according to the gradebook on
her desk, according to the card index in the principal's office, eleven years
old. There is a misconception here, one that I haven't quite managed to get
cleared up yet. I am in fact thirty-five, I've been in the Army, I am six feet
one, I have hair in the appropriate places, my voice is a baritone, I know
very well what to do with Miss Mandible if she ever makes up her mind.

9 December

Disaster once again. Tomorrow I am to be sent to a doctor, for observation.
Sue Ann Brownly caught Miss Mandible and me in the cloakroom, during
recess, and immediately threw a fit. For a moment I thought she was actually going to choke. She ran out of the room weeping, straight for the principal's office, certain now which of us was Debbie, which Eddie, which Liz. I
am sorry to be the cause of her disillusionment, but I know that she will
recover. Miss Mandible is ruined but fulfilled. Although she will be charged
with contributing to the delinquency of a minor, she seems at peace; her
promise has been kept. She knows now that everything she has been told
about life, about America, is true.[12]

Barthelme's language is perfectly inoffensive, the story is not offered as
realism but as an amusing satire on many aspects of society, and the diarist — as so often with stories told from this point of view — shows himself
as a bit cracked, however perceptive some of his observations may be.
The two diary entries quoted above did not occur back to back, as presented in the ad (without indication of elision). By skipping over the
many other entries dealing with social satire, the protesters create the
impression, again, that the selection deals exclusively with sex. Whether
or not one disapproves of the sexual references themselves in "Me and
Miss Mandible" the story simply cannot honestly be called "pornographic" — or even "filthy" because "filthy" to most people is a synonym
for "pornographic." The passages quoted in this chapter were the worst
that the protesters ever cited from any of the textbooks to support such
terms as they bandied about in rumors and meetings and accusations in
the media. Recall that the coalition of ten ministers of various denominations defended the treatment of sex in the textbooks (see chapter 1). Even
Citizens for Decency through Law (formerly Citizens for Decent Literature), for whom Robert Dornan was public relations representative, "has
expressed the view that the books adopted by the Kanawha County
School are not obscene or pornographic."[13]
    While it has been necessary to deal roundly at the outset with the two
blanket charges of conspiracy and pornography, because the absence of

supporting evidence doesn't become apparent simply by examining the following objections, I don't mean to say that other objections were equally unfair and unwarranted. Some I actually agree with. Many quotations support the point being made, in which case they concern some difference in values, or at least the protesters honestly misunderstand what they are quoting. I would be naïve and the perpetuator of naïveté, however, if I did not point out downright deception and misrepresentation.

Illumination requires the effort to distinguish misrepresentation from misinterpretation, subtle as that task becomes at times. In order to clarify the thought underlying censorship and bigotry we need to assess what is deliberate and what is unconscious in the objections to the books. Dishonesty no doubt occurred as part of the zealot's conviction that the ends justify the means, but certain emotional premises may cause authentic distortions of perception. It is possible that at times the protesters really thought that things were included or omitted from the books when in fact these perceptions can easily be shown wrong. I am not so concerned about deliberate falsification as I am about unwitting falsehood.

9

McGuffey Rides Again

The report made to the Kanawha County School Board by those seven members of the Textbook Review Committee who had split off from the original eighteen constitutes a good typical sample of both objections often made nationally to textbooks by conservatives and of the terms in which they cast their objections. This is especially true because, as we saw, this Textbook Review Committee consulted with the Gablers, who had also sent to the protesters the bills of particulars they had written for Texas on these same books. In some cases, as shown farther on, the committee simply repeated objections written by the Gablers. All further references to objections in this book are taken from this unpublished, unpaginated document, a copy of which was sent to me in 1974 by someone in the school district who thought I ought to know exactly what protesters were saying.[1]

A photocopied typescript of some 450 pages, this report is the same that Superintendent Underwood called "The Death of American Education." It states objections to one book at a time of the major programs adopted by the county, citing particular selections and page numbers and often quoting portions of the texts. It recommended removing 184 of the 254 titles reviewed. It opens with a list of the seven members who submitted it, five men and two women. None, I understand, has a college education, but though worth noting, that should not be regarded as of the greatest significance. One member, Nick Staton, was the one already mentioned who was subsequently elected to the United States House of Representatives. Another man, William Seaman, was PTA council president.

Included at the front of the report was the following "Review Procedure."

> In order to insure the proper frame of reference in which to view this report, we offer the following guidelines which were used in its preparation. If an objection is listed, we have also attempted to link this objection to one of the guidelines. Please keep these in mind as you read this report.
>
> 1. Any request for information, either verbal or written, that constitutes an invasion of privacy.

2. Any statement or question that is derogatory in any manner to any ethnic, cultural or religious group.

3. A preoccupation with subject matter of a cruel, depressing, violent or amoral nature.

4. The use of profanity, either written or spoken.

5. Photographs or written material depicting disrespect of authority figures of a family, civil or religious nature.

6. Any question, comment or photograph that can be classified as a treatment of situation ethics.

Three phrases occur here that you will find repeatedly employed all over the United States as set terms in the literature of censorship — "disrespect of authority," "invasion of privacy," and "situation ethics."

As preface to the report there appeared this quotation.

If you can induce a community to doubt the genuineness and authenticity of the Scriptures; to question the reality, and obligations of religion; to hesitate undeciding, whether there be any such thing as virtue or vice; whether there be an eternal state of retribution beyond the grave; or whether there exsists [sic] any such being as God, you have broken down the barriers of moral virtue, and hoisted the flood gates of immorality and crime. I need not say, that when a people have once done this, they can no longer exsist [sic] as a tranquil and happy people. Every bond that holds society together would be ruptured; fraud and treachery would take the place of confidence between man and man; the tribunals would be scenes of bribery and injustice; avarice, perjury, ambition, and revenge would walk through the land, and render it more like the dwelling of savage beasts, than the tranquil and happy abode of civilized and Christianized men. (McGuffy's Reader, 1854)

This statement, written over one hundred years ago, correctly mirrors our position concerning the dispute over the Language Arts adoption. We believe that continued exposure to the materials, to which we object, would irreparably damage the moral fiber of the students of this county.

We do not ask that you concur in our objections as we fully realize that diversity of opinion does exist. We only ask that you honor our right to hold our opinions and protect our children from that which we feel would do them harm. We ask that you reject those items of instructional material, whether they be written or spoken, to which we object. By so doing you will not be submitting to mob rule, as it has been stated; you will not be violating laws or the democratic process, as it has been stated; but, rather, you will be demonstrating that you respect that most sacred precept of all — the rights of the individual citizen.

It has been said that this adoption is relevant, timely and offers to the student a view of our nation and world "as it really is." We would agree that this statement is partially true, however, we feel that the view that is offered is distorted and surrealistic. Even if it was totally true we ask that you consider this; do not merely show America "as it is," but give our children hope and promise that with God's grace and wisdom they may one day see our nation and world "as it should be."

I don't disagree with all the basic values underlying objections to follow. I too think that positive, idealistic thinking is essential. I do disagree with interpretations of the selections that falsely set the books at odds with these values. And besides the fact that many Americans are not by faith and heritage Christian (and are not all men!), the McGuffey credo fails also to do justice to this nation's pluralism in another way: even those people who can identify completely with "civilized and Christian men" can solemnly nod in assent and then promptly start fighting among themselves over how their children should be taught, because they do not understand the same thing by this phrase.

If we limit our sampling of objections to *Interaction* books alone, we will miss an important distinction that became apparent in the Kanawha objections — between textbooks that are straight anthologies and textbooks in which the program authors themselves talk to the student. I have already pointed out that even anthologies may differ in how much they get into trouble according as they clump reading matter by forms or by contents. The latter, the thematic approach, lays the program creators much more open to the charge of editorializing. Some textbooks are anthologies that include all sorts of study suggestions, commentary, and questions on the text. Some other textbooks that are not anthologies treat language, grammar, communication principles, spelling, literary appreciation, and semantics by *expository* means, that is, by describing, explaining, illustrating, listing rules, prescribing, and so on. Naturally, in doing this the program creators are authoring in their own voice, except when quoting, and therefore have to take responsibility for the endless opportunities they set up, and utilize, to express their own values.

I decided early that *Interaction* books would contain no commentary, questions, or study paraphernalia. Even the teachers guides avoided directions for treating individual selections. Directions to students were placed on activity cards and concerned only repeatable activities such as writing a fable or working up an oral reading of a poem, not particular selections in the anthologies except to cite one sometimes to illustrate a form. I remember that on emerging from a publisher's lunch with me in one of those ubiquitous seafood restaurants near the Boston Common, the man then in charge of Houghton Mifflin's school department stopped on the sunny sidewalk, squinted at me in sudden puzzlement, and asked, "But how would these be *text*books?" He had been listening to me describe the sort of materials I would be willing to do if we signed on together, which had sounded good to him, then as he mulled this over while paying the check it hit him that such books would almost exactly resemble "trade" books that you buy in regular bookstores. My reply was that *Interaction* books would be textbooks because he would be publishing them and he was a textbook publisher. Later, in fact, *Interaction* was sometimes billed as "the nontextbook program," because it sought to teach through realistic practice in using the language what programs usually try to teach through expository lessons embodied in series of spelling/grammar/language/composition/communication textbooks separate from the literature or reading series, itself usually heavily larded with pedagogical paraphernalia.

In my view the learner does not need information or others' prescriptions *about* language; he or she needs copious occasions to *use* that language. Under individualization, students log far more practical experience in speaking, listening, reading, and writing than by doing all those expository lessons together in lockstep fashion from the textbooks. Our approach did depend, however, on many nonbook materials such as the activity cards, recordings, and learning games that Kanawha County did not purchase or mention therefore in the book of objections (except for some recordings). Although concern for censorship did not enter into my decision to put out only anthologies as the textbooks of *Interaction*, the learning philosophy having dominated the conception, the practical upshot in Kanawha County was that the only charge we might be liable to, legitimately, was biased selection — which turned out to be severe enough! — whereas most of the other programs got heavily scored for material the creators had themselves authored. Of no small interest is the fact that Kanawha County bought the series that were heavily freighted with teaching paraphernalia as their "basic" texts and allotted *Interaction* to the "supplementary" status.

This distinction between compiling and authoring did not, in fact, hinder the single-minded thinking behind the Kanawha objections, which consistently fail to distinguish between what program creators utter and what the speakers in the selections utter. If an author treated the subject of riots, or a character referred to riots, then we compilers were thought to favor and promote riots. This confusion becomes more understandable in the case of the other programs, which continually interwove the voices of the program authors with those of authors they were quoting or of characters in the literary selections. What results, in the objections I will cite here to selections from other programs, is a mixture of fairness and unfairness in which it seems to me that a third party might indeed agree sometimes, as I do, with certain objections that these texts attempt undue direction of youngsters' minds. If *Interaction* is less vulnerable to this charge, it is, as I say, simply that we took a wholly different pedagogical approach that kept our own voices out of the texts.

For too long textbook creators have used reading selections as things to ask questions about, either to test for reading comprehension or prompt certain thinking. I had an agreement with Houghton Mifflin that our books would contain no "questions at the end." George Hillocks, Jr., says in the article cited before that Alice Moore told him their real objection to "Jack and the Bean Stalk" was not to the content of the story itself but to the questions attached to it in one series.[2] These other programs did not deserve what happened to them, were done intelligently with good intentions, and certainly were not participating in some conspiracy to take over the children. But this costly lesson indicates how much we educators have traditionally overdirected students. Whether intentional or not, any program or approach that features specific directions to masses of students in a standardized format, whether it is "modern" and "open-ended" like these programs or whether it is a "no-nonsense" programming of phonics and language facts pandering to back-to-basics factions, will almost certainly be guilty in some measure of propagandizing just because it is manipulating students too much.

If this is true of language arts textbooks, how much more true it is for textbooks in other subjects such as history, government, and economics. Social studies, and sometimes even the sciences, are much harder to present impartially than literature, which can be about anything at all and is not meant to have the same function. Textbook creators, furthermore, do not usually write literature, whereas textbook authors in other subjects *do* write the main body of the texts themselves. They "present" much more directly out of their own minds.

It happened that English did not reflect its changes in textbooks until after the other subjects. This means that by the time the Gablers and other textbook reviewers turned their attention to language arts textbooks they were raising objections of the sort and in the way that they had learned to raise during years of screening books in social studies and the sciences. I think this affected considerably how they treated literature even though literature is a very different mode of discourse. Since their predecessors exerted powerful influence on the Textbook Review Committee, I believe that the Kanawha County objections we are about to survey contain responses more inappropriate than they might have been if the censors had not been sharpening their knives during their scrutiny of other discourse that more directly reflects and affects actuality.

Of course texts for English do include things besides literature, some of which is also factual, but language arts and English classes do not exist to get across a particular subject matter as history or biology courses do; practicing the language as speaker, reader, and writer is a more general mission, and for this purpose many kinds of content will do. The difference in the nature of literature as an art and the difference in the purpose for which even nonliterary texts are read in English courses were lost sight of, I feel strongly, in the reviewers' application of the methods and criteria they inherited from the censorship network, which still perpetuates today inappropriate expectations about literature and a generally misguided mindset about courses of language learning as distinguished from courses developing a certain content. This is to say that whenever I read conservative criticisms that a history book ignores the spiritual setting of this nation's founding or that an economics text overemphasizes the role that the federal government should play in regulating the economy, I feel the reviewers make a much stronger case than they do in some of the following objections, which seem to me to try to treat English texts as if they were just so many more civics or physics books.

I beg the reader to keep in mind as we now survey some of these official objections that the purpose is neither to defend the books nor to pillory the objectors. You may agree with some of the objections, or you may become incensed at this sort of censoring. I merely wish to sample the objections, comment on them, and later use all this as a base for some more general observations. It is one thing to rail against some bigots who banned some books. It is quite another to hear what the objectors themselves say about particular offending selections. We have to hear their voices and follow the thought and feeling, tune to their frequencies. I have often found that in listening to their outrage I shed my own.

Kanawha's main elementary language arts adoption was D. C. Heath & Company's all-purpose series *Communicating*, which mixed literature, language, and composition.[3] Objections hit it harder on its directions in the teachers' guides than on its reading selection. For example, to follow up a depiction of bullying, the first-grade teachers edition gives these directions and receives this objection:[4]

Unit 1, page 7, column 2, paragraph 4 and 5

Use this occassion [*sic*] to discuss personal experiences that could in some way be similar to the pictured experience. Ask the pupil such questions as the following:
1. Have you ever had a bully stop you from doing something that you wanted to do?
2. How did you feel?
3. What happened?
4. Why did the bully do what he did?
Try to reserve a period for personal story telling time. Encourage the children to recall how they felt, and why they and others behave the way they do in their stories.

Objection: Why should six-year-olds be encouraged to talk about bullies? Surely something more constructive could be discussed. And also, we object to the child being asked, "How do you feel?". This is similar to sensitivity training and has no place in a classroom situation. Education in the class-room should be based on facts and skills.

The response to the following directions, from the same book, typifies the resistance mounted against efforts to engage children in communicating their own experience.

Page 17, column 2, paragraph 4

Find an appropriate time to shift the discussion to personal experiences. The questions that follow will help the children recall a significant event and find something about the event that is interesting and meaningful to them. No matter what the subject is, let the children talk freely about it. As soon as the children are ready to talk, small groups may be formed so each child can have an opportunity.

1. Has anyone ever broken a toy, a chair, or some other article the first time he was visiting an unfamiliar house?

2. Has anyone ever awakened and found a stranger looking at him?

3. Has anyone ever awakened in a strange bed and been scared?

4. Has anyone ever had a dream in which he talked with some animals?

5. Has anyone ever seen a deserted house? (Did you go in?)

Objection: A child should not be forced to discuss his own personal feelings. This constitutes an invasion of privacy. This is also a behavioral change. Why should a six-year-old be subjected to questions that will implant fear and frustrations in his mind? Why not have questions on pleasant and wholesome attitudes?

This objection and the one before were directly taken by the Kanawha County reviewers from Mel Gabler, Bill of Particulars in the form of a letter to Dr. M. L. Brockette of the Texas Education Agency, August 3, 1974, pp. 6–7.

Here's what happened to a fifth-grade lesson aimed at dealing with color prejudice.

Level 5

Unit 11, page 194–195

Telling the fable creatively.

Question 1. Pretend that the hunter who has three eyes and no hair wants to live in the town. The people who are afraid of him want to make a law forbidding this. Other people disagree and say that the law would not be fair. Tell what might happen.

Question 2. Pretend that the people of Wardsback are all different colors: red, yellow, green, etc. When the hunter decides to stay in the town for a while, he is told that his skin color has to be changed. He wants to know why. What will the people answer him? How will it all end?

Objection: Again the student is asked to make intelligent commentaries concerning the racial issue in America. Questions like this again tend to reinforce the feelings of racism and cause those students who are white to experience feelings of guilt, while those students of minority races may feel feelings of superiority or some other attendant feeling.

Of course it's probably true that such a teaching unit *does* attempt to change some children's thought and behavior away from home instruction. My own feeling is that the textbook authors are trying too hard here and the approach is too manipulative. A particular lesson on color prejudice probably doesn't dispel such prejudice and isn't necessary, anyway. A constantly expanding acquaintance with the lives and works of many different sorts of people, and continuous opportunity to think new thoughts of all sorts, will naturally free the mind from restrictive early conditioning. We shouldn't aim students' minds at particular issues we adults are hung up on.

Consider also the following direction to students. Does this effort to engage fifth-graders with ambivalence push too directly? Do you sustain the objection of the censors here? Or do you doubt the instruction for another reason?

Unit 12, page 225

Telling your own tale. Second section, question 1. Do you know a real person whom people admire even though he is bad in some way? Maybe you can tell an interesting story about this person.

Objection: Evil and wrong doing should not be presented in an admiring light, but rather should be presented as evil and should be punished.

Do you agree with the judgment made on the following story ideas?

Unit 16, page 294

Telling your own story. Think of an experience in which everyone believes something to be true. But it turns out not to be true. Here are some examples:
1. A big dog will attack you.
2. A woman is very mean to kids.
3. A house is haunted by evil spirits.
4. Witches come out on Halloween.

Objections: A continued and unrelenting focus on violence and fear. There must be more calm, peaceful and friendly ideas that the publishers or authors of this book can put forth as opposed to having a big dog attack someone. Why don't they say "a friendly puppy followed me home"?

It seems evident that telling such stories is intended to *release* children from fears by giving them an occasion to symbolize and deal with them. But the dissenters consistently refuse to recognize the defusing of negative emotions through confronting them. They seem to feel that talking about such things makes them materialize or makes them worse. Now, I would agree that focusing the mind *gratuitously* on negative matters that are not already a problem should be challenged. I myself avoid stipulating topics for students in favor of students finding their own subject matter. In this way subjects come up if and when students need them to. But the objection here, endlessly repeated throughout the document, seems to confuse the word with the thing, as if symbolizing something conjured it. If Halloween represents violence, then every grade school teacher in the nation stands guilty in the docket.

Here are some micellaneous objections to items in the sixth-grade text of *Communicating*.

Chapter 1, page 22–27

Marshall McClune [sic] and "The Technological Embrace."

Objection: Marshall McClune is first of all a blue sky thinker with little to do with absolutes or reality. Secondly, this particular article is a very poor example of writing for an English textbook. It takes five pages and only uses three paragraphs.

Chapter 2, page 53

Poem: Emerson's "Brahama" [sic].

Objection: Object to the premise of the poem itself. That God is both the appearance of good and the appearance of evil.

Chapter 2, page 53

The book of Ecclesiastes.

Objection: This is referred to as an unorthodox book implying that it has no meaning.

Unit 1, page 1

"or shuffling Holy Rollers at an all night inspiration".

Objection: This is a derogatory term for members of the Pentacostal [sic] Holy Church. It should be deleted.

Unit 2, page 20–25

"The Use of Force."

Objection: This is a terribly sadistic story. I would hope that this is not a representative example of the medical profession. The doctor in this story would appear to be in dire need of psychiatric help. The story is classified as a realistic story, however, I cannot think of any case that it would appear real to me.

"The Use of Force" recounts how a doctor has to force open a young girl's mouth, with the help of her parents, to discover if she has a seriously infected throat, which indeed she has—in the days before sulfa drugs were available. She fights bitterly, but the job has to be done, because she can die if not treated. The author is poet William Carlos Williams, himself a doctor.

A lesson that tried to get children to think about war by means of discussing a myth provoked this reaction.

Unit 8, page 149

Discussing the myth. The actions.
   Question 2. When does trouble first come into the world?
   Question 3. The soldiers fight a war to bring love into the world. Why does Kintu oppose this war? Do you agree with Kintu or the soldiers? Why?
   Question 5. Would Kintu's law of love solve the problems in today's world? Are there some things worth fighting wars for? Or could you always apply Kintu's law of love?

Objection: Questions 2, 3, and 5 are far beyond the scope of a normal sixth grade student. Questions like this, while certainly thought provoking, could only tend to cause confusion and doubt, and thereby destroying [sic] the faith in government leaders. The recent issue over the Vietnamese War is still fresh in the student's mind and questions concerning war and love, and etc. could only further the doubt that already exists. While there are a few people who actively support fighting and warfare, there are times when warfare is justified, and the student should be made aware of that.

Now comes a summary of the whole Heath series, grades 1–12.

These series of books are undoubtedly professionally prepared and scholarly works. Their objective is clearly defined and relentlessly pursued. It is this objective to which we take great exception. The Heath English program, grades 1–12 is a systematic attempt to change the thinking, perceptions and behavior of the American school student. It is increasingly subtle and crafty. It is therefore, a danger in the worst form.

In the guise of English, new linguistics, oral communication and relevancy for the student, it seeks to seduce the child and change his thinking and behavior patterns already established or it establishes and indoctrinates its own philosophy.

Specifically, basic grammar or how English works is avoided and replaced by linguistics [sic] even the new grammar is secondary to literature in the Heath program. Heath is literature that indoctrinates in the guise of grammar. The Heath philosophy through continued editorializing by the authors in a subtle choice of examples for the student replaces grammar with literature in books 1–12 and why? Of course, it is to indoctrinate. The philosophy includes a study of folk tales, myths, legends, realistic stories and new grammar. . . .

Through examples, and editorializing again myths are linked to reality until the student is unable to determine which is which. The myths in books 2–6 set the stage for the undermining of absolutes and for the undermining of organized religion. The building blocks are carried into grades 7–12 for the purpose of rejecting the biblical accounts, the origins of language, the biblical accounts of moral absolutes.

Throughout the entire Heath series, there is systematic development of a subtle rejection of democracy and of the American free enterprise system. This is handled under the guise of rhetoric.

Although it is clear enough that the objectors want to fill the curriculum with rules for correct grammar — the new, descriptive grammar not being as good as the old, prescriptive and proscriptive grammar — this summary only implies about literature what specific objections elsewhere make explicit, that the inclusion of literature into a series they felt should comprise only language facts provided unwelcome opportunities for crosscultural comparison as, for example, with creation myths, folk literature especially being multiethnic and international. When a whole book was devoted to language information, however, like McDougal, Littell's *Dialects and Levels of Language* in its *Language of Man* series,[5] it received this condemnation.

Although this book is not objectionable from a moral standpoint, it is a finished product in itself. It has no real value in an English course of study. There is very little value studying dialects which change from time to time. Neither is there value in studying specialized professional dialects for these have value only to those involved in that profession.

Similarly, the *Interaction* booklets *Codes, Maps, Charts and Graphs*, and *Tongue Twisters* were judged unfit for English classrooms despite their illumination of language or their practical utility.

Of course, the overt objection to the study of dialects is relativity. The dissenters wanted all language study to drill on correctness and to pretend that English has an absolute form. The fear arises over and over again in various ways: if youngsters know of alternatives, standards will crumble, whether in morals or language. And dialectical variation goes with variation in people and their ethnic groups or milieus. Dialect is always a hot issue because individuals can be identified as members of acceptable or unacceptable social groups by how they talk. Fear of slipping into "bad grammar" correlates directly with one's social insecurity or with one's past struggle to overcome a social stigma. Professional grammarians and language specialists know that facts about language go vastly far beyond mere knowledge of what conforms to the majority or "standard" dialect, but censors, typically, are not interested in any other information about language than that regarding status or identity.

10

Anyone for the Classics?

Let's go on to the literature or reading material itself. A secondary school book in Scott, Foresman's *America Reads* series, called *Counterpoint in Literature*,[1] contained the following chestnuts, which have been anthologized for generations for school. The objectors claimed that "brutality and gruesomeness dominated this text." This is how they dismissed them.

> "The Highwayman," Alfred Noyes – Girl shoots herself through the breast.
> "Lord Randall," traditional ballad – The main character is poisoned.
> "Danny Deaver," Rudyard Kipling – Poem concerning a military hanging.
> "The Tale-Tell Heart," E. A. Poe – A man cunningly contrives to kill an old man whom he loves, carries this out and dismembers him.
> "To Build a Fire," Jack London – A man freezes to death.

Any of us could play a game describing world classics in the most negative way possible and produce a list exactly like this one.

After a similar negative description of selections in an *Interaction* book of ballads for high school, the objector asked, "Is it so strange to wonder why a selection of ballads for school-age youth cannot include subject matter content that is cheerful, pleasant, happy, and inspirational?" Actually, to anyone who is conversant with the literature of ballads this *is* a strange question, because few ballads fit this prescription. The older, traditional ballads, such as one finds in Francis James Child's classic source, *The English and Scottish Popular Ballads*, tend to commemorate dire events or to poetize the strange – "Barbara Allen," "Mary Hamilton," "Henry Martin," "Lord Randal," "The Three Ravens," "Sir Patrick Spens," and so on. One can lighten such a book, as we did, with "Scarborough Fair," a version of "Get Up and Bar the Door," and "Robin Hood and the Butcher," but certain forms of literature have an affinity with certain subjects or tones. Should, then, high school students be denied such a form? (Farther on, you will read of what happened when we editors bent the definition of "ballad" to allow us to include, for variety," The Cherry Tree Carol.")

A teacher who had been invited to add her commentary to the criticism of the literature series *Man* (McDougal, Littell),[2] wrote:

> I think these books stink! What do they mean? I failed to find the obscenity and atheism in them that has become the issue in the fight between the factions. *What I Found* was a want of anything meaningful. The entire outlook is one of pessimism and dreariness — of "What's the use?" We have Babette [sic], Deutsch, Nemerov, Levertok [sic], Chekov [sic], Soroyan [sic], Faulkner, E. E. Cummings [sic]; but what of the names that have illuminated the lives of young scholars for generations? We have the modern concept of disrespect for authority, renegation [sic] for the elderly, the giving over of power to the poor, the out-at-the ass, the foreigner and the renegade. Why throw the baby out with the bath water? Why can't we take it a little at a time and not decide immediately that *White is Ugly?*
>
> I believe that children need a period to live in a world of fantasy — they will learn that there is no Santa Claus; but they will learn in their own way what this is symbolic of — it will be no rude awakening. I believe that young people need to believe in the *ultimate* beauty and goodness of human nature as long as possible, even though they are of necessity subjected to reality every day. I think the books have a definitely "Leftist" lean, and of course, that is abhorent [sic] to me. I could never vote for any textbook which only offers one side of any problem — and that the negative one. I think we have enough badly written literature now; without adding to the mess. I think we need go back to the classics and the fundamentals of education — many fine people came of this training.

Interaction was loaded with classics, if by that one means long-acclaimed writings of earlier periods. It is important to bring out just how strong the textbooks were in traditional reading matter in order to understand what lies behind the charges that it conspired against accepted values. Considering prose only for the moment, some representatives were: from antiquity, Sophocles, Cicero, Mark Antony, Pliny, Plutarch, and Suetonius; from the Renaissance, Christopher Columbus, Benvenuto Cellini, Michel de Montaigne, Leonardo da Vinci; from the seventeenth and eighteenth centuries, Francis Bacon, Daniel Defoe, Jonathan Swift, Lord Chesterfield, James Boswell, Samuel Pepys, and Benjamin Franklin; from the nineteenth century, Ralph Waldo Emerson, Henry David Thoreau, Edgar Allan Poe, Herman Melville, Nathaniel Hawthorne, Mark Twain, Ambrose Bierce, Stephen Crane, Washington Irving, Bret Harte, Thomas Bailey Aldrich, Sidney Lanier, Charles Lamb, William Hazlitt, Thomas Babington Macaulay, Walter Pater, William Hickling Prescott, Abraham Lincoln, Davy Crockett, Frederick Douglass, Booker T. Washington, Robert Louis Stevenson, Alexis de Tocqueville, Guy de Maupassant, Nikolai Gogol, Ivan Turgenev, Feodor Dostoyevsky, and Leo Tolstoy.

This does not include Shakespeare and many novelists for the simple reason that anthologies don't usually include whole books, and most schools already have editions of Shakespeare. We did manage to include shorter stories of novelists like Hardy and Conrad. A list of *Interaction* poets or of twentieth century "classics" would run in the same vein but much too long to enumerate here. Also, we devoted an unusually large amount of space to folk literature — parables, myths, legends, fairy tales, fables, and proverbs — that include many classics ranging from Aesop and the Bible to familiar orally transmitted folk tales and sayings from England, Appalachia, and countries all over the world.

If what is meant by classics is children's classics, good coverage must range from the Brothers Grimm, Charles Perrault, Hans Christian Andersen, and Andrew Lang, who wrote famous personal renditions of inherited tales, to modern folklorists like Richard Chase, Maria Leach, and Harold Courlander, to those authors of modern children's stories and poems such as Lewis Carroll, Beatrix Potter, Christina Rossetti, Hilaire Belloc, Else Holmelund Minarek, Eve Merriam, Marilyn Sachs, Laura Ingalls Wilder, Elsie Locke, Roald Dahl, and Lafcadio Hearn. All of these authors appear at least once in *Interaction* and many several times.

A sampling of stories for primary school includes, besides numerous nursery rhymes and Mother Goose tales, "Henny Penny," "Jack and the Bean Tree," "Tom Tit Tot," "Mr. Miacca," "The Three Pigs," "The Elves and the Shoemaker," "The Bremen Town Musicians," "Johnny Crow's Garden," "The Old Woman and Her Pig," "The Three Billy Goats Gruff," to list some of the better known ones in this culture. Traditional folk literature in upper elementary included Arthurian and Beowulf material and such myths as those of Thor and Pandora; fairy tales like "Rapunzel," "Beauty and the Beast," and "Rumpelstiltzkin"; the legends of Pecos Bill, Paul Bunyan, William Tell, and Hans and the Dutch dike; animal stories like "Charlotte's Web" by E. B. White, "Rikki-Tikki-Tavi" by Rudyard Kipling, and others by Gerald Durrell, Farley Mowat, and Sterling North.

This goes on into juvenile literature for secondary school that includes vast amounts of neutral types and subjects — having virtually nothing to do with sex, politics, religion, race, or other taboos — such as mystery, adventure, humor, science fiction, and sports, all of which were heavily represented in *Interaction* by several separate books devoted entirely to each one at a time. Among these authors were Saki, Sir Arthur Conan Doyle, Agatha Christie, Anthony Boucher, Zane Grey, Thor Heyerdahl, William Pène du Bois, James Thurber, Ogden Nash, Howard Pyle, Jack London, G. K. Chesterton, Wilbur Daniel Steele, H. G. Wells, Richard Connell, Ray Bradbury, Arthur C. Clarke, Isaac Asimov, and Zenna Henderson. This sampling risks even making the program appear overly traditional, but I have of course deliberately stocked the lists with the more familiar or "classical" works and writers.

What got us into trouble in Kanawha County was not really any exclusion of the classics or of traditional or neutral reading material but the *inclusion*, besides this, of works and writers not usually represented at that time. This is true of probably all the reading programs to which objections were raised. The others were well stocked, like *Interaction*, with literary chestnuts and expected kinds of selections by well regarded authors. No major publisher, regardless of philosophy, would dare market books purporting to constitute a literature or reading curriculum without this kind of insurance.

On the authors' economic side, it is much cheaper, I realized during the course of working out these anthologies, to compile older texts because anything over fifty-eight years in copyright at that time belonged, with some exceptions, in public domain, which is to say that it could be reprinted *free*. I began to perceive that one reason earlier textbook programs comprised so many old selections and lacked contemporary readings concerned not necessarily a stand for the "classics" but rather a stinginess in paying permissions rights. It's time the public knew more about the coarse finances that operate in the sensitive area of their children's learning. Normally, the publisher does not pay for these permissions but merely advances the costs to the textbook authors by paying the rights-holders for them upon publication and charging the amounts to the authors' royalty accounts.

Interaction co-authors ran up a debt of nearly a quarter of a million dollars in reprinting and recording permissions, more than our earnings ever paid off before *Interaction* went out of print. We paid top dollar to get the very kind of *total* coverage that our detractors deplored. We could have made them very happy by publishing only what was old enough to be public domain or hackneyed enough to cost very little. The market in reprinting is interesting. Even giant writers that were still under copyright, like James Joyce or Joseph Conrad, cost only a fraction of the price to reprint something of popular contemporaries like Flannery O'Connor or Kurt Vonnegut or minority writers like Maya Angelou or Piri Thomas. Well anthologized famous moderns can simply not bring the price of newer writers and, especially in the early seventies, Third World authors, who were enjoying a bull market. As did also our competitors in Kanawha County, I'm sure, we co-authors ran up a big bill to ensure a broad representation of periods and points of view. We paid for just what the objectors didn't want. By being cheap about reprints, conventional compilers can make higher profits while appearing to stress "our cultural heritage" and thus pleasing bigoted school constituencies.

In other words, the charge that the offending programs neglected traditions and classics in order to bias their presentations is false, but what is important here is why the book opponents had, or gave, this impression. Obviously, the publishers were banking on *both* — traditional representation plus conspicuous addition of writing by minorities, women, and other comtemporaries who dealt with today's realities and did so in a style children could relate to easily. Had we offered only the conventional textbook fare, *then* we would have biased our books. It is perhaps only natural that including what has not before been included made the objectors truly feel that what they were used to was being left out when in fact it was only being supplemented.

Their *perception* concerns me in all this, because this is what we all need to understand. It is not as a complaint that I say the dissenters ignored our traditional literature and screamed in outrage about the new writers, new subjects, and new styles. I believe that the emotions aroused by today's realism, minority dialects, the casual profanities in dialogue, sexual frankness, black humor, multicultural viewpoints, and new-age desperation about changing quickly a very sick world, so overwhelmed the objectors that they really could no longer see the totality of the books — *all* of what was in fact there. It was precisely the totality that posed the problem for them. They wanted a highly selective, not an eclectic, package. So to them *Interaction* looked diabolically biased. Perceptual difference is a serious matter, especially when one group is seeing quite differently from another group. It can make for war.

In the objectors' view it was not mere name-calling to say of one of our senior high books called *Monologue and Dialogue*: "Cover to cover, Trash." Besides a couple of opening bits of whimsy — Richard Brautigan's poem, "Gee, You're so Beautiful that It's Starting to Rain" and one of the droll Don Marquis pieces from *Archy and Mehitabel* — this book contains Walter de la Mare's "The Tryst," Robert Browning's "Soliloquy of the Spanish Cloister," William Blake's "The Clod and the Pebble," John Keats' "Ode to a Nightingale," Matthew Arnold's "Dover Beach," Richard Wilbur's "Two Voices in a Meadow," and T. S. Eliot's "Journey of the Magi." This makes up roughly half the number of selections — some major poems in the English language and several lesser known but respectable selections of the sort that have appeared in many anthologies without creating a stir.

Actually, as we'll see, the objectors are not happy about many of the classics themselves, but for now let's note simply that five of the remaining items in the book are by blacks. One is in "plantation dialect" ("Jealous" by Paul Laurence Dunbar, an older black poet), one is a Barbadian telephone conversation in which the two black gossipers unwittingly satirize themselves, one is in West African pidgin English, and the other two are standard-dialect poems by black writer Welton Smith. Monologues by John O'Hara, Anthony Hecht, J. F. Powers, and playwright August Strindberg account for all the rest of the book except for two cartoons, by Rob Cobb and Jules Feiffer. (Powers' "The Eye" is the selection Elmer Fike was so exercized about.)

Multicultural representation does not account entirely for the harsh judgment on this book. Drawing on evidence, again, from objections elsewhere, I believe that the dissenters really are appalled by many of the classics themselves. Looked at negatively, Keats' "Ode to a Nightingale," Blake's "The Clod and the Pebble," and Arnold's "Dover Beach" are all negative—"morbid," "depressing," "hopeless," and quite possibly "anti-Christian" if you are compelled to look for that too. Blake, or rather the pebble, says,

> Love seeketh only self to please,
> To bind another to its delight,
> Joys in another's loss of ease,
> And builds a Hell in Heaven's despite.

Keats' soliloquist says

> Darkling I listen; and, for many a time
> I have been half in love with easeful Death. . . .

Arnold's lover says to his beloved that the Sea of Faith has withdrawn, and the world

> Hath really neither joy, nor love, nor light,
> Nor certitude, nor peace, nor help for pain;
> And we are here as on a darkling plain
> Swept with confused alarms of struggle and flight,
> Where ignorant armies clash by night.

The fact is that most literature deals with negative emotion, even often when it is funny. (Freud said wit is a defense.) All tragic plays end in death. Emphasizing the classics means amassing what can be construed as negativity. Consider carefully even *Alice in Wonderland* and *Huckleberry Finn*. There are atrocious scenes in both. As for books attacking authority, consider that the Alice books and the *Wizard of Oz* are big exposés of adult incompetence, the Wizard even being shown finally as an outright fraud. Book burners calling for the classics do not mean what they say. They may mean that they want taught in school the same books they were assigned in school themselves, because those are familiar and hence "classic." They may not regard books they read as a child as negative, but classics they did not read as a child may strike them as violent and morbid. By "classics," some simply mean certain patriotic chestnuts or even certain lines like "Give me liberty or give me death."

Presumably a classic is a classic because it deals with important human experience in a very artful way, so that catharsis, insight, and pleasure are produced perhaps even *because* the material is painful or fearful. Art transforms experience in the mind and does so, in the case of literature, by playing a pleasing game with words. It is both coping and sporting at once. Book-banning people may become so hypnotized by the subject matter, especially if it is something they're waiting to red-flag that they cannot respond to the form or manner or technique in which something is written and thereby miss its real function, to lift us beyond negative emotion, to take it and transmute it.

11

The Innocence
Is the Crime

I have outlined *Monologue and Dialogue* in particular not only because it illustrates how a broader representation rankles some people to the point of dismissing some of the acknowledged gems of English literature but also because it evokes a complex of reactions from such people that I want to explore. Although the one-sentence condemnation, "Cover to cover, *Trash,*" does not of course fully itemize the objections, I think it's quite fair to infer them from the many other explicit judgments made on similar selections in other books. A surprisingly large number of *Interaction* books got off scot-free of objections, sometimes because their particular form happened to steer them naturally away from controversy, so that it is interesting to note which books came in for a heavy drubbing.

Usually the books that were branded "morbid," "depressing," "negative," "un-American," "anti-Christian," "racist," and so on were those which because of the nature of their form or topic tended to contain more material by minority writers or by majority writers in a critical or satirical vein. Black or Chicano authors do not gravitate toward science fiction and adventure or mystery stories, nor will you find these authors in collections containing a lot of writing from earlier periods of history. You will find them in contemporary fiction and poetry and in essays, reportage, memoirs, and it was books containing these that were most condemned.

In contemporary, realistic writing youngsters want to read about the lives of people whose trials they can identify with and whose triumphs they can aspire toward. They want to read about the world they know in a way that helps them to understand and master it. This does not at all mean that they don't enjoy and project themselves into reading matter set in other times and places or in make-believe worlds, but it does mean that where realism is involved readers want to be able to identify with what is familiar. Eventually, we would expect youngsters to grow to identify with people different from themselves, but the less experienced and developed they are the more they will for the moment have to identify with their own kind. For minority children this means writers, material, styles, and view-points of their own kind, just as it does for other children.

The splendid advantage of mixing pluralistic reading material is that at the same time each youngster can find his or her own kind he or she can also discover other kinds. Such a mixture cannot be apparent from one book alone. Some of our books were loaded indeed: we knew that stories featuring minority athletes, entertainers, political leaders, or central fictional characters would interest minority children especially if told in a voice they could recognize as one of their own. So the *Interaction* books for secondary school called *Autobiography*, *Memoir*, *Biography*, *Chronicle*, and *Essays in Reflection* abound in minority writing. Our breakdown of books by types of form or popular genres naturally unbalanced some books, which was necessary to offset other books naturally unbalanced away from minorities.

Good teacher strategy, however, would consist in helping children to move on from one book or type of reading to another so that their range of acquaintance widens and they become consequently able to identify more and more broadly. A pluralistic reading curriculum exists not merely to sort each into his or her own kind but to familiarize each with the other kinds. There's no reason blacks shouldn't acquire a taste for science fiction and haiku and penetrate Greek and Norse mythology nor that Kanawha Valley children shouldn't learn what black history has been and how blacks live and feel today. But if you do not believe in a pluralistic or multicultural schooling, on principle, you can claim that it is biased against your values.

One of the *Interaction* books called *Biography*, for secondary school, contained the life story of "Bessie Smith, Empress of the Blues" by Studs Terkel. The rest of the book comprised biographies of Crazy Horse, Archimedes, artist Marc Chagall, Langston Hughes, and Queen Elizabeth.

Objection: This biography rather matter-of-factly presents the life and career of a jazz singer and entertainer. This story lends approval to the honky-talk [*sic*] lifestyle of the jazz musical entertainer. It is not wholesome material for presentation to school youngsters. It is a discredit to the Negro race. There are many wholesome and respectable Black Americans, whose biographies would make much better reading and reflect considerably more favorably on Black Americans.

In one of the secondary books called *Autobiography* we included "We Weren't Bad, Just Mischievous," an excerpt from *I Always Wanted to be Somebody* by black tennis champion Althea Gibson. This is the readout on it:

Page 6: Damn bucket
Page 10, Line 25: "I beat the hell out of her."

Page 11, Line 27: "Pig-tailed bitch"
Page 11, Lines 30–31: "Honest to God" — God's name in vain
Page 13, Line 3: "What the hell"
Page 12, Lines 17–20: Gang type violence
Page 13, Line 18: "Damn you"
Page 13, Second paragraph: Description of stealing

Objection: This story includes unwarranted profanity and presents crude and uncouth behavior and attitudes in an ambivalent context. Likewise, gang violence and stealing are also presented in an ambivalent context with no allusion to the wrongness of such behavior. A matter-of-fact indifference to profanity and wrong doing — even an implicit approval of such behavior — appears to pervade the context of the story.

I think "ambivalent context" simply means that the author made no effort to denounce the routine fighting, snitching, and skipping school that everyone growing up in Harlem got involved in. Althea Gibson assumes, I believe, that no one thinks this is a great way to live, and it is clear that through tennis she worked her way out of it. She does distinguish between serious crime and these street habits that all the kids fell into amid the destitution.

> Like I said, we never got in any real trouble. We were just mischievous. I think one good thing was that I never joined any of those so-called social clubs that they've always had in Harlem. None of my girl friends did, either. We didn't care for that stuff, all the drinking and the narcotics and sex that they went for in those clubs — and we didn't care for the stickups that they turned to sooner or later in order to get the money for the things they were doing.[1]

She also tells how she learned responsibility from losing a job she very much liked merely in order to take the day off with girl friends. (They went to see *their* idol, singer Sarah Vaughan, at the Paramount.) Youngsters growing up in an environment of despair and desperation need very much to read how others just like themselves learned to take charge of their lives and rise above the futile street life Gibson recalls.

In the same book we included an excerpt from entertainer Dick Gregory's *Nigger: An Autobiography*, "Not Poor, Just Broke." It is significant that in this title and "We Weren't Bad, Just Mischievous" the authors make an effort to offset the hard circumstances of their youth by rather humorously substituting a word of greater self-respect for the word that might be used to describe their early days. Gregory's piece got this response.

Page 29, Line 35: "I pissed in my pants" — how crude!
Page 30–31, last paragraph on p. 30: Violence
Page 32, Line 19: "Get your ass over here."

Page 33, Line 18: "Get your ass over here."
Page 34, Paragraph 7: crude, ugly talk

Objection: The foregoing passages specifically cited, and indeed this entire story, present cynical, blatant accounts of the crude, uncouth, vulgar, and violent. It is written in such a way as would seem to intentionally offend the sense of decency and good taste of many persons for whom the writer has repeatedly expressed a cynical disdain.

The objection typically ignores the main point of this selection — to show what it was like to grow up black — and focuses on the language, which for the ghetto is considerably toned down.

The violence referred to (on page 30) occurred during one of numerous Tarzan movies Gregory saw as a boy:

Used to sit there and laugh at those dumb Hollywood Africans grunting and jumping around and trying to fight the white men, spears against high-powered rifles. Once we had a riot in the movies when Tarzan jumped down from a tree and grabbed about a hundred Africans. We didn't mind when Tarzan beat up five or ten, but this was just too many, a whole tribe, and we took that movie house apart, ran up on the stage and kicked the screen and fought the guys who still dug Tarzan.[2]

For upper elementary, one equivalent in *Interaction* for memoirs and biographies was *True Stories*, in which we put a mixture of various nonfiction accounts. In one book of this title we included "True Stories by Slaves," transcriptions of actual slave recollections that we had drawn from B. A. Botkin's *Lay My Burden Down*. Dissenters objected: "Admittedly whites should not forget the cruelties of slavery, but there seems little point in including these recollections in a book entitled 'true stories.' " What lies behind the inconsistency of this sentence, which starts out apparently objecting to including slave accounts at all but then shifts the basis of the objection, in midsentence, by implying that the stories are not true? The memoirs constitute as legitimate a part of history as any other documents, all of which are ultimately founded on personal testimonials of what happened, some firsthand accounts by participants or observers. But I doubt that the objector questioned the truth of the stories. Rather, the incoherence expresses, I believe, the emotional and irrational aspect of the objection, which contains two half-points thrown together as the objector cast about for some reason to give for the feeling of recoiling that these stories aroused.

Not all ethnic objections occurred in the nonfiction books. Among the few good selections we found to go in *Adventure Stories* for upper elementary black children was John Steptoe's "Train Ride," about some small black boys from a New York borough who dare to take a subway trip into Manhattan and have a great adventure worth the price of the punishment they receive on finding their way home late. The story is told in black urban dialect but without any profanity, as the opening sentences illustrate.

You know how it be in the summer time, all hot. Everybody be sittin' around on the stoop. We be playin' out in the street. Me and my friends. I gotta lot of friends.[3]

Upper elementary is the time when children either really master reading or become so overwhelmed by the failure to that they soon drop out or endure school in misery. We included a few stories in black dialects to give less academically developed blacks every chance to find reading matter they could readily relate to because both subject and language would be familiar. The narration of "Train Ride" more or less sounds as if a peer is telling the story. The objection:

Exceptionally poor grammar used in this story. Dialects make for difficult reading and to include this as reading for poor students shows faulty thinking.

Recall that Alice Moore's original reason for asking the School Board to delay a vote on the books concerned "relativity" in language usage, dialects. Then later she and followers brought out the full charges based on their notions of "civilized Christians." Because our speech identifies and sorts us, if it varies much from a majority standard, language usage always holds the stage in school confrontations over curriculum. The real issue of course is tolerance of differences. Correctness poses as the issue, but since this mainly comes down to dialectical differences — people rarely make *personal* mistakes in grammar — the real issue is the fear that white children will be influenced to talk like blacks (and black children like whites) and so break an important identity definition, one of the chief fears of segregationists.

Interaction contained few selections in nonstandard dialect, because we knew that every child has to focus on standard speech, as virtually every parent, white or black, agrees. But part of the richness of English literature is its dialectical variation in both white and black communities — Irish, Scottish, and Australian, or African, American ghetto, or West Indian. Some inclusion of dialects, then, aimed at literary diversity, not at literacy.

But it is always precisely this *comprehensive* approach that so embittered the dissenters. Since they could hardly put forth racism as an objection, they had to give other reasons like corruption of the language, obscenity, morbidity, immorality, sacrilege, and subversion — all of which truly represented their values but did not often apply to the minority selections in question. In other words, the objections to ethnic pluralism had to be cast into the form of the other objections they were making about nonethnic selections. This is why the remarks they make on minority writing seem much more trumped up than in some other areas of dispute.

One of the more frequently used accusations was racism itself. Black poet Al Young's "A Dance for Ma Rainey" (the blues singer of the twenties) was branded "more racist maso-sadistic [sic] ideology," which was the sole comment. After addressing Ma Rainey, Young expresses what she hid but sang from,

> that pain that blues
> jives the world with
> aching to be heard

then closes the poem with this extended phrase:

> our beautiful brave black people
> who no longer need to jazz
> or sing to themselves in murderous vibrations
> or play the veins of their strong tender arms
> with needles
> to prove that we're still here.[4]

All black writing that alludes to the oppression of its people is of course called racism in reverse by the censors. This focus on suffering, and the references to the wounds blacks have sometimes inflicted on themselves in their frustration, no doubt accounts for the idea of "maso-sadistic."

I think that the objectors really don't understand what blacks have been through and also don't understand how literature can function to deal in a nondestructive way with otherwise overwhelming pain, not the least of which has been the loss of so many of their brothers to drugs, crime, and hatred. While paying tribute to Ma Rainey, who made blues a way to transform her pain, Al Young is telling himself and other blacks that if they gather their spirits together as a self-respecting people, they don't need these awful alternatives.

In the same book, *Lyric Poetry*, which ran a very broad gamut indeed of types and tones of poetry, appeared "Black Warrior" by Norman Jordan. The objection said, "This poem advocates racist violence and justifies secretive, vengeful, cowardly destruction of 'Whitey's' property. Advocates law breaking." Here is the entire poem.

> At night while
> Whitey sleeps
> the heat of a
> thousand African fires
> burns across my chest
>
> I hear the beat
> of a war drum
> dancing from a distant
> land
> dancing across a mighty
> water
> telling me to strike
>
> Enchanted by this
> wild call
> I hurl a brick through
> a store front window
> and disappear.[5]

To the extent that the poem may be partly addressed to Whitey, I think it aims to explain why some blacks have hurled bricks through windows, so futile a gesture. Coming after the evocation of proud ancestry, the act is made to appear paltry, a far cry indeed from the vision of his once powerful people. The title "Black Warrior" has to be ironical. To anyone who can listen, this poem says that this "secretive, vengeful, cowardly destruction" is not what blacks want. They want to restore the unity and identity and power they had before stolen into slavery in a foreign land. Actually, these are the same things, I'm sure, that their attackers want.

One of the most perceptive writers about black-white relations has been James Baldwin, whose works were represented a number of times in *Interaction* because we felt he is not only an exceptionally good writer of any race but also a person uncommonly able to suspend himself between the two races. No Uncle Tom, he can spell out, chapter and verse, the chronicle of white scourging of blacks, but he also doesn't stop there; he goes right on to call on his brothers to feel compassion for whites. He pulls off an extraordinary interweaving of denunciation and reconciliation so exquisitely and deliberately double-edged that I think our dissenters couldn't believe what he was saying. It is typical of rigidity that when two channels are beamed to it at once it can receive only one, the one of course that it expects and fears. Baldwin's unified double-attitude comes across never more movingly perhaps than in "My Dungeon Shook: Letter to My Nephew," which appeared in *Interaction*'s *Letters* for advanced high school.

> *Objection:* This man's letters and articles appear throughout this series of books, he obviously is a mentally scared individual who believes in no one or nothing but himself. He appears to be anti-everything and reading this letter seems to prove the point. Enough of this type of thinking could bring about racial uprisings everywhere.

Here are some excerpts, in order. It is typical of Baldwin that he calls whites his "countrymen." He is addressing his brother's son.

> . . . You can only be destroyed by believing that you really are what the white world calls a *nigger*. I tell you this because I love you, and please don't you forget it. . . . I know what the world has done to my brother and how narrowly he has survived it. And I know, which is much worse, and this is the crime of which I accuse my country and my countrymen, and for which neither I nor time nor history will ever forgive them, that they have destroyed and are destroying hundreds of thousands of lives and do not know it and do not want to know it. One can be, indeed one must strive to become, tough and philosophical concerning destruction and death, for this is what most of mankind has been best at since we have heard of man. (But remember: *most* of mankind is not *all* of mankind.) But it is not permissible that the authors of devastation should also be innocent. It is the innocence which constitutes the crime.
>
> Now, my dear namesake, the innocent and well-meaning people have caused you to be born under conditions not very far removed from those described by Charles Dickens in the London of more than a hundred years ago. I hear the chorus of the innocents screaming, "No! This is not true! How bitter you are!"—but. . . . I *know* the conditions under which you were born, for I was there. . . .

There is no reason for you to try to become like white people and there is no basis for their impertinent assumption that *they* must accept *you*. The really terrible thing, old buddy, is that *you* must accept *them*. And I mean that very seriously. You must accept them and accept them with love. For these innocent people have no other hope. They are, in effect, still trapped in a history that they do not understand; and until they understand it, they cannot be released from it. They have had to believe, and for innumerable reasons, that black men are inferior to white men. Many of them, indeed, know better, but, as you will discover, people find it very difficult to act on what they know. . . . In this case, the danger, in the minds of most white Americans, is the loss of their identity. Try to imagine how you would feel if you woke up one morning to find the sun shining and all the stars aflame. You would be frightened because it is out of the order of nature. Any upheaval in the universe is terrifying because it so profoundly attacks one's sense of one's own reality. Well, the black man has functioned in the white man's world as a fixed star, an immovable pillar: and as he moves out of his place, heaven and earth are shaken to their foundations. . . . But these men are your brothers — your lost, younger brothers. And if the word *integration* means anything, this is what it means: that we, with love, shall force our brothers to see themselves as they are, to cease fleeing from reality and begin to change it. . . .

We cannot be free until they are free. God bless you, James, and Godspeed.[6]

Now please look back at the objection. I have quoted Baldwin at length here because I think the extravagantly negative reaction to this piece — more hysterical than unfair — may signal that it hit very close to home indeed.

A Chicano in another selection makes a point remarkably similar to Baldwin's extension of sympathy to whites.

"It is hard on Anglo, too. His own history made him what he is. He's caught in a web of tradition, prejudice, and misinformation. He must get out of that web. So must we."[7]

The speaker here is a drugstore owner quoted by Bill Moyers in "Mathis, Texas," a section of his *Listening to America* excerpted for one of four *Interaction* books called *Reportage and Research*, aimed at college-bound senior high students. The objection to this selection was a single word — "Racism."

The subject is indeed racism but is treated with remarkable impartiality. Moyers, an Anglo reporter, mostly just pieced together official reports, eyewitness accounts, and interviews, narrating a continuity but very scrupulously not taking sides. Several clashes and the long-standing conflict are told and described by people of both sides. It is a model of objective reportage, and one can see friendliness and progress in the relationships as well as ugly trouble. Unelaborated, the objection is ambiguous. Racism which way? It would be impossible to make a charge of bias stick. It could also cover the possible meaning that focusing on racism is bad. I think ambiguity was a convenient dodge; objecting to racism looks like a virtuous — liberal — way of dispensing with a selection aimed at illuminating racism. The real problem is that the selection *does* present both sides.

Similarly condemned, at the elementary school level, was an excerpt from Ruth Franchere's biography of Cesar Chavez for juveniles, which we had included in another book of *True Stories*.

> *Objection:* This story projects Mr. Chavez as a kindly man working solely for a noble cause. Many farm owners may take exception to this being entitled a "true" story.

Franchere tells her story in a pretty innocuous way, emphasizing its political aspects only as much as necessary for a "leader of the people." It clearly aims to give young Chicanos a figure they can identify with, admire, and be inspired by. In fact, it does for Chicanos what all those stories of George Washington and Abraham Lincoln have done for Anglos. Hero stories don't dwell on the moles and warts, a fact that cuts across ethnic lines. But this account is quite straightforward enough and not at all designed to incite anything more than ethnic pride. Again, it is the sheer fact of equal representation that seems to earn the rejection.

I am not trying to prove hypocrisy. The phenomenon is more subtle than that, usually at least. But I must point out what we can certainly call an inconsistency and let the reader make of it what he or she will. It occurs in the same book of *Reportage and Research* referred to shortly ago. From the renowned cultural psychologist Erik Erikson we had drawn a selection, "Hunters Across the Prairie," a portion of his monumental *Childhood and Society*. While describing the Indian attitude toward birthing in white hospitals, he writes, "Older Indian women expecting the birth of a grandchild would quietly wail like the Jews before their sacred Wall, decrying the destruction of their nation." The response to this was, "Belittles Jewish beliefs."

Forty or so pages farther on in this book appears Mel Ziegler's "Biography of an Unwanted Building," a factual account from *New York* magazine of the typical financial problems of a large declining Manhattan apartment house. All that the objectors said about this selection was, "Say the names in *Bold Type* together." The names, those of the chain of owners of the building, are Morel J. Fuchs, Max Steinberg, Anthony Miano, George Hahn, and Les Evens.

12

Man's Head, Beast Body

Intolerance is rejection of what we do not identify with. It may direct itself against a wide array of things, but race and religion seem to be the two main targets. *Informative Articles* was the title of two books for secondary school containing an extremely miscellaneous collection of factual and how-to-do-it articles from many different sources. We included in one of these books an excerpt from *Yoga for Americans*, an early and well known book by Indra Devi, an American woman who had taught Gloria Swanson. At the very beginning of this long article, the author says, "Many people still think that yoga is a religion. Others believe it to be a kind of magic. . . . *Yoga is a method, a system of mental, physical, and spiritual development.*"[1] Then in a question-answer session:

Q: *What religion does a yogi profess?*
A: A yogi can belong to any religion or to none at all. In this case, he usually forms his own relationship with the Ultimate Reality once he has come closer to It.
Q: *Can a Catholic take up yoga?*
A: Certainly, since yoga is not a religion. In fact, a Catholic association has recently been formed in Bangalore, India, in order to introduce the Yoga asanas to the Catholic young men there, and to integrate them into the Catholic way of life.[2]

Despite these obvious efforts to head off misconceptions, the three pages of general introduction to yoga that included these quotations was objected to as "religious indoctrination."

The rest of the 25-page article is taken up with descriptions of bodily postures, breathing exercises, and daily health care that typify a course in hatha yoga. Since no yoga teacher could conclude an account of physical practices without returning to the main goal, spiritual illumination, the last half page deals with meditation. I am going to reproduce that half-page because of the school dilemma embodied in it and the response to it.

You may now get up and go about your business or you may have a period of meditation. Simply sit down in Lotus Pose, or else cross-legged, close the eyes and take a few deep breaths. Then sit very still, trying to direct your thoughts to the Infinite Light which is God, Truth, Love, and is beyond form, beyond our understanding. Try to realize that It is everywhere, both outside us and within us; that we, as human beings are the carriers of the Divine Light here on earth, that it dwells in our hearts, that our bodies are the Temple of the Living Spirit, and that we should let this Spirit shine through our eyes, speak through our words, be felt through our deeds.

Then send a thought of peace and love to all those around you, to your family, your friends, those whom you love, those whom you don't love, to all living beings on this earth and beyond. At the end you can say aloud:

> From the unreal to the Real
> From the darkness to Light,
> From death to Immortality
> *Om*
> Shanti, shanti, shanti.

Om is the sacred sound of the Hindus, and *Shanti* means peace in Sanskrit.

You may also say any other prayer, or use your own wording—this is up to you. But I suggest that at least once a day you remind yourself that you are of divine origin and that you are on this earth to bring love, peace, and goodness to all living creatures.[3]

Since this passage is preceded by innocuous relaxation exercises and concludes the article, it surely constitutes the entire text referred to below.

Objection: On *page 61* are detailed religious and psychic exercises to be performed in the practice of Yoga. There is even a ritualistic incantation of this heathenish religion cited on this page. Additionally, there is religious doctrine promulgated here, which is repugnant to New Testament Christianity.

Lest the foregoing be misunderstood: no state-supported propagation or teaching of the Christian religion is being advocated here. But it is likewise incumbent upon state-supported education not to advocate or teach any other religion either. The inclusion of this material is a violation of the First Amendment Constitutional guarantees of freedom of religion and separation of religion and state. Students have a basic right to study the Language Arts without being subjected to Eastern religious indoctrination.

That the selection appeared, among some other do-it-yourself pieces, in a book called *Informative Articles* should count for something, as well as Indra Devi's own efforts to leave to the reader the option of omitting the meditation portion and of substituting some other "prayer" for hers. Is there reason to doubt the ecumenical spirit in which this selection is offered? People of all conceivable religions study and practice yoga, and chants, mantras, or prayers of all traditions may be used, including Protestant hymns, secular poems, and Catholic kyrie eleisons. Most yogis, even if Indian, know the Bible quite well, feel perfectly at home with Christ and the Christian God, and in fact regard all the world's religions as expressions of the same truths. Finally, the First Amendment argument would be more logically carried out if the last sentence of the objection ended "without being subjected to *any* religious indoctrination."

Nevertheless, I think the dissenters have a stronger case here than with any of their other objections, at least on technical grounds. Christians who have been trying for years to get prayer into schools feel especially bitter if a prayer from another religion seems to get the privilege they were denied. The two Sanskrit words can be construed as part of some Hindu liturgy (although *Om* and *Amen* derive from a common source, *Aumen*, and *Shanti* simply means "peace"). And the idea that each individual carries the Divine Light within does represent a doctrinal point not shared by all creeds. So, depending on one's interpretation of "religion," that half-page of the selection may with some justice be interpreted as violating the separation between church and state.

But did the authors of that constitutional principle mean by "religion" *any* universal beliefs about the nature and purpose of life, or did they mean "religion" as a particular church, organization? I think definitely the latter. Consider their background and intentions. The founding fathers wanted church and state separated in order to prevent the perversions of government and the persecutions of individuals that had occurred in Europe and England because temporal rulers became heads of church and spiritual rulers heads of state. Their forefathers had come to America as much to avoid religious intolerance as anything. Furthermore, they were virtually all students of the Enlightenment, the Age of Reason, which stressed tolerance of differences and, more than that, the perception of similarity across the differences, the universality of humankind's spiritual needs. The great majority of the founding fathers were Freemasons and Rosicrucians as well as Christians.

This means that they believed that in essence all religions seek the same thing, that all people share fundamental commonalities, especially before God. They thought in cross-cultural and ecumenical ways. Certainly their goal was not to discourage spirituality in school but to avoid a takeover by one church or sect. These authors of the Constitution would agree with the Kanawha judge who ruled (see chapter 1) that the First Amendment does not declare that religion shall not be mentioned in schools. If it did, students would be prohibited from learning about the many religious and metaphysical ideas that arise throughout the fields of history, art, social studies, and philosophy. It is precisely because religion and culture are so intermingled that we cannot study one without the other. What schools may not and should not do is adopt, promote, or favor one religion — indoctrinate.

Representing the Bible itself is a matter of hell if you do and hell if you don't. In *Parables* for high school we included only one of Christ's parables, just one to connect the parable tradition most familiar to American children to similar stories in other traditions. We assumed some knowledge of Christian parables and concentrated on ones we knew few children in this country would be familiar with. We also wanted to show how individual professional authors had taken over and utilized the form. Parables represented Ghana, Turkey, Ethiopia, Japan, Indonesia, Denmark, Scotland, and Russia.

> There are parables in this book which are good, the parable of The Prodigal Son, parables by Robert Louis Stevenson, and Leo Tolstoy. Most of the other parables represent a poor selection for a book of parables. Surely, better selections could have been made, while still doing justice to the principle of multi-ethic. Only one of the parables of Jesus is mentioned. Since the Judao-Christian [*sic*] ethic is the most significant philosophical principle permeating Western civilization and American culture, why could not a more proportionate representation of parables from the Bible have been included? Multi-ethnicity does not require a disproportionate, lopsided representation of ethnic groups and culture in educational material.

The objection to our *Proverbs* voiced a similar complaint.

> Again, as in the case in the book of parables in this series there is a very disproportionate selection of proverbs from among cultures, civilizations, ethnic backgrounds, etc. insofar as the proportionate make-up of American culture and society is concerned.

We were trying to represent the makeup of world cultures, not just American culture, as is appropriate for an ancient, international folk form. Also, it seemed reasonable to us to assume students had already acquired familiarity with religious and folk material of their own culture. To people imbued with chauvinism, who associate self with fatherland and mother tongue, missing an opportunity to assert your own ethos over others' — and exposing your children to the risky attraction of other cultures — seems inexcusable.

Because of the very principle of separation of church and state invoked in the objections, publishers feel that the only way an excerpt from the Bible can be anthologized is as some form of literature. In *Legends*, for high school, we included the story of Samson from the Revised Standard Version of the Bible, prefaced by a straight historical summary of preceding events.

Objection: The story of Samson as recorded in the book of Judges in the Old Testament is historical fact. To include this historical account in a book of "Legends" is to cast doubt in the minds of young people upon the veracity of the Holy Scriptures. Moreover, this is at variance with and is calculated to undermine the religious beliefs of young people whose families have taught them to believe in the divine inspiration of the Bible. This is one more example (among many others) of how the editors and publishers of these books take unwarranted and unconstitutional liberties which affront the religious beliefs of fundamentalist youth in the public schools.

This results from an unfortunate misunderstanding about the nature of legends and myths. Now, in popular parlance, a story may be called a legend or a myth to indicate that it is made up, but in serious erudition these forms are not at all equated with fictions. Professional folklorists and the most highly regarded scholars of the forms, like Northrop Frye or Joseph Campbell, consider them as embodiments of the highest truths of a culture.

Some historical veracity partly defines legends, which are stories about people who probably really lived and often have been proved to have lived. Other stories in the book, for example are about William Tell, Robin Hood, American Indian heroes, and figures from King Arthur's court, all of whom are regarded as based on actual people, however embroidered or amplified the stories may be as retold for generations. But even these accretions and exaggerations are considered by the curators of legends not just as fiction but as expressions of the hero's significance not evident in a simple telling of physical events. The epic cycles of Charlemagne and Roland and of the Trojan War heroes are collections of legends generated around real people and events.

The story of Samson and the other stories of the Old Testament are just as historical as those recorded in other ancient documents, and the inclusion of Samson in *Legends* implies nothing less. One does not have to be a Christian or orthodox Jew to accept the chronicle portions of the Old Testament as actual history. The defensiveness of this objection is unnecessary on two counts: the historicity of the chronicle portions of the Old Testament is well accepted, and the classification of "legend" does not disparage a story or imply it is not based on truth.

To criticize textbooks both for not including Biblical material and for placing it under literary headings puts publishers in a double bind, because there is no other way to get Biblical selections into language arts books. It is very important to clear up misunderstanding about both this and the historicity of legends and myths, because fundamentalists take this necessary way of handling Scripture as part of an effort to say the Bible isn't true, including the very existence of Christ. Since I think the Bible contains truth at many levels — some biographical and historical, some spiritual and metaphysical—I for one would not want to present it as idle tales.

Some objections were made to particular points of ideology or to particular people standing for those points. For example, in *Fictional Diaries* we included one of Ring Lardner's humorous stories told by an immature adolescent. The objection first stated that, "Ring Lardner was a leftist sportscaster, his son Ring Lardner, Jr., was one of the infamous Hollywood 10, who were known Communists." This refers of course to the blacklisting that occurred during the extremist campaign directed against subversives by Senator Joseph McCarthy in the 1950s. Merely recommending *The Joan Baez Song Book* at the end of a high school book of songs triggered this response:

> *Objection:* Miss Baez is notorious as a writer and singer of social protest songs, The [sic] themes and content of which are usually critical of our country, its institutions, traditions, and moral values.

Interaction and the *Man* series included a piece by Margaret Mead, the late, much acclaimed anthropologist. Objection was made to her as a person: "Margaret Mead is an atheist and evolutionist who accepts anything as right or good if it is the practice and accepted customs for that particular society." Three charges are made here—atheism, evolutionism, and relativism (see "situation ethics"). Interestingly, all three of these stances are imposed on the scientist, for better or for worse, by traditional mainstream science. That is, the scientific investigator has been expected to keep her belief in God, if any, out of her work and act as an atheist; to assume some version of Darwinian evolution as an hypothesis; and to observe and describe nonjudgmentally the customs and practices of different world peoples. (The right to atheism, by the way, is guaranteed in the Bill of Rights as part of religious freedom.)

Here is a typical objection to evolution. In *Charts and Graphs* was a chart called "Early Man and His Tools," depicting four stages of man from lower to upper Paleolithic, going from 750,000 years ago to 15,000 years ago.

> *Objection:* This presentation presupposes in a matter-of-fact way that the *theory* of evolution is a proven fact. This is scientifically inaccurate. It is contrary to the religious beliefs of many persons, and consequently, is inadmissible material for inclusion in public school curricula when implied as fact.

The First Amendment does not forbid the inclusion in school teaching of some material contrary to someone's religious beliefs (consider how far *that* claim could be taken!). But the point that Darwinism is scientifically inaccurate and only a theory, not fact, deserves consideration, not because it is a reason to keep the concept of evolution out of schools but because it touches on legitimate and profound issues of what constitutes knowledge. "Science," after all, simply means "knowledge." It does not stipulate how we come by knowledge.

Esotericists have long spoken of a "spiritual science" and were among the first to denounce Darwin's theory, though poles apart by nature from fundamentalist Christians. Theosophists and Rosicrucians, for example, teach a cosmogenesis and anthropogenesis totally different from both conventional Biblical interpretation and modern Darwinism.[4] Esoteric doctrine does not contradict modern science but says that it conceives of evolution in such material terms that it garbles it badly for lack of a larger (metaphysical) framework. In other words, other people than fundamentalists — very thoughtful, well educated, sophisticated people — also insist on the shortcomings of Darwinism and material science. Indeed, there is a basis on which the theories of this kind of science may be challenged, but this basis concerns the essential nature of knowing itself, not a mere maneuver like "Creation Science," which claims falsely to compete with modern science as an alternative theory.

The creationists' efforts to introduce religion into school disguised as science brought on beneficial airing of the subject. The Public Broadcasting System showed in 1982 a program called "Did Darwin Get It Wrong?" that reviewed the evidence and showed through interviews that even those scientists who criticize Darwinism assume his general theory and reject hotly the fundamentalists' exploitation of their criticisms. Likewise, in a 1982 issue of *Science* Boyce Rensberger wrote:

> Unfortunately, the debates within evolutionary biology are often confused in many people's minds with the attack of the creationists on public schools. The creationists, in their attempt to force the teaching of a supernatural creation, often talk as if the debates are a new and startling challenge to some misguided scientific orthodoxy. Actually, Darwin's theory of evolution, like all good theories, has faced tests and challenges ever since it was put forth in 1858.
>
> The history of the theory of evolution over the last hundred years is a stunning testimony to the theory's power. A century after Darwin's death, it is clear that every major advance in biology — from the discoveries of naturalists to the formulas of molecular biologists — fits beautifully into the broad outlines of the picture that Darwin drew. Where new discoveries have conflicted with Darwin's theory, the theory has been modified to accommodate the findings. This is exactly how all scientific theories are built. One result is that the theory of evolution, even with the question marks that remain, stands today with more authority and reliability than ever.[5]

Seventy-two Nobel Prize winning scientists testified before the United States Supreme Court in 1987 that creationism was not a science. In its landmark decision afterward, on June 19, the Court struck down a Louisiana law requiring schools to teach creationism, ruled that creationism was a pseudo-science employed to find a place for religion in schools, and thus reaffirmed in legal circles the Court's previous stand for the separation of church and state.

When objectors demand that Darwinian evolution be labeled in school as an hypothesis, and that alternatives to it be included as well, I believe they are thinking only of including their version of Genesis. I wonder if they have considered just what other alternatives might be presented in school to be really fair. Certainly among the strongest contenders would be those of the Theosophists and other esotericists, whom fundamentalists would detest. Then what about the variety of creation myths that have issued from virtually every civilization and culture known? Schools will be sorely charged indeed to represent on an equal-time basis all these alternatives to Darwin, and the attempt would require exactly the multicultural program that so antagonizes the objectors.

And what are we to do with the host of other still unproven scientific hypotheses that are being taught as fact because they provide predictability and permit the creation of technology? Electricity and magnetism are still mysteries, just names for still unexplained phenomena. So are most of the main concepts of modern science. In other words, the objectors make an excellent point about ticketing a theory as such and about presenting it in a context of alternatives, but since evolution is only one instance, this point poses general problems of teaching science that have simply never been faced. We let children think we understand nature better than we actually do, and this no doubt makes it harder for them to break through as adults to what we still don't know.

The importance of this issue for objectors centers on whether people are primarily spiritual or material creatures. This is a legitimate concern indeed, but it must not take the form of merely abhorring an animal origin, which even if true would be true only for the physical level and would not preclude a spiritual being as well. The popularization of science for both schools and the general public projects a far too physical view of our understanding of the world. Now that science is dealing increasingly with the invisible, the intangible, and the imponderable — probing very far out through astrophysics and very far in through nuclear physics — it seems inappropriate indeed to continue to purvey science as concerned only with physicality and never relating to what people have called metaphysics. Mathematical descriptions of nature, on which we rely the more we penetrate the universe in any direction, are really abstract philosophy, and we are borne back to the Renaissance integration of science, religion, and philosophy. In fact, it has been some time now since Einstein said that "physics leads to metaphysics."

No, the objectors are not wrong in exerting a force to keep the teaching of science from closing doors to immaterial reality. A number of selections in *Interaction* gave voice to realities alternative to the standard, mechanistic, materialistic science inherited from the nineteenth century. We excerpted from Ostrander and Schroeder's *Psychic Discoveries Behind the Iron Curtain*, Carlos Castaneda's *Conservations with Don Juan*, and Gina Cerminara's biography of Edgar Cayce, the remarkable spiritual healer who was also a conventional Christian. Had it appeared at that time, we would have drawn from Fritjof Capra's milestone fusion of current science and metaphysics, *The Tao of Physics*. The objectors usually did not comment on such selections, and I would not expect them to recognize these authors or personages as allies.

Only Christians of a certain cast of mind have felt that a theory of biological evolution conflicts with the Bible or negates spirituality in humankind. Curious enough is the defense where there is no attack, but more curious still is the almost obsessive apprehension about being classed with or reduced to beasts. For example, in a book called *Information* for upper elementary school we included "The Courtship of Animals" by well known juvenile author, Millicent Selsam, that got shot down not for touching on sex education but for mentioning in the same breath human fertilization and fertilization in animals.

Objection: The reproductive process of man should not be included with these examples of lower order life. This is an endorsement of evolution. Evolution is not to be taught in such a manner as to present it as fact. The photo on page 39 is attempting to say that there is no difference between humans and frogs, fish and snakes. Recommend rejection!

This article features the ways sperm and egg come together in the animal world and thus includes some examples of courtship. It makes comparison only at the microbiological level of sperm and egg, nothing being said about human courtship. The "photo" is not a photo but a simple drawing of the sperm and the egg for humans, frogs, fish, and snakes to convey this basic fact of sexual reproduction across the various animal families. At this biochemical level, similarity does of course exist, as it does for many other aspects of physiological functioning such as metabolism, but absolutely nothing in the text or picture implies the extravagant generalization that "there is no difference between humans and frogs, fish and snakes." Nor does the article deal with evolution; the only reason, I believe, that the objector brought it in is that evolution means for him or her that people are dragged down to the level of beasts. Surely there is more to humans than their sperms and eggs.

Snake*

Theodore Roethke

I saw a young snake glide
Out of a mottled shade
And hang, limp on a stone:
A thin mouth, and a tongue
Stayed, in the still air.

It turned; it drew away;
Its shadow bent in half;
It quickened, and was gone.

I felt my slow blood warm.
I longed to be that thing,
The pure, sensuous form.
And I may be, some time.[6]

"Objection: Insinuates belief in reincarnation."

Reincarnation did not occur to me when I approved the poem for *Lyric Poetry*, except perhaps as one of several potentialities Roethke wants the reader's imagination to play with. He could perfectly well be talking about becoming "pure, sensuous form" in this lifetime, through magical or imaginative transformation, by role-playing the snake, by creating poems, by voluntarily descending from time to time to his reptilian "old brain," etc. Part of a poet's business is to shake up staid perception and help us entertain unlimited possibilities.

I think it right enough indeed to see reincarnation as one of these possibilities, but among those who seriously believe in reincarnation, reappearance of a human as an animal is a repugnant trivialization of a central spiritual doctrine. People reincarnate as people, and generally as a higher being than they were before, because the purpose of returning is to use the material plane as a school for further soul growth. It is part of a belief that souls evolve from lower to higher consciousness. Reincarnation of a person as an animal is a superstitious degeneration of the idea, but it has recurred enough during history to become a solid popular prejudice that may partly account for why the Christian church put it under the table early in its course of gaining state acceptance and wider membership.[7]

Reversion to animality runs as a motif throughout typical fundamentalist thinking and connects inherently with racism, since a racist's hierarchy of lower to higher strains of human beings usually anchors the

*Reprinted by permission of Faber and Faber Ltd. from *The Collected Poems of Theodore Roethke*.

lower end in the animal world. Thus Europeans (Christians) looking
down on Africans and Amerindians as "barbarians" and "savages" meant
that they were little better than animals. These are in fact precisely the
epithets that Darwin himself applied to the Tierra del Fuegians, whom he
compared to lower animals, partly because they showed no religious
feeling, which was clearly one of his main criteria of civilization.[8] Notions
of racial purity generally assume that purer races have removed themselves farther from bestiality. This view in turn implies, curiously, an
acceptance of some sort of continuity between animal and human such as
evolutionists assume.

Part of the curiosity I'm tracking here concerns how differently Darwin and his theory have been villainized than fundamentalists villainized
him. In a chapter of *The Origins of Totalitarianism* called "Race-
Thinking Before Racism" Hannah Arendt points out how Darwinism,
though politically neutral itself, was pressed into the service of various,
even opposing, ideologies such as rule by race or by class, pacifism or
imperialism. Its notion of inheritance could justify aristocracy; of survival of the fittest, colonial domination; of struggle for survival, revolution by the masses; of individual mutation, takeover by bourgeois
upstarts; of gradual scale between humans and animals, racial discrimination. What endured into the twentieth century, she says, was the
movement toward eugenics, which implied the possibility of creating
racial purity and breeding a master race of supermen.

> The process of selection had only to be changed from a natural necessity
> which worked behind the backs of men into an "artificial," consciously
> applied physical tool. . . .
>   But before Nazism, in the course of its totalitarian policy, attempted to
> change man into a beast, there were numerous efforts to develop him on a
> strictly hereditary basis into a god. Not only Herbert Spencer, but all the
> early evolutionists and Darwinists "had as strong a faith in humanity's
> angelic future as in man's simian origin."[9]

Any concept of evolution must have, after all, two ends of a scale —
angelic as well as simian. Regardless of whether one accepts Darwinism
or not, it is a kind of negative thinking to look only downward to the ape
and not upward to the angel or perfection implied in any evolution. Darwin was describing an *ascent,* so that, among all the other doctrinal possibilities it can be used to support is the one that humans are engaged in a
spiritual evolution and that we are in transit to God, perhaps after some
kind of fall. (Unfortunately, he used the genealogical term "descent" as in
"descended from.") Because it is possible to see in Darwinism whatever
one likes, it is significant what interpretation a given party does read into

it. (It should be refreshing for us all to regard Darwinism as a sort of Rohrschach test.)

Supposedly, some Christians attack Darwinism because it denies humanity's spiritual origins as told in Genesis. But this assumption of contradiction is unnecessary and not made by most Christians. I feel there is another reason, and it has to do with apprehension about one's animality. By no means does the theory of evolution equate people with beasts, but we will detest this theory if we have a low self-esteem and hence fear that we are little better than an animal. In other words, how we react to a scale of apes to angels depends on where we feel we stand on it. This determines the negative thinking that sees in Darwinism a denial of spiritual origins.

Racism is a displacement onto others of bestiality suspected in oneself. It implies exactly the apes-to-angels hierarchy that threatens people of low self-esteem, who may consign to the lower rungs those not of their own kind. The more of these others rank below me, the farther I must be from the bottom. Opposing intermarriage to maintain racial purity aims to gain or maintain higher standing in the hierarchy. As the Nazis knew so well, however, the backside of eugenics is genocide, the ultimate in racial discrimination.

So doubt of one's worth underlies both racism and the repudiation of evolution. People brought up believing in angels but made to feel they are falling amid apes are especially haunted by apprehensions of animality. Believing in God but not in oneself sets up an intolerable chasm that one crosses not by finding others inferior but by identifying with divinity. As a final note upon this subject at this point, consider the objection made to a picture in *Using Figurative Language* of the *Language of Man* series: "Man's head with a beast body is obnoxious."

13

Reading Comprehension

Let's return now to particular ideological stands in the objections. One of these concerned militarism. Coming out shortly after the end of the Vietnam conflict, the Kanawha textbook programs contained a great deal of material produced by that war, especially about incidents raising moral issues, like the massacre of civilians at My Lai. Questioning of the reasons for American presence in Vietnam, conscientious objection, and reportage on military misconduct were routinely condemned.

An *Interaction* book for senior high school called *Transcripts* contained an interview from the *Evergreen Review* with five veterans who had taken part in the My Lai episode. With unusual understatement an objector merely wrote, "Not necessary for education." Similar material in another book called *Transcripts* for lesser advanced secondary students consisted of short excerpts from the trial of Lt. Calley, the officer immediately in charge at My Lai, and from an interview CBS newsman Mike Wallace did with paul Meadlo, who admitted to killing a number of civilians and who gave an account interesting to compare with the one his officers gave, as recorded in the transcript of the trail. The Kanawha reviewer said,

> The remainder of this book is filled with the trials of Sacco and Vanzetti and of Lt. Calley, and with interviews with Paul Meadlow [sic] and Capt. Medina. I question why this type of literature is important for students unless it is to make them feel guilt and shame.

(Captain Medina appeared as a witness during the trial, not in an interview.) These Vietnam selections occupied one-tenth of the book totaling 120 pages and including also three sports selections, interviews by folklorist Alan Lomax and oral historian Studs Terkel, a radiocast of the explosion of the *Hindenburg*, some humorous debate from the *Congressional Record*, and a couple of other nonideological selections.

Consider the implications of lumping together the My Lai selections with the excerpt from the trial of Sacco and Vanzetti. Both may be regarded as challenging authority or criticizing the government. If the trial was unjust or My Lai immoral — or Vietnam unjustified — then such selections would point to derelictions on the part of America or some parts of "our way of life." Self-scrutiny is among the biggest taboos of the mystique we are examining. "Hawks" eager to renew the war on Communism say that we no longer have to hang our heads and inhibit our policies because of some lingering guilt about Vietnam (as if moral self-examination had been a sick phase). Students nearing the voting age need to think about the actions of governments.

Interestingly, the objector does not challenge the veracity of these selections. One of the virtues of verbatim transcripts is that they constitute a kind of hard facts, on the one hand, being recorded verbal events, and stand clearly, on the other hand, as the views and experiences of those who utter them, devoid of authorial commentary or presentation. For this reason we regarded transcripts as a fine medium for engaging students with certain controversial subjects as well as with an important mode of discourse covering interview, trial, debate, newscast, panel, etc. Referring to this raw, dialogical mode as "literature" may be a subtle effort to offset the realism of these selections, which forced the objections into a subdued vein.

Although we as editors could create bias by collaging snippets or selecting a passage in which one party develops a view to the exclusion of his adversaries, the fact is that these My Lai selections might well arouse sympathy for the killers as well as the killed, because one effect of a transcript can be to capture, through its spontaneity, some of the truth beyond the individuals speaking. Who cannot be moved, for example, on hearing Lt. Calley say, in his statement after being convicted of premeditated murder:

> When my troops were getting massacred and mauled by an enemy I couldn't see, I couldn't feel and I couldn't touch — that nobody in the military system ever described them as anything other than Communism.
> They didn't give it a race, they didn't give it a sex, they didn't give it an age. They never let me believe it was just a philosophy in a man's mind. That was my enemy out there.
> And when it became between me and that enemy, I had to value the lives of my troops — and I feel that was the only crime I have committed.[1]

His crime of ordering the massacre of civilian men, women, and children may not be so great as that of leaders who put him in this hopelessly ambiguous situation. His government had told him the enemy was "Communism," but they also told him it was these people "out there" in front of him. But which ones? Some are supposed to have a certain bad "philosophy" in their heads and some not. The ones you are supposed to be defending against Communism look exactly like those who killed your buddies yesterday. They're all called "gooks," which surely means sub-human animals. Since the real effect was to kill a huge number of "gooks," perhaps it's naïve to talk of ideological conflict; perhaps Vietnam was just another race war. The Them-and-Us square-off between capitalism and Communism shifted over into the Them-and-Us of white vs. yellow, or American vs. Asiatic. (Remember Pearl Harbor!)

In another *Interaction* transcript that did give voice to only one view, the voice was that of a judge explaining to a Vietnam draft evader why, despite his respect for the defendant's sincerity and good character, he was sentencing him to prison, according to the law in cases where a person has refused even to file formally as a conscientious objector. Like Calley's post-trial statement, this one too opens up a bigger perspective than either of the opposed views. Kanawha reviewers made no comment on this selection, even though the draft evader was much praised by the judge. His rare ability to sentence and praise at the same time stymied, I believe, their customary mode of reacting.

Here is the objection, however, to a one-inch column ad by an organization offering advisory service to conscientious objectors, which appeared among dozens of selections in the booklet titled *Advertisements* (the only such book in the program, by the way), surrounded, in a kind of amusing juxtaposition, by ads for pistols, burglary locks, Charles Atlas muscle-building, and several others reflecting America's heterogeneity.

> *Objection:* Given the current context of controversy concerning the avoidance of military service for a variety of dubiously contrived excuses, this advertisement is a "natural" pedogological [sic] springboard for the advocacy of radical ideology concerning hatred for the military and justification for rationalizing cowardice and other alledgedly [sic] "conscientious" reasons for avoiding one's obligation to serve his country, when called upon to do so.

Fortunately, *this* objection was not so understated as to prevent our getting a good look at what's bothering the dissenters.

A book in the *Man* series contained an article in which the statement is made, "What is absurd and monstrous about war is that men who have no personal quarrel should be trained to murder one another in cold blood." The objection read: "Killing in war is not murder. Defending one's nation is not choosing war any more than killing in defense of one's home and family is choosing murder." It is assumed that any war is in defense of the homeland, which is of course the impression instigators of war always take pains to create. Feeling obliged to apologize for war in general is symptomatic of the militaristic attitude, where war becomes an equivalent of patriotism and group loyalty, to the point that pacifism means just the opposite, dislike of one's country and disloyalty. Thus for the dissenters it was self-explanatory to object to a selection as pacifist, because this was their synonym for traitors and cowards.

For example, in the secondary school book *Fables*, a retelling in modern dress by Lenny Jenkins of Aesop's "Birds, Beasts, and Bat" was rejected with this sole remark: "This moral could appear to be a pacifist view if expanded." Actually, the fable in this case does not at all draw a pacifist moral, though I would think it perfectly all right if it did. I point this out because it shows a characteristic tendency in these objections to read into selections the ideas the reviewers are prepared to defend against.

The moral that the author concluded his fable with was, "If you try to sit on two chairs at once, you'll end up on the floor between them." This moral expresses logically and straightforwardly what the preceding action suggests. When a hawk and a bear quarreled over a fish, they set off a full-scale war between the birds and the beasts. Bat says, "I'll see which side looks like it'll come out on top, and join that one." The author says, "He knew that with his leathery wings he could easily pass for a bird, and with his ears and claws he could pass for a beast." Bat fights on one side at times and the other at other times, reversing for each occasion a special uniform he had made showing bird and beast on opposite sides. After the war is over, both sides reject him because he fought for the other. Ever since, Bat sneaks around at night and lives a confused, unhappy life. "Nobody knows exactly what kind of creature he is, and nobody cares," ends the story.[2]

It never occurred to me that this fable had anything to do with pacifism or militarism. It is about being two-faced to the point of losing identity. Have our objectors made a simple equation between a turncoat and a pacifist? Or are they playing with texts as pretexts for inflaming themselves?

It is time we shifted the focus of this examination from ideology to reading comprehension, though it will remain difficult to tell issues of one from those of the other. Objections presented so far have featured differences in *values*, whereas now I would like to emphasize differences in *interpretations*. This distinction must ever remain imperfect, for one sees what one wants or fears, or fails to see what one cannot afford to see or dare to want. Nevertheless, the deliberate effort to separate the ideological conflicts based on different values from the comprehensional conflicts based on different interpretations helps to bring out, if nothing else, just how much we read things in and out of texts according to our previously acquired belief systems.

Censors tend notoriously to repudiate this variation in interpretation itself as being one of the forms of relativity that in fact they want to censor. Instead of having a stable, absolute meaning, they feel, then a text can "mean any old thing you want it to" and hence become meaningless. I don't say that most texts *should* elicit different interpretations but simply that they often *do*. I will try to point out instances where the objectors have misinterpreted a text from the way I think the author intended it to be construed. I do this not to fault the Kanawha readers but to hold out the possibility that vehement disputes such as happened there may stem from real misunderstanding as much as from true differences in values. It sounds fatuous or sentimental to hold that all conflicts are really just some sort of misunderstanding, but it may well be that *at some level of analysis or depth of truth*, all conflicts do indeed hinge on misunderstandings, depending on how well we succeed in discovering the less obvious similarity among people as well as the blatant differences.

If some titles in the *Interaction* breakdown of reading matter tended, like *Memoir* or *Biography*, to bring out ethnic variation, other titles tended to create special thinking problems affecting reading comprehension. Thus the previously mentioned *Dialogues and Monologues* failed to get rave reviews among the objectors as much perhaps for the sophistication of the unusual sort of literary technique it featured as for the representation of black thought, style, and dialects. As I've indicated, all the selections in it, even the two cartoons, placed on display, as on stage, a created character not to be confused with the author.

They were meant to show students that many texts besides play scripts may be performed — poems, short stories, and eventually even non-literature — because they contain personas, invented or found characters, who *utter themselves* and speak for themselves. The author who made up or discovered these speakers may or may not agree with what they say and in any case could hardly be represented more than very partially by them. The technique is a natural for satire, especially of the sort where speakers betray themselves, hang themselves, or make fools of themselves.

At any rate, a serious cognitive issue lurks within this sometimes giddy, sometimes dark technique, sophisticated in its assumption of irony but primitive too in being essentially an aping of real life behavior. As in the theater, it throws the reader or viewer into a point of view, a mind, without a hand-holding guide or narrator or cozy authorial host. As in real life, it poses a problem of comprehending on your own what you behold.

Objectors to the books frequently misunderstood selections throughout the program where ironic meanings were involved or where created characters held the textual stage. What shows this is the attributing to the author — or even the compiler of the anthology! — of thoughts uttered by his characters. It's as if we were to ascribe to Shakespeare the sentiments uttered by all the dolts and rogues and murderers in his plays, or uttered even by his kings and wits. So behind the objection "trash" to *Monologue and Dialogue* (and we offered three other books of that title) lay not only revulsion to the content of some selections but great discomfort with a technique that makes the reader judge for himself. I think the objectors did not fully understand what was going on in the soliloquies by Strindberg, O'Hara, J. F. Powers, Browning, and Eliot or at any rate did not know what they were supposed to think.

The speakers in all but "Journey of the Magi" are *intended* to earn our disapproval or scorn. The self-revelation of a gullible or vicious person seems to give voice to evil, but clearly the one who is creating such a voice — the author — is trying through the irony to put across a very moral view. (One kind of irony is to say the opposite of what you mean in order to say better what you do mean, as in the expression, "Fine friend you are!") To be irritated by irony goes with an intolerance of ambiguity and partly characterizes the highly restricted thinking that emerges as the hallmark of book banning. The college-bound youngsters to whom this book was addressed seem quite capable of seeing how to take this technique. In fact, I have often had teen-agers *write* stories of this sort, and one result was included in the book, a monologue spoken by a nosy neighbor intruding on a new apartment tenant, written by a ninth-grade girl.

It is difficult to know when the censors misunderstood selections because of insensitivity to literary expression and when because of oversensitivity about particular subjects. Poems on Christ they consistently regarded as sacrilegious and blasphemous, whereas none I have ever read, in or out of the condemned programs, would I regard as such. Theirs may be a case of militance impairing intelligence. Many modern poets ranging from A. E. Housman and Ezra Pound to recent and often little known poets have retold the story of Christ in vernacular language and contemporary dress. It is very clear to most readers that far from disparaging or ridiculing Christ, as charged, they want to put across the message of the Gospels in an entertaining way to people of today who may not read the Bible or may otherwise feel that Christianity doesn't have much to do with life as they know it.

In a high school book called *Narrative Poetry* we included two such poems. Charles Causley's "Ballad of the Bread Man" begins with a colloquial version of the Annunciation. Mary is standing in the kitchen baking a loaf of bread when an angel flies in and says, "We've a job for you." In this light style the poem goes on to tell the Nativity as it might happen today, but through the breezy manner we hear a reverential note that sounds the real meaning of the poem. Christ is imagined as a bread man who, with a paper crown on his head, goes around offering everybody bread from his father. But nobody is interested, nobody sees "the god in himself/Quietly standing there." The objectors called this "A mockery of Christ's birth and life."

In "The Ballad of the Carpenter" Ewan MacColl characterizes Christ as a friend of the working man.

> Now, Jesus walked among the poor, for
>   the poor were his own kind,
> And they wouldn't let the cops get near
>   enough to take him from behind,
> Yes, to take him from behind.
>
> So they hired a man of the traitor's trade,
>   and a stool pigeon was he.
> And he sold his brother to the butcher's
>   men for a fistful of silver money,
> A fistful of money. . . .

The ballad ends:

> Two thousand years have passed and gone,
>   and many a hero, too,
> And the dream of this poor carpenter, at
>   last it's coming true,
> Yes, at last it's coming true.[3]

This too was judged as "Mockery of Christ's life and death on the cross."

One modern classic of this genre was anthologized by several of the programs purchased in Kanawha County. It is a monologue by one of the three Magi telling of the journey to Bethlehem and of the effects of experiencing the Nativity. This is the concluding section.

All this was a long time ago, I remember*
And I would do it again, but set down
This set down
This: were we led all that way for
Birth or Death? There was a Birth, certainly,
We had evidence and no doubt. I had seen birth and death,
But had thought they were different; this Birth was
Hard and bitter agony for us, like Death, our death.
We returned to our places, these Kingdoms,
But no longer at ease here, in the old dispensation,
With an alien people clutching their gods.
I should be glad of another death.[4]

Objection: "Journey of the Maji" [*sic*] by T. S. Eliot. This poem is a take-off on the Bible. The birth they say was "Hard and bitter agony for us like

*Reprinted by permission of Faber and Faber Ltd from "Journey of the Magi" from *Collected Poems 1909–1962* by T. S. Eliot.

Death, our death." It is poking fun of [sic] the birth of Jesus. (This is teaching religion, indirectly.)

Deleting valued moments of great literature on such grounds constitutes a danger that can be frightening indeed if we consider that such objections have increased nationally at a rapid rate since 1974.

The chief objection repeats the chronic fear that the life of Christ is being used as a subversive vehicle to make negative statements about Christianity. This is not so of course. This Magus or Wise Man is saying that after the stunning advent of Christ's presence in the world, his life and that of others was changed so profoundly that the witnesses in one sense die. In fact, all the word play on birth and death expresses the "born again" idea so dear to fundamentalists. Physical birth and death are played off against spiritual birth and death, as the capital letters help to indicate. One who has witnessed Christ can no longer live the old life and would just as well let it die.

The reasons why the objectors missed the meaning touch deeply on the concerns raised by this whole Kanawha case. Thinking overconcretely typifies so-called fundamentalist thinking. Death and birth are construed only as physical and hence the poem as negative. They think the poem is saying that the birth of Christ made people want to die! The objectors did not recognize the born-again aspect—spiritual rebirth after the death of "the old dispensation"—because in their view the born-again Christian doesn't suffer afterwards: Christ redeems you by taking past sin and suffering on his own head, and you become light and free, as Graley described. It is all taken care of for you, whereas the view of Eliot, like that of many other Christians, is that "You must work out your salvation with diligence," as Eliot has the spiritual figure say to the couple in *The Cocktail Party*. The Wise Man understands from the appearance of Christ's new spirituality in the world that people have to take on a new responsibility and can no longer act like children who don't know any better and who do right only because some patriarch commands them. The objectors did not understand the poem because their view of Christ as Savior does not prepare them to expect the individual to take on a responsibility so awesome that it entails the death of the old self. "Jesus Saves" indeed.

I invite the reader to explain for herself or himself why the reviewer misinterpreted the following text, "The Cherry Tree Carol," which we included in a book of ballads. Here is the full text of the version we published in *Interaction*.

1. When Joseph was an old man,
   An old man was he,
   He married Virgin Mary,
   The Queen of Galilee.

2. Then Mary spoke a few words,
   So meek and so mild,
   "Joseph, gather me some cherries,
   For I am with child."

3. Then Joseph flew in anger,
   In anger flew he:
   "Let the father of the baby
   Gather cherries for thee."

4. Then Jesus spoke a few words,
   A few words spoke he:
   "Give my mother some cherries,
   Bow low down, cherry tree."

5. The cherry tree bowed low down,
   Bowed low down to the ground,
   And Mary gathered cherries
   While Joseph stood around.

6. Then Joseph feared and trembled,
   Bowed low down on his knees:
   "What have I done, Lord?
   Have mercy on me."

7. Then Joseph spoke a few words,
   A few words spoke he:
   "Oh, tell us, little baby.
   When thy birthday will be?"

8. "The sixth day of Januare
   My birthday will be,
   When the stars and the elements
   Will tremble with glee."[5]

"*Objection:* The lyrics of this song are subtly sacrilegious and can be construed to cast aspersion on the scriptural account of the virginity of Mary the Mother of Jesus."

Numerous songbooks for the home contain this carol, a standard that seems to enshrine a folk legend like many others inspired by the life of Christ but not told in the gospels. Since so much folk literature is born of the effort to understand spiritual things, I think that this carol uses Joseph to represent the common man's reaction to hearing that Mary is with child. In chastising Joseph's cynical assumption it teaches us all to stay alert for divinity, to recognize spirituality behind familiar appearances.

In a book of fables for secondary school we included "The True Christian" from one of the newspaper columns of satirist Arthur Hoppe, whom I have read for years in the *San Francisco Chronicle* and never known to turn his perceptive humor against basic human values or true

Christians. In his fable a faddist son hopping on one bandwagon after another — "Gestalt jogging, transcendental massage, elementary Zoroastrianism, advanced astrology" — prompts his father to ask what's wrong with Christianity. Turning his enthusiasm on this new religion from his parents, the son joins Juniors for Jesus and pushes his parents into giving so much to the poor that the family itself teeters on the brink of poverty. Only the son's sudden shift of interest to "Ecumenical Taoism" saves the situation. At the end the mother blames the father for "telling him he ought to be a Christian," and the father says defensively, "I meant a Christian like us." Clearly, *both* generations are satirized. Hoppe's moral is, "Don't worry about today's generation gap. It could be worse."[6] The objection: "Sarcastic and cynical of the Christian religion."

Many poets write antihunting poems, and many youngsters like such poems because they identify strongly with animals, even well into adolescence. Rural places like the bulk of Kanawha County, however, go big for hunting. Although this conflict of values underlies Humbert Wolfe's ironic poem "The Gray Squirrel" and probably underlies some of the antipathy it aroused, the explicit objection to it assumed again that the target was Christianity. Actually, like Hoppe, Wolfe holds up Christian ideals as the criteria against which the real target is judged. Here is the whole poem, from a secondary school collection called *Lyric Poetry*.

> Like a small gray
> coffeepot
> sits the squirrel.
> He is not
>
> all he should be,
> kills by dozens
> trees, and eats
> his red-brown cousins.
>
> The keeper, on the
> other hand,
> who shot him, is
> a Christian, and
>
> loves his enemies,
> which shows
> the squirrel was not
> one of those.[7]

Objection: This poem cynically derides Christianity, supposedly because the person who shot the squirrel was a Christian. Apparently, no matter or context is so remote or obtuse that it cannot be made a pretext for heaping abuse upon Christianity and Christian people. Granted, professing Christians have their fair share of human frailty. It is nonetheless remarkable to observe a textbook publisher of reading materials for public school students leaving no stone unturned in an absolutely frantic effort to heap scorn and abuse on Christians, the Bible, and Christianity at every conceivable opportunity. This mood and attitude permeates this entire series of textbooks, and for this reason (among other reasons) the books containing such material are by no means acceptable for use in any tax-supported school system.

Serious Christian moralists have always pointed, as Wolfe does here, to contradictions between belief and behavior. The reader may object that hunting does not violate Christian doctrine, but to interpret the poem as the objector does is to confuse, at the least, the fallible members of a church with the teachings of that religion. The irony of the last stanza is admittedly more complicated than the irony in "The True Christian" because "those" refers ambiguously to both "enemies" and "Christians." One might argue that if adults interpret the poem as anti-Christian, so will youngsters. I think youngsters are more inclined to defend animals and so less prone than adults to look for offense against religion.

The poem has been anthologized several times for school use, perhaps because of its discussion value. Students can talk about whether killing animals is wrong or un-Christian. Some young readers may well feel that the poem is unfair because squirrels, not being people, are neither friends nor enemies and don't come under the cover of Christian charity. Fine. Since the poem would have provoked such students to make their religion more their own, if they're Christians, or to refine their moral understanding about conflicts in values, challenging the poem would satisfy some educational reasons for including it.

But the objectors do not approve of supplying students with literature that might prompt them to think further about inherited ideas and values. This disapproval implies that thinking further will more likely weaken than reinforce what parents have transmitted to children. Why this lack of confidence that their values will stand the test of thought and experience? This matter is central to the whole controversy. To the extent that we textbook compilers included selections that either invited students to think about their home heritage or that supplemented that heritage with ideas not taught at home, we were "subversive." Fike is right that the conflict is about – in my words now – whether school is to offer only what the student already has from parents or something new from outside.

Let's take another subject but one also loaded – socioeconomic class. Miners, mountaineers, policemen, and hardhats usually share some similar working-class values with each other and with many of the Kanawha dissenters. I have strong sympathies with these people, as do many of the writers whose work we represented in the *Interaction* anthologies. One of the more painful ironies to issue from the whole drama of the controversy was the realization that the dissenters construed as adverse even selections championing the cause of working people. It's as if they don't know who their real friends and enemies are. A high school *Interaction* book called *Reportage* will serve as a case in point. It drew this verdict from the book protesters: "All of the stories in this book propagate radical ideology which advocates hatred for one's country, lawbreaking, racial strife, etc."

First, less than half of the 26 diverse selections could conceivably be construed as broaching some political or ideological issue on behalf of *any* side. The emotion aroused by a few articles causes the objectors to read ideas into other innocuous items or to ignore the rest of the book. But mainly — and this constitutes the core of the problem — articles taking the side of working people will usually seem disloyal to the American system, because taking the worker's side so often means exposing some injustice to which he or she is subjected. The censors may mutter curses themselves about low pay or bad working conditions set by the government or large companies, but when a spokesman articulates their viewpoint publicly, they either don't recognize their feelings or disapprove of such criticism.

In *Reportage* we included four selections that, naïvely perhaps, we would have expected these people to see as protective of their interests or sympathetic to their situations. "The Lot of a Policeman's Wife" simply relayed very directly the pain of constantly worrying for a husband's safety while at the same time enduring hostility and accusations from some of the citizenry. This received the objection that it "leads the reader to believe that a policeman's wife and policemen themselves are helpless ignorant persons who are pawns and 'lackeys' of a brutal white racist establishmentarian order," an idea neither stated nor implied in this article.

The dissenters ignored the other three selections. "Fate Deals a Last Blow to Mountaineer," tells how the United States Forestry Service buried with a bulldozer a man's home because in resurveying to make more room for commercial pine they had concluded he was living on National Forest land. "Death on a Bridge" is Gay Talese's very moving account of a hard-hat's death working on the Verrazano-Narrows Bridge. Most pertinently, "Mine Profits Leave Record of Death" asserts forcefully that company violations of mining safety regulations routinely cause the deaths of miners, and that state inspectors and union officials collude in such violations. This article was reprinted from *The Guardian*, just the sort of radical paper that miners would disapprove of despite its responsible presentation of their case. And there is the dilemma.

The people most victimized by corporations are the very ones who resent most any criticism of capitalism. They believe more in "free enter-prise" than the corporation executives, who long ago learned that they can make more money collaborating to restrain trade and fix prices or by get-ting the government to protect and subsidize them than by competing and leaving matters to the vagaries of supply and demand. Similarly, the peo-ple most at the mercy of governmental incompetence or corruption sav-agely attack anyone trying to expose these rotten spots. Fact-finding and rational analysis are regarded as disloyal tearing down of our country and "our way of life." Clear-thinking attacks on corruption get equated with overthrowing the system—a serious error. One mind-stumping effect of this favoring of slogan and shibboleths over enlightened self-interest is that working-class people abet their abusers (who scorn them for it) and persecute those who might help them. It is of course not liberals who come and "stripmine the land" and "take what they can," as the song says on Avis Hill's record, but capitalist corporations. When religious conservatives join commercial conservatives, only the latter gain. It is true that today blue-collar workers will march and demonstrate and strike in defiance of leaders and even break laws and commit violence to get their way. But they do not seem to regard this sort of actions as belonging to the same universe as talking and thinking and reading books.

As with the subject of Christianity, so with that of socioeconomic class. The objections are sometimes based on differences in how one relates a text to one's life, not actually on differences in values. The dissenters and the authors share some essential values more than it appears from the objections, where a red flag run up in the mind blocks that mind from detecting the author's overall drift and intent.

Suppose now we let subject matter fall out as it may, miscellaneously, and focus just on textual comprehension. I mentioned earlier a fictional diary by Ring Lardner, "I Can't Breathe." It purports to be the diary that a very giddy eighteen-year-old girl of the flapper era of the twenties is keep-ing while staying at a resort hotel with her aunt and uncle. She gets engaged several times a year and no sooner falls in love with one young man than a new suitor or an old beau claims her heart and, of course, her hand once again. In her diary she prates immaturely about the older generation, recounts her maneuvers with her boyfriends, and ends fantasizing a solution to her numerous engagements—a series of marriages timed so as to allow her to get what she wants from each man. After castigating the Ring Lardners senior and junior for being Communist, the objection to this story continued:

> This book reeks of generation gap encouragement, encourages deceit and out and out lies, refers to policemen in the same light as a convict, a drunkard or something queer. Teaches disrespect for policemen in two different places.

> Treats drinking to excess and smoking as the perfectly natural thing to do, and suggests that multiple marriages are the ideal situation. A marriage for every season. An absolutely ridiculous story.

Indeed it is an absolutely ridiculous story, and it is supposed to be. The girl is being ridiculed through her own words. As an example of some things the objection refers to, here is part of an entry after a dance at which her aunt and uncle expressed approval of her latest beau.

> I guess it is a big surprise to a girl's parents and aunts and uncles to find out that the boys you go around with are all right, they always seem to think that if I seem to like somebody and the person pays a little attention to me, why he must be a convict or a policeman or a drunkard or something queer.[8]

Such a story gives adolescent readers an entertaining opportunity to get some critical distance on feelings and attitudes they may actually share in a less extreme way with this diarist. Any experienced teacher, or any parents not afraid of losing their children, would never question that students will see the girl as making herself look ridiculous by showing how scatterbrained she is.

The question, and the reason I cite this objection, concerns why the dissenters took the story so amiss. What, again, are the roots of such incomprehension? Did knowing Ring Lardner was the author give the objector a mental set that turned an obviously lighthearted satire of the flapper mentality into a grim subversion of traditional values? The fact is that the satire, if we take it as serious commentary, really would be on the side of the objector, who surely views the silliness the same way Lardner does. Does the objector feel compelled to pretend to misread the story in order not to wind up a bedfellow with a "known Communist?"

Sondra Spratt's "Hoods I Have Known" is a charming, humorous story told in a mellow mood of reminiscence by a first-person narrator. It had appeared originally in *Mademoiselle*, and we reprinted it in a short story collection called *Fictional Memoir*, emphasizing by this title the resemblance these stories had to actual memoirs. The narrator was a proper, head-of-the-class girl in her urban seventh-grade class who, when punished one day for a little infraction, was moved to the rear of the room, where she got acquainted with some "hoods," older holdovers from poor street gangs. She and the leader attract each other, aware they are opposites, but after a brief puppy love that barely trails once out of the classroom, and during which she enjoys trying to reform him, she is reinstated at the front of the class and the two again go back to their separate worlds.

Objection: This is a rather sad depressing story which is illustrated by a cigarette-smoking picture of a young tough. The story ends with the author's saying he had rather someone be a hoodlum than to be a success in life.

It is hard to imagine how anyone could read a story several thousand words long told by a reiterated "I" who is a girl having a crush on her first boyfriend and still come out thinking the "author" is male. The real author's name, moreover, is obviously feminine, and the title of the book focuses on the nature of the stories as facsimiles of personal recollections. I've had occasion to observe of other extreme lapses in reading comprehension that sometimes a preconception will be so strong that it will override almost any amount of contrary information given in the text. In this case, I believe the preconception may be a sex-role stereotype to the effect that only men write books; an author is a male.

As for the photo, any adolescent will recognize the unsure kid trying to look cool by smoking. It would be totally unreal to think that either the "hood" in the photo or the one in the story would be seized on as a model. Because the objectors branded so many other selections also as "sad and depressing" and as ending with a negative moral, I quote the last paragraph of this story.

> Someone I know says she thinks she saw someone who looked like Danny in a summer theatre production in Woodstock last year. She said that he was still big and had a lot of hair but that he spoke English perfectly. She said he was sweet and looked like Marlon Brando. Despite what my friend says, I don't like to think Danny became an actor. I don't like to think that at all. It makes me sad and a little embarrassed, for that would mean after all my seventh-grade heartbreak and eleven-year-old plans somebody else had reformed Danny after all. I'd rather have him be a fisherman. I'd rather have him be a hood.[9]

Now please look back at how the objection describes the ending of the story. Had a secondary student responded on a test of the story with the interpretation voiced in the objection, we can be sure the teacher would have indicated poor comprehension.

Oscar Lewis is an anthropologist who spent years studying and living with families in the "culture of poverty," as he calls it. He transcribed the oral autobiographies of his subjects, whom he also observed, and put these accounts together as composite pictures of how poor people in places like Mexico and Puerto Rico live and feel. Selections from his work appeared in both *Man* and *Interaction* as nonfiction. Lewis' chronicle from Mexico City, *The Children of Sanchez* (made into a movie starring Anthony Quinn as father Sanchez), was represented by an excerpt from *Man in the Expository Mode, 2.* The first sentence of the objection below summarizes accurately a part of the behavior pattern of Sanchez.

> The father Sanchez is strict, beats his boys, etc. But when they turn out wrong, he rationalizes.
>
> *Objections:*
> 1. The story is deliberately concocted to belittle parents and their knowledge about how to raise children.
> 2. This story belittles discipline.
> 3. Does this story place the entire blame of failure on the part of the parent? Doesn't the school have some responsibility?
> 4. If the editors or author understood children and the "process of education" they wouldn't need to blame the parents. They would know what to do!

The phrase "deliberately concocted" cannot be applied reasonably at all to a true chronicle based mostly on the participants' own accounts and, in any case, clearly labeled "expository," not at least unless one is prepared to charge fraud. The whole commentary suggests that the objector lapsed into thinking that the account is a short story and the author has availed himself of fictional license to rig events to score a criticism.

It is interesting that this reader made so gross an error as this and yet generalized so well about Sanchez' disciplining of his boys. In the classic manner, the objector read into the text something he or she was looking for. Oscar Lewis certainly did not editorialize, "belittle" or "blame." And consider that arch last line, "They would know what to do!"

Although this objection presumably comes under the heading of "challenging authority," it seems to be essentially about parental defensiveness. The selection itself neither challenges authority nor attacks parents. It is aimed another way completely, toward anthropological description of group behavior in a certain milieu. I could assume that this misreading of intention owes to some inexperience and naïveté about modes of discourse such that the objector cannot discriminate fiction from true case history — or made-up narrator from the real author — but maybe the real problem is that the objector's defensive projection would cause misreading even if he or she had benefited from more learning experience in differentiating viewpoints in texts. In other words, suppose it is the powerful prior mind-sets that distort interpretation of a text, and maybe, without this distorting force, differentiation of modes of discourse would not *have* to be learned.

At any rate, so long as one generation forbids the next to read the sorts of selections we have been examining it prolongs its own handicap. Ironically, both *Man* and *Interaction* tried to help students gain sophistication about what authors are doing in various writings by distinctly separating and labeling modes of discourse and voices of characters and authors. If parents succeed in outlawing such texts, then they make it nearly impossible for their children either to take what someone else says the way it was meant.

14

Petrified

We move now to a kind of objection for which book censors are not generally known but which seems to me so emblematic of their concerns that I will begin to close this survey with it.

Probably few short stories have been anthologized as frequently, in *and* out of school, as Shirley Jackson's "The Lottery," which we included in a book called *Fictional Chronicle* that featured group experience. "*Objection:* An absurd story about a town which offers a human sacrifice by way of a lottery."

The story ends with the kind of shocking surprise that O. Henry or de Maupassant often deliver, but it is so widely admired, I believe, because the details leading up to the human sacrifice read like the preparations for some folksy Vermont fair and because when friends and family turn on the lottery-chosen woman the stoning comes with the force of some primitive psychological truth made all the more chilling by our having let the sociality lull us, once again, off-guard.

I don't know why the objector deemed this story "ridiculous." Since an unfamiliar act happened in a familiar setting — small-town America — one could consider it unrealistic. Perhaps the objector would say that friendly, normal folks like those in the story would not sacrifice a neighbor or any member of their own community. Police tell us that, statistically, we are far more likely to be murdered by someone near and dear to us than by a stranger.

Judging from the pattern of other reactions to selections, I would speculate that book censors of the type we are considering find this story appalling because it points to the possible price of groupiness — the sacrifice of the individual — and suggests that close community — the very lifeblood of our objectors — thrives on traditions that retain rude exactions as well as support and security. Our rationally appearing institutions reveal sometimes their substrate of ignorance and passion. Even if readers do not agree with this theme as a proposition, most are willing to entertain the idea momentarily in exchange for having been so well entertained by the story embodying it.

But even selections clearly not meant to be set against criteria of familiar realism received the objection "ridiculous." For secondary school we put together *Humorous Stories*, a zany collection that clearly signaled its outlandish intentions through title, art, and selection, ranging from older authors like Saki, O. Henry, and Mark Twain to H. Allen Smith, E. B. White, James Thurber, Art Buchwald, Mel Brooks, Woody Allen, Kurt Vonnegut, and Joseph Heller, among others. A couple of the simpler stories first encountered in the book were two parodies of "Little Red Riding Hood." Wayne Figueroa's ghetto version, called "Little Black Riding Hood," begins like this.

> As we open our story, we notice a small dark figure tripping down to High Street to the subway. Her name is Little Black Riding Hood and she is going to visit her father who works at the Cheetah Night Club on Broad and 57th Street. He is the clean-up man there.
> She's taking him his feed bag. In it she has pigs' feet, grits, collard greens, and some black-eyed peas. She's a boss little broad, with her mini skirt, a boss Afro, and a cool dasheekie.
> As Little Black Riding Hood came off the A train, she spotted someone she wished she hadn't. It was the Big Bad Banker to whom she owed money.[1]

"*Objection:* Ridiculous."

"Ladle Rat Rotten Hut," by Howard Chace, tells its version entirely, like the title, by using real words that are not the actual words but sound like them. It is of course pure wordplay. On entering her grandmother's:

> Ladle Rat Rotten Hut entity bet rum, an stud buyer groin-murder's bet.
> "O Grammar!" crater ladle gull historically, "Water bag icer gut! A nervous sausage bag ice!"[2]

"*Objection:* A so-called 'story' which is a collection of words that make absolutely no sense."

This unique story requires an interesting mental operation by the reader that can be frustrating and annoying. One has to suspend the ordinary meanings of the printed words and truly "go with the flow" of the words as sounded. Aided by one's memory of the original story, and settling for approximations of sound, one must allow the spoken words to evoke the meaningful words they somewhat resemble. It is not necessarily easy to put out of mind the normal meanings of the printed words and to recognize familiar oral words when their pronunciation is consistently off.

It is a new and disorienting experience, and if one becomes anxious or irritated about not being able to figure out some passages, the experience can, like learning a new language, be so unsettling as to leave a bad feeling. Perhaps the objector had trouble, since he or she said the story was "a collection of words that make absolutely no sense." Children love the story and may have less difficulty than some adults figuring it out, because they can more readily yield up old ways and adopt new. Reactions to this game are significant to the extent that the game entails flexibility, creativity, and an ability to hold the ordinary in abeyance until one can arrive at it by an unaccustomed route.

A bit of autobiography whipped into whimsy might describe E. B. White's "The Doily Menace," in which he recounts his mock vicissitudes with doilies. As a child he did not know what the word meant and, as he was accustomed with words he did not know, especially if they had a sound like this one, he assumed it had something to do with sex. Later, after he knew what the word meant, he failed to see doilies when they appeared in paper form at the dining table and twice in public ended by devouring doily along with dessert. *"Objection:* A ridiculous story."

It is of course one thing to call a story one found unfunny a ridiculous or absurd story; it is quite another to throw a book out of school with such words. Partly, White is poking fun at himself, because he perhaps should have known what "doily" meant, since the word was used around his house, but, as he says, he did not connect word to object, a failing similar to his not noticing doilies placed under his nose on dishes from which he was eating. Perhaps this self-ridiculing is so foreign to our objectors that they cannot see a point to the story. Actually the self-ridicule serves as a vehicle to fool around with experience and with words while making a point about repression. It is play, and that may be, most of all, why such a story seems "ridiculous."

From Carl Sandburg's classic children's book, *Rootabaga Stories*, we excerpted for *Folk Tales*, an upper elementary book, the account of the train ride by Gimme the Axe and his family through marvelous places to the Rootabaga country. One scene from this journey will convey some of the flavor of these popular tales.

> Next they came to the country of the balloon pickers. Hanging down from the sky strung on strings so fine the eye could not see them at first, was the balloon crop of that summer. The sky was thick with balloons. Red, blue, yellow balloons, white, purple and orange balloons — peach, watermelon and potato balloons — rye loaf and wheat loaf balloons — link sausage and pork chop balloons — they floated and filled the sky.
>
> The balloon pickers were walking on high stilts picking balloons. Each picker had his own stilts, long or short. For picking balloons near the ground he had short stilts. If he wanted to pick far and high he walked on a far and high pair of stilts.
>
> Baby pickers on baby stilts were picking baby balloons. When they fell off the stilts the handful of balloons they were holding kept them in the air till they got their feet into the stilts again.[3]

The objection to this reads: "This story is pure nonsense. If this is for remedial or slow reading students, it is doubtful that they could manage to make any sense of it."

So far as content is concerned, even preschool children are delighted by this story, as many a bedtime-reading parent knows. I read this often myself to my two daughters when they were quite small. The nonsense is of course part of what they like. To object to nonsense in children's stories betrays a grave incomprehension of children's minds and of the literature written for those minds (and for those parents able to share the transformations of the world that go on in the child's world).

What is strange is to think that children do not understand fancy and whimsy and nonsense. They live in a world not yet fastened down to predictable laws, like that of fairy tales and folk tales, where many more things are possible than for most adults. In fact, they resist a great deal the restriction of reality to only what one observes in the everyday world. They may already accept the adult view that these fantastic things can't happen, but they want to play with the possibilities anyway. I feel just this element of creativity and play bothers the objectors, as if they take too seriously the rearranging of reality just for sport and somehow believe that playing in the imagination will upset knowledge and leave reality up for grabs.

My final example may help illuminate this inappropriate objection of "absurdity" applied to literature that is supposed to be absurd. A book called *Short Plays,* again aimed at upper elementary children, contained a short radio play by Rod Conybeare, "A Spider Spectacular," that had been played on the "Rod and Charles Show" on the Canadian Broadcasting Company. In this droll little fantasy we hear, after a narrator's introduction that takes us close up into a spider web, a husband-wife dialogue designed to echo human domestic exchanges all while smacking of the spiders' world. The female threatens to eat the good-for-nothing male and then proceeds to catch a fly who confesses to being sluggish from eating too much chocolate cake the night before. Then she approaches another insect caught in the web with whom she chats before discovering, too late, that her interlocutor is a wasp tricking her.

INSECT: Say, you must be an *Aranea diadema* to have such glue inside you.
FEMALE: Yes, I am.
INSECT: Well, don't prolong it, honey. Give me the old stinger and let me rest in peace.
FEMALE: You're a female.
INSECT: Well, sure.
FEMALE: Females are usually the most clever insects.
INSECT: I'll go along with that.
FEMALE: What do you call yourself?

INSECT: Oh, nothing in particular. Say, you know you're going to have to
get closer if you want to paralyze me, aren't you?
FEMALE: You don't seem worried.
INSECT: Oh, maybe I'm tired of life, uh, huh.
FEMALE: Well, well if that's what you want.[4]

The objection to this variation of anthropomorphizing animals for
humor throws back to previously mentioned attitudes about people and
animals: "The subject matter of this play is almost nauseating. Most
humans have an inborn revulsion to insects and this play indicates why."
In addition to instances already pointed out of similar revulsion, an
Ivory Coast myth included in *Myths*, for elementary school, "The Giant
Caterpillar," was called a "Disgusting story about a giant caterpillar."

> Long, long ago there was a caterpillar as fat as an elephant. His mouth was
> as red as his tail. His body was covered with hair, and on his head was a
> long pointed horn.[5]

After the caterpillar swallows a child, the villagers seek it out and kill it,
recovering the unhurt child, but as they cut it up into bits, hordes of tiny
caterpillars swarm out. "And that is why, even today, we find caterpillars everywhere on the earth." This myth typifies the how-the-leopard-
got-his-spots explanatory function of mythologizing.

Children like monsters that they know do not exist. Why do they
bother some adults? Revulsion to animals may represent an effort to
break attachment to one's own animality, symbolized by fat caterpillars,
voracious and venomous spiders, or human heads with animal bodies.
But I feel that the answer has something to do also with literalness and an
anxiety about departing from daily realism and the known, safe world.
Such concern must reject play, imagination, and invention as "unrealistic" and "absurd," because these may open the mind to new possibilities
that will make it reel and lose control. Without confidence to cope with
the unknown, we feel we must restrict reality to the familiar. And, too, if
things are not what they seem, well, that's so terrifying a thought that it
seems to pretty well justify the desire to know no more.

To ban fantasy, zaniness, and absurdity is to cancel the uniquely
human powers of transforming world in mind, of envisioning from what
one has seen what one has not seen, and is hence to reduce people to animals, whose solemn adherence to things as they are prevents them from
understanding how things might be . . . and may be already. This stand
represents another form of not wanting to know, of evasion. Without the
ability to transcend appearances, how would humans manage even to
conceive of God, of the soul, and of invisible planes of reality? To banish
imagination would be to diminish our spiritual potentiality and relegate
us indeed to bestial limitation.

Imagination, then, is not only a way to play but a major mode of knowing. It is, like reason, a faculty for extending understanding beyond mere physical appearances. Practical perception requires, in fact, that people relate for themselves the known elements of reality so as to arrive at the unknown. Failing to do so may well bring on catastrophe, as dramatized in a definitive way in "The Stone Boy," a short story by Gina Berriault and a selection in the *Language of Man* series from a book called *In the Fictional Mode*. First the objection.

> This is a story of Arnold, a young boy who accidentally kills his brother while knowingly hunting out of season. He was on his way to pick peas with his brother (early in the day). After the shooting, Arnold continued to pick peas because the early part of the day was the best time to pick them!
>
> When he goes home, his father takes him to town to see the Sheriff, who questioned him as to why he hadn't gone for help. His answer was, "I come to pick peas." "It's better to pick peas while they are cool." (He felt nothing, not any grief.)
>
> The rest of the story relates his feelings about his mother, etc. (He had gone to his mother's room expecting to tell her, "He had come to clasp her in his arms and to pommel her breasts with his head.")
>
> *Objections:*
>   1. The story is abnormal. It should not be used in the classroom.
>   2. The classroom is not a "sensitivity training" laboratory.
>   3. Teachers are not trained to deal with abnormal situations. Who is dictating that this type material be used in the classroom and why?
>   (The implication in all such type material in the *Man* series indicates, to me, that those who dictate are saying that America, its people, are lost. And they are to instill a sense of equilibrium in them; perhaps, even to control them.)
>   4. Why don't the educators eliminate the problems? Why don't they do some positive research to help the student. They are failures — as well as the parents.

Perhaps the astonishing defense of parents launched in the objections goes a long way toward explaining the equally astonishing misunderstanding of the story revealed in the plot summary.

Presumably, the story is abnormal because it treats a boy who "felt nothing, not any grief" after shooting his brother, as the objector interprets. This reaction of the objector is precisely that of the characters in the story. They can understand that the young boy might have shot his older brother accidentally — the two were both stooping to pass through a wire fence — but they can't understand why he went on and picked peas an hour before telling his parents and why he shows no emotion. The sheriff says sardonically that this kid is too "reasonable" to be upset over it and, when the father asks, "You don't want him?" replies "Not now. Maybe in a few years." The stoniness of the boy becomes of course the main point of the story. The reader has to try to understand what the characters cannot. We are given, after all, more information.

This is the opening.

> Arnold drew his overalls and raveling gray sweater over his naked body. In the other narrow bed his brother Eugene went on sleeping, undisturbed by the alarm clock's rusty ring. Arnold, watching his brother sleeping, felt a peculiar dismay; he was nine, six years younger than Eugie, and in their waking hours it was he who was subordinate. To dispel emphatically his uneasy advantage over his sleeping brother, he threw himself on the hump of Eugie's body.
> "Get up! Get up!" he cried.[6]

Arnold feels very ambivalent about his brother, as many siblings do about each other. He naturally loves Eugie, and admires him, but is envious too and squirms at Eugie's derision of him. Just before the gun caught on the fence and Arnold jerked it to free it, Eugie had made a scornful remark about Arnold's puny legs. We have no right to think that, even at a very unconscious level, Arnold meant to kill him, but the fact that the shooting could express the resentful and envious part of Arnold's feeling seems to join the usual shock to make him try to deny the death happened by going ahead with what they had planned to do — pick peas. The adults don't have access to indications of these and other feelings, and in their laconic country way they simply size up the situation as a case of a "stone boy," unfeeling, and turn from this abnormality the way animals do, by instinct.

The author explicitly alerts us that their assumption is not the truth. When the sheriff asked Arnold if he and his brother were good friends, Arnold didn't know how to reply.

> What did he mean — good friends? Eugie was his brother. That was different from a friend, Arnold thought. A best friend was your own age, but Eugie was almost a man. Eugie had had a way of looking at him, slyly and mockingly and yet confidentially, that had summed up how they both felt about being brothers. Arnold had wanted to be with Eugie more than with anybody else but he couldn't say they had been good friends.[7]

The objection says that the "rest of the story relates his feelings about his mother, etc." By blanketing father, sister, neighbors, farm, and farm animals under that "etc." and by quoting the phrase "pommel her breasts with his head" the objector creates a sexual innuendo that is totally uncalled for. Since the first numbered objection immediately afterward reads "The story is abnormal," one might well get the completely false impression that the story deals with incestuous feelings. Let's look at the whole paragraph ending with the quoted sentence. Arnold approaches his parents' door that evening.

> "Mother?" he asked insistently. He had expected her to realize that he wanted to go down on his knees by her bed and tell her that Eugie was dead. She did not know it yet, nobody knew it, and yet she was sitting up in bed, waiting to be told, waiting for him to confirm her dread. He had expected her to tell him to come in, to allow him to dig his head into her blankets and tell her about the terror he had felt when he had knelt beside Eugie. He had come to clasp her in his arms and, in his terror, to pommel her breasts with his head. He put his hand upon the knob.
> "Go back to bed, Arnold," she called sharply.[8]

By directly stating the boy's feelings, the author has tried to make very apparent to the reader what the other characters cannot see — that this nine-year-old, far from being a stone boy, felt such terror on killing his brother that he could not let himself believe the truth. He is not unfeeling, he is *petrified*. Not only is the context of that sentence far different from what the objection might lead one to conclude, but the objector omitted from the quoted sentence, without even indicating a deletion, the critical phrase "in his terror," which repeats the key word "terror" that explains the boy's behavior and, incidentally, would make it pretty hard for even the most prurient reader to sexualize the passage. What this reviewer did was pluck out a physical detail from this key moment and suppress — or repress — the main point of the passage, the revelation of the boy's true state, the inner life. Please reread now the sentence as misquoted in the objection extracted at the beginning of the discussion of this story and compare it with the original sentence, especially as part of the whole scene.

It is a story of double jeopardy. The mother does not let Arnold come to her. By the time, the next morning, that she and the father make overtures to him, he really has *become* a stone boy, for a secondary reason. "He called upon his pride to protect him from them." The story ends this way.

> "Was you knocking at my door last night?"
> He looked over his shoulder at her, his eyes narrow and dry.
> "What'd you want?" she asked humbly.
> "I didn't want nothing," he said flatly.
> Then he went out the door and down the back steps, his legs trembling from the fright his answer gave him.[9]

Instead of losing one son, the family has lost two. Because the people around him could not understand his behavior, they turned away from him and *made* him a stone boy. The original problems come from the boy's stunned reaction of denial, but the tragedy is compounded by the adults' insensitive reaction. Not just from the adults; even Arnold's sister refuses to pass the milk to him at breakfast. So we have a story about misinterpretation being misinterpreted. The reviewer blocked out the boy's terror from the text as the characters did from *their* field of perception.

It is a compassionate story. No one is blamed. These are good simple people doing their best. The fact is that they are all inclined to be terse and undemonstrative, that is, to treat feeling as stoically as possible. It's part of the hard and primitive country life. "He felt nothing, not any grief" is actually a line from the story but was included in the objection without quotation marks, juxtaposed with another quotation, about the peas, that occurred somewhere else. To straighten this out and at the same time indicate the author's perspective on this fighting back of feeling, here is Arnold going to bed for the first time alone: "He felt nothing, not any grief. There was only the same immense silence and crawling inside of him; it was the way the houses and fields felt under a merciless sun." We can understand why the characters do not know what is happening in the boy. But what excuse does the reader have after getting all this privileged information about the inner life, which includes more than I have quoted?

Let's suppose that everyone resists *some* knowledge. Some things we don't *want* to know. Arnold did not want to know that he had killed the person he most wanted to be with. Such negative capability would seem to cut life off at its very roots. His family and neighbors do not want to know the underside of their apparently sturdy simplicity. They are willing to believe that Arnold lacks feeling but not that he has *mixed* feelings and extreme feelings, which are what create the problem of his strange behavior. They don't want to think that they're implicated in the death by letting a nine-year-old make so free with a gun that he carries it casually pea-picking and scoffs at hunting seasons; survival on a family farm depends on children shouldering responsibility as early as possible. They don't want to complicate their inner life by tracing and connecting everything to get a full explanation.

They feel they must resist descending into the self to understand others through understanding oneself, because they need to keep attention focused on things outside — minute details and shifts of weather, animals, plants, and the outward behavior of each other. They already have enough to cope with without having also to deal with feelings that they are afraid of. Ah, but there's the rub: if they do not go inward enough, they do not know what to make of what they see in each other. Even the mother turns away Arnold at the critical moment of emotional aftermath. The survival strategy of sticking to the physical, of curtailing knowledge, turns out to defeat itself. By not knowing what they needed to know, the family and community lost another member; maybe the sheriff *will* be wanting him later. Maybe even the first son was lost through this same suppression of knowledge: if you can acknowledge that the baby brother resents and envies his big brother at the same time that he admires and adores him — if you can harmonize apparently contradictory information — then just maybe you can head off "accidents." But in some measure we all resist this degree of consciousness.

I dwell on this story because it is a parable of not wanting to know, and not wanting to know lies very much at the heart of this study, which concerns in one arena the banning of books and in a broader theater the restriction of mind that creates conflict among humans and disconnects them from the rest of creation. Literature, on the other hand, expands consciousness and creates connections.

A popular song says, "There ain't no instant replay in the football game of life." Caught up as participants, we seldom understand well enough in the moment, which is when we need insight. Even from a simple, unedited, uninterpreted rerun we may understand more than the first time around. Literature serves much better than a rerun, because it illuminates the kinds of actions and situations we might encounter in real life. We know more about what is going on in and around the people than we do when we live such events. It is a function of literature to prepare us thus for new events as well as to purge us of bad feeling left from previous events. Almost all literature treats problems, even the stories with happy endings, precisely because storying serves to induce understanding, to raise consciousness.

But there is a serious catch: if you are resisting knowledge so severely that you miss the illumination, misread, and want to throw out stories because they are "depressing," "negative," and "morbid," then the remedy so badly needed cannot help. If receptive to the illumination, a reader can separate himself or herself from the characters while identifying with them and feel uplifted by even a story filled with the most awful characters and happenings, because illumination connects with celebration.

Becoming more conscious is a very positive experience, a "high." Besides knowing more than before, one feels better because literature is *triumphant*. It makes no difference if, in the story, everyone gets killed off or no hope exists for the *characters;* for the reader life not only goes on but goes on better because it is more illuminated. There but for the grace of God go I, but I *don't* go that way, and I feel very good about it. The author triumphs by achieving this illumination that we miss ordinarily and by converting bad news to good news. This, he or she says, is what happened or might happen but doesn't have to happen, or if it has to happen, we can make this use of it, see this truth or beauty in it.

Literature is artful, a kind of game, a construction to sport in. Somebody made something! No matter what it's about, a creation is good news, something new to play with. Artfulness delights. A well told, well worded story celebrates by its very creativity the power of consciousness, the source of triumph in life. I have never been depressed by a well wrought piece of literature. This is far from an art-for-art's sake attitude. A skillful, perceptive story like "The Stone Boy" arouses me to more compassion for people, makes me both see and feel more. For me this stirring of spirit, coming along with the enlarged understanding and the pleasure in the creative verbal contraption make a good story positive no matter what horrors it relates. What depresses me are stories that don't illuminate or celebrate — stories that flinch from either the depths or the heights and stonewall a self-belying cheeriness or feign a fashionable malady. Being undepressable by good literature makes it especially a challenge for me to try to understand the sort of objections about negativism that the books drew on themselves.

But I know that all of us ward off things we don't want to know, like the people surrounding the stone boy, things we feel will undo us if we *acknowledge* them. Some of these things are peculiar to us as individuals, some are ignored in common. ("Ignorance" contains the idea of "not paying attention to.") So whole groups may screen out certain kinds of knowledge. This avoidance of knowing I will henceforth call *agnosis*, a term I have coined to imply a self-limitation of the natural human faculties of understanding. Now, it is true that survival itself requires selective attention and hence the temporary ignoring of some things as we give priority to others. But if this process is inflexible and involuntary — beyond control — it can hurt us as readily as save us. Witness the stony people of Berriault's story. A petrified person will have a monolithic mind. That is why it is important to try to get to the bottom of the case before us.

PART 4
DIAGNOSING AGNOSIS

15

Ideology and Bed-Wetting

A case is an instance of something. What the textbook rebellion exemplified is the not-wanting-to-know that I have called agnosis. Far from being peculiar to fundamentalists or mountaineers or the uneducated, agnosis limits the thought and action of virtually everyone everywhere. But to illuminate this universal condition we have to "get down to cases." To take the case for the problem would be a grave mistake. What leaders of the book rebellion said and what the book objectors wrote have furnished ideas that allow us to explore specifically a state of mind common in some degree to the rest of the world. Extremity heightens and clarifies what may be too easily passed over ordinarily, and the blunt enactment of attitudes in Kanawha County makes it easier to follow out their consequences and trace back their origins.

Since fear increases agnosis in any type of person, the more that conflict, want, crime, environmental poisoning, and other negative forces gain strength the more the mind tends to retrench. Conservatism is rising all over the world, but conservatism is not a mere political ideology. Among other things, it is a direction in which very different types of people move when they become anxious. The defense perimeters of the mind are the parameters it places on knowledge and understanding. Book censorship is only an outer symbol for this inner state of siege.

Leaders of the textbook controversy boasted that their example set rolling a conservative buildup that swept the country by the eighties. However large their role, it is true that during the latter seventies America went their way. This was reflected only partly in censorship itself. The momentum gathering there set off alarms throughout the publishing and educational worlds that sound more insistently even at this writing (1988). In 1979 Edward B. Jenkinson wrote:

Since the battle of the books in Kanawha County in 1974, incidents of censorship or attempts at censorship have increased markedly. During the 1977–78 school year, more incidents of removing or censoring books occurred nationally than at any other time in the last twenty-five years.[1]

In 1981 Stephen Arons:

> Incoming battle reports include a nationwide survey made public April 30 by its sponsors, the Association of American Publishers, the American Library Association, and the Association for Supervision and Curriculum Development. The survey indicates that the nation is in the midst of a surge of book censorship which seems designed to cut off independent thought at its educational roots. . . . Responses . . . point to the involvement of more than 20 percent of the nation's school districts and 30 percent of its school libraries in challenges to literary works and textbooks. . . . The AAP report understates the magnitude of the movement. . . . Judith Krug, director of the ALA's Intellectual Freedom Committee, is alarmed that the number of reported incidents of attempted book censorship in school and public libraries ballooned immediately after the November 4 election of Ronald Reagan, and has continued at a record rate along with the rising fortunes of the new right.[2]

In 1985 *USA Today* reported:

> Efforts to censor books, films and curriculum in public schools rose dramatically this year with incidents reported in 46 states. . . . The liberal People for the American Way found a 37 percent increase in censorship over the 1983–84 school year. "People who used to be content trying to remove *Catcher in the Rye* or *Huckleberry Finn* have set their sights on the entire curriculum," said Barbara Parker, spokeswoman. . . .[3]

At the end of 1986 the lead article on the front page of a Sunday *Houston Chronicle* was "More Books Rejected as Censorship Effort Grows":

> "In the last year, censorship reports to us have soared by 35 percent across the country. More and more school districts are reporting attempts, and half are successful," said John Kean, anti-censorship chairman of the National Council of Teachers of English.[4]

The conservative buildup became apparent in many other single-issue contests besides censorship. Factions coalesced to lobby and get votes for school prayer and private schools and against abortion, women's rights, pornography, and gay rights. Jimmy Carter's sponsorship of the Equal Rights Amendment and his efforts to tax unintegrated private schools spurred tremendous organizing and lobbying by opponents among both Democrats and Republicans. Powerful coalitions emerged in time to help elect Ronald Reagan in 1980, someone formerly regarded as too extremist to ever bid successfully for the presidency. Armed with hit lists of undesirable candidates, these coalitions raised funds and waged voting campaigns in local and state elections as well as national.

Two such coalitions were the Moral Majority, headed by TV evangelist Jerry Falwell, and the Pro-Family Movement, headed by Washington political strategist Paul Weyrich. These joined forces with each other and some smaller organizations under the general rubric of the New Right, which had several leaders, one of whom was its fund-raiser Richard Viguerie, also publisher of the influential *Conservative Digest*. Another was popular TV evangelist Pat Robertson, who worked for collaboration between Protestant fundamentalists and conservative Catholics. Estimating combined forces at around 80 million in 1980, Robertson said, "We have enough votes to run the country. And when the people say, 'We've had enough,' we are going to take over."[5] The election of Reagan somewhat fulfilled this prophecy. In a memorandum of August 18, 1986, the Reagan administration's Private Sector Task Force recommended, as part of its antidrug campaign, that federal officials should start an "education-information program through the churches, with particular emphasis on the Christian Broadcast Network [Pat Robertson's network] and its constituency,"[6] a proposal that the American Jewish Congress criticized as unconstitutionally singling out one religion or church. In building CBN into a $182,000,000-a-year conglomerate, Robertson had set the prototype for evangelical TV ministries and for their political liaisons.

By the time Robertson became a candidate for the presidency in 1987 many preachers and politicians of the New Right were undergoing public scrutiny or trying to survive outright scandals, like the Reagan administration itself. Another pioneer evangelist, Oral Roberts, had recently drawn much satiric criticism for having vowed to God that he would die if he did not receive enough contributions to save his organization. Jim and Tammy Faye Bakker, leaders of another evangelical organization called Praise the Lord, were ousted upon revelation of sexual and financial misconduct. When Jerry Falwell took over PTL, the Bakkers and their followers engaged him in acrimonious inter-pastoral recriminations. Meantime, after setting up several victories for the extreme right in the 1986 congressional elections, New Right leader Lyndon La Rouche was charged by the federal government with obstructing investigation into possible misuse of tax-exempt funds for political purposes — an allegation also leveled at Pat Robertson himself, who was trying to protect his presidential campaign by carefully distancing himself from his beleaguered fellows in the television ministry.

This unraveling of much of the New Right paralleled of course the unveiling of the Iran-Contra affair. A typical figure linking Reagan administration activities and private efforts was Carl "Spitz" Channell, a conservative activist convicted of defrauding the government while trying to raise funds for the Nicaraguan Contras in tandem with the covert intrigues of Lt. Col. Oliver North. Two former advisers of President Reagan, Michael Deaver and Lyn Nofziger, were investigated for peddling influence, and the attorney general himself, Edwin Meese, was fighting charges of both financial misconduct and impeding justice in the Iran-Contra investigations. The long shadow that these hearings cast over the end of Reagan's presidency cast doubt also on whatever underlay his great popularity and that of the movement that helped carry him into office.

On grounds of pure economic self-interest, working-class Americans would generally do better to vote for liberal candidates, who favor unionism and champion the wage earner rather than the shareholder. Since workers number a majority, conservative candidates would have a very hard time ever winning if they could not hold out other incentives. So it is usually only through social and moral issues that conservatives can carry an election (though a bad showing by either party always helps the other.) It is this central but little discussed fact that makes the rise of the New Right so important. The Reagan victories represented a triumph of alignment between a standard Republican platform and these social/ moral issues, the equivalent of the teaming up of Elmer Fike with the fundamentalist ministers.

The social/religious constituency of Reagan became very disgruntled during his first administration because he dragged his heels on their issues and rode herd instead on economic problems and overseas policies. He tried very hard, however, to exempt unintegrated private schools from taxes, well aware that Carter lost to him partly over this issue. Significantly, as the 1984 election neared, Reagan began wooing Hispanic Catholics with talks on school prayer and abortion (knowing that his other domestic policies left them little other reason to vote for him) and then pulled out the stops on "pro-family" issues in 1984 itself, notably with his sponsorship of a bill for school prayer.

Interestingly, it was during this same decade of mid-seventies to mid-eighties that Moslem fundamentalists also became extremely active in politics. It was they who assassinated Egypt's President Sadat, took over Iran under the Ayatollah Khomeini, and began a crusade frankly called a holy war (jihad). Hard times often bring on reactionary moods and governments; that is a predictable response to anxiety about cultural changes, unemployment, inflation, and general loss of control over society and environment. The attacks in America on the separation between church and state seem to be part of a worldwide impulse to reinstitute theocracy. Whereas our deistic, Freemasonic founding fathers created America as a theocracy in the sense of government guided by universalist spirituality (consider "In God We Trust" and the mystic symbols of the Great Seal as shown on the dollar bill) but disjoined from even their own Christian church, the theocracy popular so far today is government by a particular, culture-bound religion. Inasmuch as such a trend can give a religion access to an army, it sets up the dreadful possibility of holy wars on all sides.

In fact, anti-Communist crusading, which intensified considerably under Reagan, goes far beyond the opposition of economic ideologies or even the competition between superpowers for hegemony. The most zealous "pro-family" anti-Communists say they have God behind them. In an interview in a 1980 issue of *Conservative Digest* Paul Weyrich said:

> What is behind the thrust against the traditional family values? Well, first of all, from our point of view, this is really the most significant battle of the age-old conflict between good and evil, between the forces of God and forces against God, that we have seen in our country.
>
> We see the anti-family movement as an attempt to prevent souls from reaching eternal salvation, and as such we feel not just a political committment to change this situation, but a moral and, if you will, a religious commitment to battle these forces.[7]

Let's compare this declaration of holy war with another by Robert Welch, founder of the John Birch Society, which is named for a man said to have been killed by Chinese Communists and is dedicated to all-out war on Communism. At the end of *The Blue Book of the John Birch Society* Welch places an epigraph from *The Life of John Birch:* "With his death and in his death the battle lines were drawn, in a struggle from which either Communism or Christian-style civilization must emerge with one completely triumphant and the other completely destroyed."[8] Such salvos are like those of the Ayatollah Khomeini, which justify sending scores of thousands of frequently unarmed teen-agers to suicidal deaths in a crusader war such as that with Iraq.

The Kanawha County case prefigured an increasing American trend toward a sort of de facto theocracy, an evangelical governance of the nation that, under the guise of defending freedom against Communism, feels justified in moving toward a police state at home while intervening militarily in countries abroad. During Reagan's 1984 reelection campaign, the New Right presented itself as the wave of the future — progressive, positive, and powerful. It depicted Democrats as old-fashioned, negative crybabies. Reagan's landslide victory demonstrated the appeal of this promotion, which even won over voters young enough to be Reagan's grandchildren. But this greatest conservative triumph of contemporary America represented actually a whole country running scared in the face of accumulating social and technological change, a perpetually precarious economy, and chronic dread about international conflicts.

In the Kanawha County book rebellion we can see the true heart of the New Right — its basis in fear and faithlessness — for the attitudes and causes championed by the dissenters were reiterated during the 1984 conservative tide that swept Reagan into the White House for the second time. Explicitly or implicitly, the Republican Convention of 1984 opposed the Equal Rights Amendment, abortion, the nuclear freeze, detente with the Soviets, desegregation, prosecution of civil rights violations, and federal regulation of corporations to protect the environment and the consumer, but favored high defense spending, saber-rattling against the Soviets, school prayer, the dropping of programs for minorities and the poor while increasing harsh measures against criminals (who come mostly from deprived communities), greater military intervention in Central America, strong and secret roles for the CIA and FBI, and more police powers to seize and search. No matter how elegantly argued or suavely expressed, the feelings and ideas behind Reagan's conservative triumph were essentially the same as those voiced in Kanawha County by people fearful and faithless enough to think that if their children encountered new ideas they would turn their backs on them. However much wealthy, well educated, well bred, and well groomed New Rightists may wish to disavow their country cousins and poor relations, they're all in the same ideological family.

Epitomizing this kinship is the conservative think tank in Washington, D.C., the Heritage Foundation, which played a significant part in the antitextbook campaign and in the formulation of policy for the Reagan administration. As mentioned, it sent to Charleston its legal counsel to aid in defending book dissenters arrested for civil disturbances such as blocking buses and schools. So close was the Heritage Foundation to the Reagan administration that the proposals it submitted for legislation on such matters as the budget were difficult to distinguish from drafts that the administration ultimately proposed.

> The first-term Reagan administration adopted many Heritage Foundation ideas—abolishing the Education Department, extending tax breaks to segregationist schools, limiting laws that bar colleges from discriminating against women, re-introducing prayer in school, and cutting student aid programs, among others—as its own.[9]

Among a half dozen solid New Rightists that Reagan appointed to the Department of Education was Dr. Robert Billings, former executive director of the Moral Majority (awarded a doctorate by a Tennessee Ph.D. mill later discredited by the state) and Charles Heatherly, former director of special projects for the Heritage Foundation.

After the reelection, Heritage Foundation officers boasted on television interviews of their high score in influencing policy, and it was common knowledge that a great deal of interaction habitually occurred during both of Reagan's terms between this private conservative lobby and the president's faction of the government. Elmer Fike was a member of the foundation, as he said; and as the letter from Congressman Phillip Crane quoted in chapter 3 shows, the Heritage Foundation was actively seeking to help other such censorship campaigns as the one in Kanawha County. It behooves thoughtful citizens to consider what it means to support, on the one hand, the violent and illegal tactics of people fanatically opposed to learning and thinking for oneself and, on the other hand, the policies of the president of the United States. But the Heritage Foundation merely symbolizes the deep affinity between the rowdier elements of fundamentalist conservatism and the sophisticated organizations of the New Right, which do not of course firebomb schools or make grammatical mistakes as the creek preachers did but who second their motions.

What links them across differences in style and decorum is, contrary to all New Right rhetoric, a profound lack of faith, a negative conviction about human beings, a fear of individual development, and an authoritarian reliance on a sort of group mind. The positive, forward-looking, born-again, free-spirited individualism claimed by the New Right represents an attempt to overcome this negativism by denying it and by fantasizing its opposite. The fact is, as we will see, that planks in the platform of this reactionary conservatism correspond to symptoms in the syndrome of agnosis, which in the wake of Hitlerism many psychologists studied extensively as the "authoritarian" or "prefascist" or "dogmatic" personality. A salient trait, they determined, is the rejection of self-examination in favor of crusading against evils one unconsciously wants to eradicate from oneself. The resurgence of this very dangerous tendency under an exuberant "progressive" conservatism bears looking into indeed.

But in keeping with the very principle of looking within, we must not ascribe this trait only to certain groups just because they tend to act out or betray it most evidently. Preferring aggression to self-development is a universal tendency, and it is quite clear that under stress virtually anyone may become more guarded and regressive, regardless of political affiliation. Thus many poor, working-class, and minority people voted for Reagan in 1984 because he seemed strong and reassuring even though his actual policies went against their interests. It is, in fact, the deep disturbances of today's world that account for so much retrenchment into religious fundamentalism and extreme rightism. So let's examine agnosis not as a party matter but as a malady to which anxiety makes anyone susceptible.

The last period of comparable anxiety occurred just as modern depth psychology and psychoanalysis were reaching maturity. Out of this conjunction was to come research of importance to understanding the syndrome at hand. It was the period of worldwide depression, unemployment, and bitter aftermath to World War I that led into World War II. Alarm at the appeal of Hitler, Mussolini, and Franco prompted psychological investigation of the fascist personality well before the blitzkrieg itself tore across Europe.

In his monumental *Escape from Freedom* (1941) Erich Fromm applied to history and politics such clinical concepts as that of sadomasochism and explained the German lower middle class's enthusiasm for Nazism as a longing to escape from the self-responsibility of freedom into authoritarian submission. During the decade following World War II behavioral scientists launched research into the fascist-prone personality with all the moral passion kindled by the Holocaust and by the feeling that such a close call for civilization simply could not be allowed to occur again. In our own era of chronic anxiety about international tensions, terrorism, and the possibility of nuclear incineration, a review of this research may be more than merely appropriate.

In 1950 the team of Adorno, Frenkel-Brunswik, Levinson, and Sanford broke ground with *The Authoritarian Personality*, which aimed to relate ideology to personality and which set lines of inquiry still framing major research and theory today. From the perspective of a survey of research in 1978 Goldstein and Blackman synopsized the authoritarian portrait in this way *(Cognitive Style):*

> The authoritarian individual is proper and concerned with status and success, probably stemming from his parents' insecurities with status. This parental concern and anxiety results in strict training practices. This strictness leads in turn to a repression of faults and shortcomings. Aggressive impulses that cannot be expressed against parents are displaced to weaker minority group members. The faults and shortcomings that were repressed are projected onto the minority group members, thus providing rationalizations for aggressive behavior.[10]

Another team pursued dogmatism, rigidity, intolerance of ambiguity, and other traits of the authoritarian syndrome and, led by Milton Rokeach, published in 1960 *The Open and Closed Mind*. Followed by parenthetical remarks of my own, here are principal traits they give as characterizing the closed mind:

— *General* lack of discrimination. (A tendency to lump things together has been regarded by Heinz Werner and other developmental psychologists as characteristic of less developed individuals.)[11]

— Orientation toward an extreme past or future. (This represents avoidance of the here-and-now in favor of conserving the old, associated with authority, or trying, from anxiety, to program the future.)

—Passive and forgetful. (Reliance on external, rewards-and-punishment authority naturally induces passivity. Forgetfulness may seem a less obvious consequence until one considers how an active putting together of knowledge for oneself makes the parts easier to remember because of the meaningful coherence.)

—Isolation of particular beliefs and disbeliefs from each other. (This lack of consistency owes no doubt to the fact that the person is not thinking for himself or herself but taking over from the authority a conglomeration united mostly by certain emotions, which provide consistency indeed.)

—Self-contradiction. (This must follow as a consequence of the lack of consistency among ideas. Consistency exists in the unconscious motivation of the personality but not in the avowed ideology or overt behavior, where one looks for it. Inner conflict usually leads to self-contradiction.)

—Paranoia. (In the book objections this showed as counteroffensive to attacks against parents and Christianity and America that were not made in the texts but were read into the texts by the objectors. In his classic "The Paranoid Style in American Politics," Richard Hofstadter connected paranoid traits with conspiracy theories held by zealous partisans.[12] Senator Joseph McCarthy's hot hunt for Communists in America was an immediate inspiration.)

—Belief in an unfriendly world. (Here we are getting down to basics, and to causes. This is the emotional premise from which not only paranoia but the other traits as well are "logically" derived. This may be hard to see sometimes because it is buried under an overcompensatory emphasis on "goodness.")

—Disbelief in one's capacity to cope. (Coupled with the last, this makes for a very negative and explosive outlook that explains why one might not want to know and might accuse others of morbidity, depression, and violence.)

Hypothesized for the sake of further research, these traits have been generally confirmed and extended by subsequent investigation. In another survey of research of 1978, *Dimensions of Personality*, Howard Ehrlich reports that people who scored high in dogmatism or closed-mindedness also

—had lower sensory acuity, were more dependent on external support in evaluating sensory input, and restricted their sensory experience as in tasting fewer foods;

—responded less favorably to new art and music, preferred popular to classical music and classical to avant-garde (whereas low-dogmatics as a group liked all three equally), and generally rejected novelty and change;

—as patients, took longer to accept blindness and to complete in-patient psychiatric treatment;

—as psychiatric nurses themselves, gave less effective treatment to their mental patients and responded to them more as if the patients were inferior;

—liked each other better than others liked them;

—were low in self-esteem, self-reliance, and self-confidence;

—were high in ethnocentrism, prejudice, and rejection of others, rejecting other religions in proportion to dissimilarity with their own, rejecting artists, scientists, leftists, physical deviants, and other ethnic groups;

—were more conservative and more confident in accepted beliefs, accepted the tried and true despite inconsistencies, and were cautious about new ideas;

—on certain tasks conformed more with confederates whom they regarded as high-status than with those they regarded as low-status;

—in the 1964 and 1972 elections chose more conservative candidates.[13]

"The rejection of self and the rejection of others," writes Ehrlich, "is highly correlated and probably has the same developmental basis."[14]

Some of the most telling description comes from Rokeach himself, who wrote that his team's findings confirm the assumption of similarity across "personality, ideology, and cognitive functioning," indicating very close interaction among emotion, beliefs, and intelligence. Confirmed too has been the strong correlation he found between dogmatism and anxiety, and this anxiety seems to be a factor of child-rearing. Low scorers in dogmatism

> express more ambivalence toward their fathers and mothers, report being more widely influenced by persons outside the immediate family, and report having had relatively fewer anxiety symptoms in childhood. On the other hand, the reports of middle and closed subjects are on the whole similar and, compared with open subjects, they reveal more glorification of parents, a more restricted influence by persons outside the family, and a greater incidence in childhood of thumb-sucking, nail-biting, temper tantrums, nightmares, walking and talking while asleep, and bed-wetting.
>
> All of the preceding suggest the hypothesis that when ambivalence toward parents is not permitted expression it leads both to anxiety and to a narrowing of possibilities for identification with persons outside the family. Both, in turn, are interpreted as leading to the development of closed belief systems.[15]

It is illuminating to juxtapose this earthy set of findings with an hypothesis the researchers made as stated early in their report.

> It is assumed that the more closed the system, the more will the content of such beliefs be to the effect that we live alone, isolated and helpless in a friendless world; that we live in a world wherein the future is uncertain; that the self is fundamentally unworthy and inadequate to cope alone with this

friendless world; and that the way to overcome such feelings is by a self-aggrandizing and self-righteous identification with a cause, a concern with power and status, and by a compulsive self-proselytization about the justness of such a cause.[16]

What a fascinating profile. Surely more and more of us earthlings are tending to fit it as national and international conditions degenerate. Perhaps this sketch can help to explain the current increase in censorship, racism, intolerance, factional militance, reversal of civil rights, and general repression. It has been noted that as employment goes down the membership of the KKK rises. Especially astute, I believe, is the connecting of feelings of unworthiness and inadequacy to self-aggrandizement and self-righteous identification with a cause. Censorship is just such a cause.

The striking idea of "compulsive self-proselytization" deserves thought. One way people try to control their feelings and their behavior is to keep telling themselves what it is they must or must not do. This occurs considerably as self-recitation in one's inner speech, a reversion to the child's prattle as it talks itself through some action it is just trying to master or has difficulty getting itself to do. When inclined to deal outside with inner matter, we may just keep exhorting other people to do what we are trying to get ourselves to do. We all do some of this, but the more we feel inadequate or under pressure to please an authority by behavior that seems beyond our capacity, the more we may resort to self-proselytizing, trying to convert ourselves to principles and behavior that did not arise from within, that still feel alien. If also not much given to going inward (which the researchers labeled "anti-intraception"), we may make a shrill cause out of the difficult program so that we can in exhorting, denouncing, and proselytizing others create outward drama that will rebound to activate ourselves to do as we are admonishing others to act.

I felt this phenomenon at work in the book objections on such themes as challenging authority, animality, and materialism, faith in absolutes, or seeing the good side of things. I felt I was listening to someone much tempted underneath to kick back at authority (as in the book rebellion itself), who felt ideals of spirituality were taxing his or her sensuality and self-interest to the limit, and who was having a difficult time indeed keeping faith in the absolutes held before him or her and not falling into depression over the fears of incapacity and futility. (Look again at Avis Hill's song "Give God the Glory" [at the end of chapter 6], which tells of his near-suicidal feelings before finding Christ.)

Most "born again" people I have heard of hit rock bottom in their life and escaped despair and ruin only by the feeling that Christ intervened in their negative train of acts and thoughts and saved them.

The life on the frontier did not allow for an optimistic social gospel. One was lucky if he endured. Hard work did not bring a sure reward. Therefore the religion became fatalistic and stressed rewards in another life. The important thing was to get religion, get saved, which meant accepting Jesus as one's personal savior. It was and is a realistic religion which fitted a realistic people. It is based on belief in the Original Sin, that man is fallible, that he will fail, does fail. We mountaineers readily see that the human tragedy is this, that man sees so clearly what he should do and what he should not do and yet he fails so consistently. . . .[17]

Testimonials by former criminals and drug addicts make up an important part of evangelical services or jamborees of the Billy Graham sort, as they do of Alcoholics Anonymous meetings. These examples enable the distraught to admit their own "sins" and to accept a "higher power," and this performs a valuable psychological service. Thus some people may need an external authority to guide them until they develop inner discipline and direction toward salvation.

Of great value in understanding agnosis is a psychological scale originated over thirty years ago by H. A. Witkin and refined by others ever since. It runs from "field-dependence" to "field-independence" and concerns how much one relies on sources outside one's own mind, whether things or people, for knowledge and judgment. The main idea of it may best be gained from visualizing the original experiments that gave birth to it. The subject was asked to indicate when a pole he or she was holding within a simple frame was upright. To the extent the subject relied on kinesthetic sense of gravitation and verticality — on inner reference — he or she was deemed field-independent. To the extent the subject relied on visual alignment of the pole with the frame — on outer reference — he or she was deemed field dependent.

Researchers wondered if a person tending one way or the other in this purely perceptual situation would also tend to refer inwardly or outwardly in, say, problem-solving or social situations; experiments expanded into cognition and interpersonal relations. "The dimension reflects the degree to which people function autonomously of the world around them,"[18] says Donald Goodenough in *Dimensions of Personality*. The field may be either the physical environment or other people. "People who are oriented toward external fields in perceptual-intellectual functioning also tend to be oriented toward external (interpersonal) fields in social situations."[19] "People are self-consistent in mode of field approach across a wide variety of situations."[20]

Goodenough says that one pole of the dimension is as good as another: an airplane pilot might do better to orient from instruments or horizon line sometimes than by inner gravitational feel, and a field-dependent person is more out-going. But he says too that "The evidence indicates that the individual moves from a state of relative field-dependence to a state of greater field-independence during the course of development from childhood to young adulthood."[21] Field-independence increases between ages eight and seventeen and then levels off. If we assume that maturation consists of growth toward better functioning, then field-independence would seem more mature.

The fact that the child is most egocentric but also most field-dependent is worth thinking about. This paradox really means that the child *confuses* internal with external orientations and that it *must* orient toward the field but does so *subjectively*. The key concept, after all, is *dependence*. To be oriented toward the field is not the same as to depend on the field.

Perhaps the bipolar model misleads; perhaps we do not have to acquire one at the expense of the other but may, rather, retain external orientation when it is appropriate — in ministering to others, for example, or when perception may be disarranged and unreliable — and yet be able to operate autonomously when that is most appropriate. It is this factor of deliberateness, of will and consciousness, that should perhaps be joined to the current concept of this dimension to clarify its relationship to maturity. Some people orient to the field by necessity and limitation, whereas others may orient more freely both ways. People classified as field-independent, on the other hand, may include actually two kinds — those who *cannot* switch to field-orientation when that would be most appropriate and those who are not limited to the one pole but may will either way because of a consciousness of both at once.

Nomadic hunter-gatherer cultures, which have only a loose structure outside the family and require individuals to function self-reliantly, foster field-independence by their child-raising, which is permissive. Farmer-herder societies, on the other hand, which are sedentary and elaborately structured, and require that people get along well and obey rules, foster field-dependence by a strict, authoritarian upbringing. So historically, cognitive style has shifted with cultural evolution but shifted in the opposite direction from the individual's growth toward field-independence.[22] (In other words, ontogeny does not recapitulate phylogeny in this case.)

This understanding casts the permissiveness of one faction of modern American culture into a different light from that of the stereotype of lawless degeneracy. Since much of America has evolved beyond the sedentary agrarian society with its need for field-dependency to a society resembling hunter-gatherers in respect to mobility, confrontation with constant change, and the need for improvisation, the shift back to permissiveness probably represents a further adaptation to cultural conditions putting a premium on self-reliance. But of course we have to distinguish some parental indifference and haplessness from this purposeful permissiveness. Allowing children to wise off becomes something very different when combined with making them fight their own battles and with punishing them for babyishness and passivity, all of which parents do in many nomadic and hunter-gatherer societies. Perhaps, however, many Americans have moved intuitively with their subculture in this direction but do not understand the real function of permissiveness and therefore mix up the kind that produces independence with a kind of anything-goes resignation to today's cultural confusion (which drives others to attempt greater severity).

The research evidence seems to show that an authoritarian upbringing plays a major role in limiting thought and behavior (given the special meaning of "authoritarian" as developed across the studies reviewed here).

> Some investigators have argued that authoritarian child-rearing styles are conducive to the establishment of authoritarian government that, in turn, help perpetuate an authoritarian nationalistic style (cf. Erikson, 1942; Fromm, 1936, 1941; Reich, 1945). Brown (1965) noted that authoritarianism is characteristic of low-socioeconomic, less-educated individuals. For example, Stewart and Hoult (1959) postulated that authoritarianism is negatively correlated with the number of social roles an individual is able to play. They reviewed a number of studies showing that high authoritarianism is found among the less educated, older people, rural residents, the disadvantaged, members of more dogmatic religious organizations, members of lower socio-economic groups, and social isolates, as well as among people reared in authoritarian families. In each case, the potential for mastering a variety of roles is limited. Stewart and Hoult postulated that individuals with limited role experience cannot take the roles of others outside their reference group, that they cannot understand or sympathize with such outsiders, and that they feel hostile toward, and reject, members of such outgroups.[23]

The earlier researchers' assertion that "people who are high in political and economic conservatism tend to be high on ethnocentrism and anti-Semitism"[24] receives partial confirmation in this finding: "A number of studies have indicated that individuals high in authoritarianism have a rightist political orientation (Hanson, 1975). For example, Thompson and Michel (1972) found authoritarianism related to political conservatism and Christian traditionalism" (Cognitive Style).[25] Dimensions of Personality also reports that authoritarianism is associated with conservatism, but the conservative-liberal dimension is complex. Studies do not show, for example, that Republicans score higher on authoritarianism than Democrats, the respondents differing only on particular issues or candidates. Working-class Americans are liberal in economics but conservative on social and moral issues.[26] Both Republicans and Democrats embrace a broad band of the liberal-conservative spectrum, and in some localities one has to register with the dominant party simply to enjoy a significant vote (in primaries).

After saying "The prefascist authoritarian should be especially responsive to conspiracy theories of social, political, and economic events," à propos of Hofstadter's theory of the paranoid style in public life,[27] Dillehay goes on to point out in *Dimensions of Personality:* "Given that the paranoid style seems to be especially associated with right-wing causes on the American scene, we can still speculate that susceptibility to the appeals of this style increases with the general stress of bad political, social, and economic times."[28] As an example of hard times influencing people toward authoritarianism he cites the study of

Sales (1972), who examined rates of conversion to authoritarian and nonauthoritarian churches during economic good times and bad times in the United States. He studied the period 1920 to 1939 since it contains a period of economic prosperity (1920–1929) and one of depression (1930–1939). He found that conversion to authoritarian churches (the Southern Baptist Convention, the Church of Jesus Christ of Latter-Day Saints, the Seventh-day Adventist Church, and the Roman Catholic Church) increased during economic bad times and decreased during better periods. For the nonauthoritarian churches (the Presbyterian Church in the United States of America, the Congregational Christian Church, the Northern Baptist Convention, and the Protestant Episcopal Church) the findings were just the opposite: Conversion rates for these churches decreased during bad times and increased during good times. The implication is that authoritarian appeals of certain churches were more successful during periods of elevated anxiety with everyone, not just with the especially susceptible authoritarians. Sales' classification of churches as authoritarian or nonauthoritarian, it might be added, seems to be based on a careful consideration of the content and style of belief in the different denominations. The denominations do differ in terms of such matters as submission to authority, condemnation versus toleration of outgroups, and emphasis on sin and transgression.[29]

By no means is research in psychology itself a favored authority. But some investigation does convey how much family and social relations and cultural norms shape thought and feeling and influence the political and religious convictions that determine public policy—which in turn influences the family and individual and stirs the circular forces on around again.

The wisest use of research findings would surely be to help understand what opens and closes the heart and mind in ourselves as individuals and to recognize these causes and effects when multiplied into social forces. In modern America most child-rearing blends permissiveness and strictness in subtle ways that make either-or discussions absurd. Some parents spoil their children rotten between beatings, while other parents cruelly criticize their children for not having used their freedom as the parents had intended. Coldness has a way of cutting across research parameters, and anxiety has a way of flourishing throughout human community. Either will *make* a child stupid—which is the main thing we need to keep in mind—and no I.Q. test will tell us how intelligent that child *might* have been. Fear cripples, and any upbringing that relies on it for control will brutalize and stupefy. But anxiety induced in adulthood by hard times will also feed the bigoted, dogmatic, censorial potentiality of personality that everyone bears within.

We may want to believe that our ideology comes from on high—as indeed it should—but we can learn from some of this psychological correlation just how much it comes instead from personality, and personality from culture. At least this is so until we transcend personal conditioning. And there is the rub: to the extent *I think as I was treated and reared*, I suffer from partiality and some degree of ethnocentrism and dogmatism. *Any* human and material conditioning produces limitations of the sort that turn up in these research findings. (And who has grown up free of fear?) The more we base our ego on certain localized identities—of family, church, race, nation—the more strongly do we bind our mind to the limitations of each of these human partialities.

16

Group Rule

In the looking-glass world Alice meets the boyish twins Tweed-
ledum and Tweedledee. What they stand for in Lewis Carroll's whimsi-
cally logical representation of reality—the playoff between similarity
and difference—prompted me to begin a book for teachers celebrating
the twins' duel.

> Like their names, they resemble each other to a point and then diverge.
> Tweedledum and Tweedledee represent all of us. We are similar in a general
> way and different in particular ways. And our differences, like theirs,
> emerge from the similarity itself. Only things that share a common origin
> can diverge. Our common humanity is like white light that, passing through
> the prism of heredity and experience, separates itself into the colors of indi-
> vidual variation. Out of one, many.
>   But at any time, the possibility remains of emphasizing the similarity and
> becoming one again. Tweedledum and Tweedledee *agreed* to have a battle,
> but when a "monstrous crow" flew down and frightened them, "they quite
> forgot their quarrel." Pushed to essentials, we forget our differences. The
> democratic slogan *e pluribus unum* emphasizes this reversal toward similar-
> ity. Out of many, one. We have the choice to stress similarity and unity or
> difference and multiplicity. Likeness and unlikeness are in the eye of the
> beholder and hence at the center of conceiving and verbalizing.[1]

The conceptual option people play in deciding what shall be like and
unlike determines what or whom we identify with. How do people classify
themselves? How do we classify others? And of course self-classification
and self-concept form a circle. Examining the process of identification
allows us to relate people's logic to their emotions, to detect the one buried
in the other. Though classifying and abstracting belong to logic, they serve
passions and build on emotional premises inherited from a community or
acquired from early experiences. Intelligence alone does not prevent or
resolve conflict and can, indeed, rationalize it endlessly.

At the same time that we explore the process of identifying, let's attempt
to find some common denominator in the objections made to the text-

books. Surely, some unity of much significance to us all threads through and ties together the diverse vociferations, views, and values we have heard in preceding chapters. Some connections are easy to make, as between chauvinism and militarism, or authoritarianism and absolutism, and I have already suggested some. But what about racism and phonics? Or anti-Communism and antifeminism? Fundamentalism and "invasion of privacy"?

We have on our hands a mixed bag indeed, considered at one level, at face value, but since the movement that includes such censorship manifests extraordinary coherence — as in the New Right and Pro-Family campaigns — we can assume that at some level all these Dums and Dees stem from a common Tweedle. These forces, after all, are acting powerfully on whole states and nations today, in both Christendom and Islam. But I will refer to factions only to anchor discussion in today's realities; it would be singularly inappropriate to examine conflict so as to increase it. We are not so concerned with particular groups as with phenomena in everybody.

People classify themselves by how broadly or narrowly they identify. Imagine various possible identities scaled by broadening scope: family, neighborhood, local club, sports team, profession, ethnic group, social class, region, race, church, country, language, and so on to the largest conceivable identities such as the whole of humanity, "citizen of the universe," all living things, and finally, cosmos or entire creation. Clearly, the abstractive faculty plays a part in one's ability or inclination to identify beyond the local and tangible, that is, with entities well extended over time and space and very different from oneself — or at any rate from one's obvious manifestation.

Different identities set up conflict. The narrower one's identity the less it overlaps with others', includes others, and the more possibility therefore of conflict. Not many people in the world belong to my street gang or wear my school tie; more belong to my Protestant sect or my income bracket or level of education, but not nearly enough. But so what? — I can be a "Mercedes owner" and "a William and Mary alumnus" and a member of the Southwestern Abernathy County Hibernian Senior Citizens Rose Growing and Archery Club and still not conflict with other Americans or human beings. This may very well be true, depending on how one wears this identity psychologically. If broader identities subsume more concrete ones in a person — I am an Earthling or child of God *before* I am an American or Christian — then the broader identification should not allow conflict between the lesser.

The crux of the matter, then, lies with a person's *top* identification and with the strength of it. How many things does a person identify with? How far beyond the individual's locale and concrete circumstances do these go? And what is the priority of them among broader and narrower?

Probably no one ever deliberately establishes a system of identities, but to understand the more hidden sources of conflict underlying obvious "conflicts of interest," such as economic competition, territorial dispute, and choice of school books for children, we have to clarify the identity relations that explain why people allow lesser differences to overshadow the more important similarities, to the point that everyone loses. Rationally, the collaboration gained by subordinating lesser loyalties to truly universal needs would more nearly permit everyone to gain whatever the material competition and disputes are about.

The logic of classification always requires exclusion as well as inclusion: the class of A implies another class of Non-A. Hence the name-calling of "Un-American" and "Un-Christian." Constantly calling attention to Non-A consolidates the identity of A. This is why rulers of all epochs have inveighed against and attacked other countries, races, or sects. Find a foreign enemy and you can always gloss over domestic problems and rally unity around the flag. So a conspiracy theory naturally accompanies divisive emphasis on concrete identities. Anti-Communism goes hand in hand with Americanism, as necessary as Non-A to A.

Because enemies help us to define and reiterate who we are, the more vigorous the action taken against them the surer we cinch our limited identity. Hence militarism goes with patriotism. If the enemy also builds character structure on narrow identities, then of course they may indeed really threaten us, partly from doing the same thing we're doing and partly from reacting to our menaces. Since males usually run government, a factor of sexual identity plays in here too; brandishing weapons and talking tough are macho acts to affirm virility. The case made for militarism and pugnacity on grounds of defense really glances off the truth, which is the psychological need for identity maintenance that causes groups to threaten each other in the first place.

Within this framework pacifists must be excoriated and branded "unpatriotic." Saluting the flag each morning in school is necessary to ensure that children grow up defining themselves as members of the identity group. Emphasizing *membership* naturally leads to a desire for a school dress code — as close to a uniform as you can get in democratic public schools — and for other uniformizing conditions such as a stereotyping curriculum that will submerge the individual in the group and imprint children so that they all know and think the same identity-limited things. This makes the identification take hold and work far better than if cohesion is jeopardized through variant dress and thought. The rule is an ancient one from primitive times.

Knowledge authorities go with group identities. In fact one tends toward one or another authority and identity according to the stage of consciousness one has attained. Psychologists may like to speak of an "authoritarian character," but everyone of us is authoritarian in the sense that we have something or someone that authorizes our knowledge, however unconventional or personal. We may not follow a traditional, collective, centralized, external authority such as the "authoritarian" personality pledges strict obedience to, but we put our faith in *some* source.

An authority is one's source of knowledge and hence of guidance in action, since action depends at least partly on one's knowledge, and since any source deserving faith for knowledge deserves it for conduct as well. Do you believe scientific evidence, peer lore, ancient wisdom, your own observations, scholarly research, visions, newspapers and popular books, sacred scriptures, eminent contemporaries, logical deduction, auguries and card readings, intuition, or something else? The ways people differ in where they put their faith, what knowledge authority they believe in, may be the most important human variation we can become aware of, because such variation relates directly to stages in evolution of consciousness, which progress from a sort of group mind to individually acquired understanding.

Analyzing the identifying process in terms of classification and knowledge structures risks making it seem more logical and intellectual than it is. Far from it of course. This is gut stuff. The ratiocination comes afterward, as rationalization. First comes the identifying. In fact, we no doubt first learn to classify from feeling and observing social separations. This starts when we become conscious of ourselves as separate from the surroundings — me from other — and proceeds to behavioral learning of the differences between one family and another, between neighborhoods, and eventually between larger communities and countries with all their myriad enclaves and subdivisions. Very early, children become sensitized, from a million clues of action and speech, to social classifications in action. Indeed, these separations then serve as prototypes for intellectual distinctions. Identifications are made before the development of reason — which is part of my point — and when reason does become a conscious faculty, it is put into the service of maintaining a system of classification and identification generated emotionally and unconsciously.

Inasmuch as agnosis begins in childhood, it results fundamentally from parents' holding on to their children, whereas freedom of mind results from parents' releasing their children. More specifically, fearful techniques of child-rearing combine with exaggerated reverence for hearth and ethos to tie the child emotionally within a very exclusive and limiting world. In some measure this happens to every child, but in acute agnosis the view of knowledge is as follows.

What one should know has been divulged some time ago by a patriarchal authority and is transmitted within one's group as part of membership itself, implicitly through behavior and more explicitly through oral teaching. The connection between knowledge and group identity is critical. One does not acquire knowledge, one inherits it from one's group. The individual does not learn on his or her own and know things others of the group do not. People know collectively and know the same things (a standardized curriculum). Not wanting to know means not wanting to know more than the inheritance, than fellow members know, than fits into the group knowledge. What is fit to know is known already. Anything else spells danger or disloyalty. This limitation places a premium on collective unity, uniformity. Individuals who know other things may act other ways and go other ways. They "err" and "sin." They lose identity and endanger the continuance of the group. The purpose of all this is to ensure group survival within which to provide individual security.

Let's not be judgmental about this: such an authority is sensible given a certain stage of development that might make other authorities downright dangerous — or perhaps I should say, even more dangerous. Fanaticism and bigotry have been necessary for whole peoples in history and still are for some individuals and groups. And some part of virtually all of us is drawn to such an authority in the more stressful courses of our life.

Conventionally, one thinks of authority as warranting law, not knowledge, but it is precisely the confusion of rules with knowledge that we are dealing with, the taking of laws of man for laws of nature. When we don't want to know, it's because we want to fall back on rules and not have to sift through all the indefinite, ambiguous, incomplete, uninterpreted information of ordinary life and try to distill from it some conclusions that we can feel confident to act on. We long for a Supreme Codifier who has predigested life's possibilities and converted endless intricate experience into a set of simple laws. But we can't short-cut in soul school. And no one else can take the course for us.

Now actually, scientists and philosophers would like nothing better than to apply so well their principle of parsimonious thinking as to produce brief, elegant laws that cut through the clutter and crystallize a maze of information in a few symbols. But the book banner in us rejects *these* laws. It wants laws in the other sense, of directions and orders. It does not want a law that enables you to get on top of a lot of knowledge; it wants a law that makes it unnecessary to know a lot in the first place. The difference here is between simple and simplistic.

If you are chiefly concerned about doing the right thing according to a group code, you do not want a lot of knowledge, because it will only make more difficult the task of living up to the code. If, on the other hand, you are trying to perfect yourself and evolve through growth, you are committed to learning all you can, and knowledge — even when it's bad news — is your best friend. Clearly, a crucial division among people

—and within a person—concerns whether one should obey a group authority or the individual's own authority. Most of us fluctuate a great deal between the two, berating ourselves for listening so much to other people but doubting ourselves too much to act consistently on our own understanding.

Much of the usual school censorship attacks equal representation, the doing justice to the pluralism of this country and this globe. Anything international, ecumenical, or universal seems wrong if knowledge is tied to a group identity that is never planetary. The censors do not want their children to know how other people live and think, because they do not want them to know about *alternatives* of any kind—other customs, other beliefs, other values, and other courses of action.

Nor about other interpretations. "Situation ethics," "relativism," pluralism, ambiguity, symbolism, and irony all violate the first rule of agnosis—to suppress alternatives because all these present more than one point of view or possibility or message or meaning. It is in the nature of knowledge based on group or patriarchal authority that it detests and resists alternatives, because alternatives permit individual decision making, whereas the whole point of limiting thought is to limit behavior. Dogmatism may be defined as admitting no alternatives; its goal is to enact and enforce conformity.

Such is the direct link between a "literal" interpretation of the Bible and collective control of individual action. Granting no alternative renderings of the text, no symbolism, no multiple meanings at historical, moral, philosophical, and mystical levels corresponds to the removal of options for action. One who cannot envision plural pathways cannot choose. (Suppose that evolution calls for each person to grow to God on his or her own, not to be blindly herded without acquiring personal knowledge or exercising personal choice.) As a factor of action, choice points in a practical way to the common denominator of the agnosis syndrome—the limiting of knowledge and identity according to the dependence of the individual on the group.

An important link between identity and agnosis is choice. Conforming to some social identity, as we all do, limits alternatives in thought and action and amounts to repudiating some personal choice. This may go unnoticed within a homogeneous culture. Conflict occurs—and consciousness rises—when cultural pluralism forces acknowledgment of alternatives and exposes individuals to choice. Ironically, seeing choices comes from the same ability to see differences that lies behind social separations and conflicts. Thus a tremendous tension arises between the differentiating we are taught in order to distinguish insiders from outsiders and the plurality of alternatives implied by these very differences. "Other" people embody other options in thought and action. In singling out "those" for our children we are also pointing out to them those other options. Look but don't see.

If the Upper Valley of Kanawha County had had its own school district it would not have been involved in a book dispute. If consolidation and bussing did not mix children, as Fike said, each subculture could transmit itself to the young through school in tranquillity. But, in a multicultural country forced by technocracy if nothing else toward increasing integration, keeping one's culture intact and discrete becomes very difficult indeed. Even distant cultures invade the home through television. National textbooks were just one more invasion into the Upper Valley, bringing cultures such as the black and Hispanic hardly represented otherwise even in Charleston.

Public schools not only mirror society but also provide a theater for enacting society's conflicts. In the school district come together all the factions of a community that otherwise might not have to deal with each other. For business, religion, recreation, and social life a populace can go different ways, but unless families opt out of public schools at their own expense, education remains the exception. As the central meeting place where differences are smoked out, the classroom becomes an arena for contending over divergent ways of life and modes of thought. Trying to educate a pluralistic populace by a single curriculum neatly focuses the dilemma implied in our national motto. "Out of many, one," we read on American coins — *E pluribus unum.*

Efforts of even well intentioned leaders usually reflect rather than solve the dilemma. The conventional political way is to try to salve conflicting parties by halving the difference between them. Typical of this way was the response of United States Commissioner of Education Terrel Bell to the Kanawha County dispute. On December 2, 1974, when the controversy was still boiling, he said in an address to the School Division of the Association of American Publishers:

Parents have a right to expect that the schools, in their teaching approaches and selection of Instructional materials, will support the values and standards that their children are taught at home. And if the schools cannot support those values they must at least avoid deliberate destruction of them.

One of the real problems in the production and selection of instructional materials is that parents and communities differ so widely in what they consider appropriate. We are probably the world's most polyglot nation, with many subcultures increasingly interested in maintaining or re-establishing their identity in the larger society. We come from many socio-economic backgrounds. We have many divergent religious viewpoints. Our positions on politics and education and other things that matter run the gamut from ultra-conservative to ultra-liberal.[2]

Here Bell seems both to realize and to ignore the fact that the pluralism of the population does not really gibe with the expectation that schools will reflect parent values. Rather than really confront the dilemma, he ends with this recommendation:

> So I think the children's book publishing industry, and the schools, need to chart a middle course between the scholar's legitimate claim to academic freedom in presenting new knowledge and social commentary on the one hand, and the legitimate expectations of parents that schools will respect their moral and ethical values on the other.[3]

It may be demagogically advantageous to pretend that the conflict is between scholars and parents, but Bell has already said that parents disagree among themselves. Falsely shifting the conflict elsewhere distracts us from the dilemma of parents differing and makes the usual businessman's negotiated compromise look possible. Actually, Bell does touch on a real solution in the next breath when he says, "Certainly wider uses of individualized instruction for each child will give his or her parents the opportunity to rule out an objectionable book or film without affecting other children."[4] This was in fact the approach of *Interaction*, which substituted a classroom library for a syllabus. But it is not honest to toss in "individualized instruction," which was a conjuring phrase then, while clearly telling publishers at the same time "to chart a middle course," that is, continue to publish class sets for all but to make sure nothing offends anyone.

Patently, compromise will not work: the very omissions that placate some parents infuriate others. Publishers hearing Bell's talk would recognize the old business-and-government strategy of waffling. He told them very clearly to tone it down, boys, you see what's happening. Instead of offering thoughtful leadership, he sidestepped the contradiction facing publishers, namely, that adoption practices require standardized materials whereas community factions require variation. Furthermore, the rigid production procedures in these large corporations definitely militate against varying materials to achieve the individualization Bell so debonairly recommended. (Not surprisingly, Reagan recalled Bell to serve as secretary to preside over the planned demise of the Department of Education, which was indefinitely deferred.) Offering a self-contradictory solution to fit the original self-contradiction inherent in a single curriculum for a pluralistic public typifies the conventional political approach to solving problems brought over from the Old World. It is not the American way, which is a new way. In this case, that would be to go behind the dilemma to some underlying commonality among people.

The beleaguered Superintendent Underwood of the Kanawha County Schools was quoted in the press saying,

> I'm sympathetic 100 percent with the genuine protestor. If people truly want to narrow the gap of literature, that's why we have private schools. I hope they're successful.[5]

But sticking the protesters off by themselves is not public education for all students. Of course he felt personally injured, but the advice of the National Education Association was similar. They suggested giving the dissenters their own classes or schools but acknowledged this risked widening schisms. Now, this is essentially what the voucher system as now being proposed in some states would do — allow various factions to take their share of taxes and enroll their children in private schools or start their own schools.

Proposals like these are unacceptable. "Cool it and find a safe middle way," simply cannot be implemented. "Let them go off and do their own thing — and good riddance" sets a time bomb for the future. Letting subcultural groups split off and form their own private schools will seriously deepen community and national divisions. We have already experienced this sort of solution in the "white flight" from public to private schools that not only fail to afford the white students adequate resources or faculties but certainly enhance racism among all. Voucher systems would fiscally facilitate "white flight" and other splintering off into separate schools. In fact, it would not be necessary to found private schools, since most voucher systems currently under consideration permit, as one option, establishing new public schools, that is, reorganizing present schools into specialized campuses.

Such solutions are wrong because they encourage disunity and finesse the original problem of pluralism. Separation during the formative years prolongs for one more generation the intolerance about differences that is the root issue. Children who grow up apart will probably fight as adults, whose fates will become increasingly intertwined by economic, environmental, and psychological factors affecting everyone. Not having grown up learning to share resources despite personal differences, they will be unable to live, let live, and unite to solve common problems. Not speaking the same language they will not talk together. America needs to accommodate plurality *within* unity so that various parties can pursue, on the same sites, the ramifications of their goals and values and discover where these lead.

To pursue the logic of real individualized learning of the honest sort that would result in different children reading different materials and benefiting from different methods would have led Bell, Underwood,

NEA, and other commentators on the Kanawha controversy to something more like a solution, but all parties seem to have balked at the serious reorganization of schooling and publishing that this would entail.

How *do* you give parents what they want when they don't want the same thing? You individualize the curriculum, but you keep everybody together. Now, alternatives may be made available at four levels of a school system. Students may (1) go to differently specialized schools, (2) follow different "tracks" within the same school, (3) choose different "elective" courses within the same track, or (4) choose different things to do within the same classroom.

The last is best because only then are students working within each other's presence, where they can learn with each other, from each other, and about each other. A voucher system institutionalizes conflict rather than reducing it. Tracking within a single school results in de facto segregation of all sorts, schools within a school in the wrong sense. Electives permit more choice but still do not individualize enough and yet segregate some. For the younger learners at least, the one-room schoolhouse is the best model, whereby different working parties of somewhat mixed ages do different activities at the same time as chosen by the children under the guidance of the teacher.

As children mature, the time-space compass within which they work may expand beyond the classroom to the whole school and then to the community as a learning site but always without losing the mixing process of the original multifarious classroom. Thus even when going later to specialized learning sites in school or in town they will always be mixing, because as individuals make different decisions within the same system of sites and resources they will cross paths and influence each other. Authoritarian and fundamentalist parents will not at first like the mixing itself, but because it is incidental to the individualization and parents can still force their child to choose as they say, they will prefer it to mixing without a choice of activities and materials.

What kind of textbooks would go with a classroom thus organized for individualization? No textbooks, actually. I have always argued that the teaching of reading and writing would improve if schools could wean themselves from textbooks, which merely dole and standardize and take time away from the actual practice of the language arts. Books of course, lots of them, but any and all books—a diverse classroom library, not a single lock-step set.

If I don't believe in textbooks why did I direct a program containing 172 of them? Because the atrocious truth is that schools do not create their curriculum; they buy it. This is atrocious because to the already crippling institutionalism of school systems it adds all the crudity and selfish impertinence of for-profit corporation practices. The most important decisions about teaching are made in commercial houses, which have constraints of their own far stronger than the contractual rights of the academic people they sign up to "author" their materials. These companies will surely say that they simply put out what schools want, but schools have for so long relied on them that teachers automatically look to commercial materials for guidance, and even schools of educations rely on them too much in training teachers. In other words, few educators are capable of thinking about curriculum independently of published materials and of the tests toward which they are directed (itself a huge industry).

In history, economics, government, and other social studies, text-books have often been biased, as the Gablers and other critics have charged, because these are subjects about which impartiality is virtually impossible and which reflect the reigning vogues of the time. School adoption not only gives a monopoly to whatever biases the adopted books contain but, as we saw, puts irresistible stress on publishers to cater to popular predilections no matter how narrow or ignorant these may be. The lock-in of a mass public bureaucracy and a large private corporation is so deadly that it may well be better to drop textbooks in all subjects, not just in the language arts.

At any rate, I decided that since schools were buying their curriculum prepackaged from publishers, then, to effect change, a publisher was where I had to place myself. At least books that were straight anthologies would entail the least risk to integrity. My strategy was to put into classrooms just such a diverse library as real individualization called for — no single set of anything, only six copies of many different titles (six so that partners could choose and read something together if they wanted). This still necessarily limited library would serve as a model for other reading material that could be brought into the classroom from all sources and organized by students and teacher together. In referring to *Interaction* as the "uncola" program Houghton Mifflin employees were acknowledging that these were trade books in effect, not textbooks. What was most radical about the program was not the subject matter of the reading material but the replacement of unison reading by individualized reading.

But this feature was wasted in Kanawha County, where it could, ironically, have offered a solution to the conflicting wishes of parents: children putting together their own reading program do not all have to read the same books or selections. Like most places, Kanawha County was not yet ready to individualize in such a staple, thoroughgoing way, so parents were not expecting classrooms to contain texts their child would not have to read.

In order to offer a broad enough array of materials and methods to make choice real, the whole community will have to become the school system. Parents will be teaching each other's children both in school, as

aides, and in town as masters to apprentices. Child and adult education
would also mix. Cross-teaching and rub-off occur among different community factions for the practical reason that in order for everyone to get
access to every sort of learning, all resources have to be pooled and
shared. Rather than requiring more special expenditure for education,
this community pooling would actually become more necessary the
worse the economic situation became. What would justify all this mixing
is that it is the only way to give everyone enough choices to make individualization come true. Ultimately, then, the urge to assert differences
and to resist imposition by others would bring everybody together: we
all want the same thing—to go our own ways.

Such a learning community would maintain unity across plurality. *E
pluribus unum.* But it entails so thoroughgoing a reorganization of school-
community relations that we should not be surprised that school superintendents, teachers' associations, and the United States secretary of education do not propose it.

> The only way in which a school system could approach neutrality would be
> to offer students a random multiplicity of literature and ideas and values,
> and permit them to select and read randomly with no guidance from
> teachers; and no one is proposing this.[6]

This in fact is just what I am proposing. But teachers *can* guide students
by helping them find reading matter for their interests and needs. And individualized reading is not random reading.

In other words, the best way to avoid conflict over reading matter is
also the best way to teach reading—break up the standardization and get
students reading around in a rich variety of material not produced especially for schools, which simply must quit buying curriculum in a commercial package. But parental attitudes and teacher training will have to
change also. Solutions that are resolutions are revolutions.

The revolution in this case moves us away from group rule of thought
toward a kind of social unity that acknowledges and accommodates individual differences as variations of a basic human likeness. A standardized curriculum is a holdover from an earlier stage of human evolution
when individuals were not developed enough to function in autonomy
from a cultural group-mind and when, consequently, these loyalties
caused cultures to clash. "Out of many, one" does not refer to conformity
and standardization and cultural chauvinism, which caricature this ideal.
The founding fathers drew this saying from ancient mystical traditions,
kept alive in Freemasonry, where it referred to the unity in spirit behind
the plurality of material manifestations. According to this teaching, the
reason that it is possible to make many out of one is that the many came
from the one in the first place.

17

Playing with I.D. Cards

Whatever blurs distinctions blurs the classifications upon which identity is built. We have to consider what ideologies and movements represent to people — the women's movement and racial integration, for example. Sex and race are perhaps the first two main ways of categorizing people. "Racial *discrimination*" is an apt term, because it brings out the classifying act.

Equality for women and integration of races subordinate sex and race to humanity, as Communism supposedly does nationality (its anthem is "The International") and as ecumenicalism does religion. One of the vices attributed to the "liberals" in "Ballad of Kanawha County" is that they bring in a "one-world plan." In one article and pamphlet after another the John Birch Society blasts the United Nations, which it believes should be abolished (and is part of the Communist conspiracy).[1] What, if not a burning need for *lesser* identity, explains the failures of the League of Nations and United Nations?

The more comprehensive a classification the less desirable it is for most people as an identity. One world, humanity, or citizen of the universe — the concepts are too vague, faceless, and unanchored. Submerging sex and ethnicity into a larger category seems to remove markers so important that disorientation results. Who am I if there is nothing out there to be separate from or against? When Christ asks his disciples, "Who do men say that I am?" he is testing their understanding of his supreme or cosmic identity, which is not based on separation and opposition but on the oneness of all.

Opposition to the Equal Rights Amendment came, predictably, from both the moral and commercial right, that is, from working-class traditionalists and business people. Again, we have to consider what this coalition means, since it yokes together blue-collar workers and corporation executives, factions that from a purely economic point of view should be voting differently.

Equality for women may be perceived as a menace both to survival of the family and to male sexual identity in particular, two explosive psychological issues. Family, blood kinship, stands as the primal group and source of knowledge and identity. Right-wingers who have organized under the rubric "pro-family" know what they are doing! That has powerful appeal and provides, interestingly, an umbrella for most of their causes, including one we have slighted so far—opposition to abortion.

Without taking sides in the intense combat over abortion—and I believe a strong case can be made for each side—we may link it here with preservation of the family identity. Although antiabortionists argue mostly on grounds of murder, a legitimate issue, much of their support comes from fears of further liberating women and thus endangering the family. If women acquire financial independence through equal pay and job opportunities at the same time they achieve total control over birthing, then—it appears to those who have a distrust of women and no faith in the intrinsic worth of the family—women will kick over all the traces, and we can kiss motherhood goodbye. Are, then, inequality and unwanted pregnancy what is holding the family together?

The family represents normalcy. It is a natural rallying point, therefore, for defending a whole complex of traditions from which identity is constructed. The patriarch needs to possess firearms in order to protect the hearth. Conservatives oppose child advocacy ("kiddie lib") even in the form of federal laws against child beating, because it might weaken patriarchal rule and role. The "right to bear arms" goes with the "right to spank" (though the federal laws aim at treatment much harsher than traditional spanking that state laws don't dare to outlaw). Similarly, conservatives lobby against spouse-abuse legislation such as the Domestic Violence Bill. Banning most abortion effectively takes a decision about women's bodies out of their hands and turns it over to society, which is male-governed.

The ironic fact that an increasingly large percentage of fathers abandon the patriarchal role and leave their family no doubt accounts for some of the frenetic efforts to shore up the father image by those whose identity is interwoven with familial imagery and thought patterns. Much of the force behind censorship of textbooks owes to fear that outsiders are undermining the family by stealing children's minds and undercutting its authority. Much criticism of schools in general attempts to displace elsewhere the blame for social ills more reasonably traced to family conditions (which may be partly traced in turn to the culture). Actually, if the family is crumbling, schools are not the cause (being little changed anyway from decades ago) nor will child- and wife-beating and firearms hold it together.

The real issue is that many people of mating age don't want to marry or don't want to stay married. The complex reasons for this range from the possibility of nuclear annihilation any moment—which "pro-family" proponents increase by their militaristic insistence on maintaining an enemy to maintain identity — to crises of self-confidence and self-esteem that traditional bigoted identity has helped to bring about. Why is it, in fact, that so many young people have abandoned marriage, religion, and patriotism at about the same time even though family, church, and state seem to be necessary centers of identity? Even if a Communist conspiracy aimed to do just this, and successfully exploited schools as a medium, how could they succeed if family, church, and state did for the individual what they should do or have been thought to do?

Some women as well as men worry that liberated women will increasingly resemble men as they take on the jobs, roles, clothes, attitudes, personality traits, and even executive diseases that have defined men. The fact that the sexes will still differ biologically (*"Vive la différence!"*) seems to count for little alongside the slippage in *social* definition. Or do we have here another lapse of faith? The more primitive a culture, the more strenuously it distinguishes sexual roles, often raising the sexes differently, initiating them by special puberty rites, and sharply demarcating their adult roles in courtship, family function, and community duties. It is as if a cultural underscoring of sexual identities — pink for the girl, blue for the boy — is thought to help people *perform* fully as male and female. We are told today that as women's liberation advances, more young males suffer impotence. Does identity, including that of sex, depend so much on the group that without its support even the physiology of sex is impaired? Is this why Latin countries so relentlessly drum up the "macho" mystique?

At any rate, we can be sure that identity permeates every sort of human functioning, because we are what we think we are, and any adjustment of the roles and powers of one sex will affect the others' self-image, this being in the nature of any two reciprocally defining things. Women's liberation, in short, puts identity in double jeopardy, if one thinks this way, because it threatens membership in both biological groups — one's family and one's sex.

Homosexuality threatens the identity of the family for some of the same reasons women's liberation does, through obliterating distinctions and roles by which the ego defines itself. Turning to one's own sex could destroy the two-sex system of reciprocal definition; it implies that one sex can be complete in itself. And so even the unisex dress and life style of heterosexuals may also be disapproved. It is no apology for homosexuality to say that hermaphroditic figures have in most cultures symbolized the spiritual achievement of transcending the bipolarity of being, which sex represents most arrestingly. Homosexuality can turn as vicious as heterosexuality. All we need note is that the unisexual implications of homosexuality strike the same blow to identity as does any other univer-

salism or egalitarianism like the United Nations or the Universal Church
or the simple pre-Marxist notion of communism (communalism).

I suspect that one reason anti-Semites hate Communists and homosexuals as well relates directly to the fact that Jews (like "Gypsies") are international—that is, for centuries, not until the founding of Israel after
World War II, had no country of their own, and hence adopted the languages and cultures of many nations throughout the world. But countries
adapt to being adopted, and any such Hebraicizing of a society may be
perceived as similar to the spread of the "Communist cancer" and to other
"conspiracies" to take over. As Communism disregards national and cultural boundaries, and as racial integration dissolves color distinctions,
homosexuality disdains sexual differences.

Furthermore, like women's liberation, the movement for gay rights
could seem to endanger the very existence of the traditional family. Not
only do homosexuals not reproduce, they lobby for the recognition of
other live-together units, other families, than the one based on reproduction. Nature, it is true, in its own conservatism places a premium on
reproduction in order to ensure survival of species. In following suit,
human conservatives fall into the primitivism of treating humankind like
other animals, as if we had in our cultural repertory and higher understanding no course but to persecute people coping with the plight of being attracted to their own sex. Some Amerindians have not only toler-
ated but fostered homosexuals for the sake of the deviance itself. That is,
certain individuals were allowed to differ in every way—to walk backwards, to prefer their own sex, to clown with unusual license (like the
monarch's "fool")—because this deviance reminded the rest that their
human normalcy does not exhaust or represent the whole of the Maker's
various and wondrous creation.

The link between sexual and racial identities is white male supremacy.
Since lording it over women culturally defines malehood to some degree,
why should Republicans oppose ERA and integration more than Democrats? Why should extending political and economic equality to women
and blacks cause more alarm among *conservatives?*

Obviously, whoever wants to conserve things the way they are holds
advantages in present circumstances. These advantages may consist of
traditions on which aspects of one's identity are built. Or one may enjoy
membership in a club that holds the upper hand and owns the most property. One is in. Being male and white are two clubs that have bestowed
automatic supremacy. Anyone who is in has something to lose by
change. The haves more naturally want to conserve than do the have-
nots, who stand most to gain from any change. Older people usually
possess more earthly goods and status than the young and so are, as a
group, more conservative. Not all people think this way, but to the ex-

tent we are materially motivated we don't give away advantages to those who are out (*materially* motivated precisely because we don't identify with them). Women's equality and racial integration challenge white males in economic competition at the same time they deal a blow to psychological security by blurring identity boundaries.

Though because of their double supremacy white males form the core of American and perhaps Western conservatism, *anyone* who enjoys benefits from things as they are now will think and act as a conservative to the extent he or she does not feel membership in broader categories of beings. Someone who is poor but white, or female but white, may seize more greedily onto racial supremacy than a rich white man, who may feel insulated from economic competition and can bask in the cultural support of his ego. Hence the vehement racism of many working-class whites of both sexes, who not only have to scramble more for money in an egalitarian society but are thrown increasingly together with those to whom they used to be able to feel superior — lumped together in housing and schooling and also, reluctantly, in their own thoughts. And they will often vote the same ticket as the wealthy, who also have only to lose by change.

However blatantly and pervasively racial discrimination may manifest itself in thought and deed, racism is not the real issue. It is only part of a pattern. Scapegoating, yes, but who is ever a scapegoat except the Other as defined by one or another sort of grouping? And as we have seen, grouping may be based on sex, nationality, religion, and many other differences among people. Color is just especially conspicuous. As sex breaks down only two ways, color breaks down only about five main ways. Thus both represent the grossest discrimination, but they do not for all that differ in kind or function from other social categorization. James Baldwin spoke directly to the whites' use of blacks to define themselves and to the virtual panic occasioned among some whites by the prospect of obliterating this distinction.

People inclined to oppose minority and women's rights will probably vote for gun freedom and capital punishment. The "right to bear arms" may be construed as part of "our American heritage" and hence associated with Minute Men and patriotism. Defense is the reason given, as it is for colossal weapons expenditure. (After the truly defensive war was over, World War II, we changed our "War Department" to the "Defense Department.") Just as we used to build cars with more horsepower than could be used on the road — extra, symbolic power — we arm beyond defense to take on the attributes of weaponry, to invest ourselves with a borrowed power we don't feel in our being itself, exactly as primitive peoples take on the power of the tiger by wearing its skin or claws. (To appeal to this totemic mentality today, cars are called Jaguars and

Lynxes.) Moreover, guns and cars are notorious symbols of sexual potency, which overlaps with power generally.

One of the components of the Fascist Scale, a measure used by early researchers in authoritarianism, was "toughness," which of course does not really correspond to courage and endurance but rather to a show of hardness that covers the fear that one is soft and weak. If I am for gun freedom, capital punishment, "law and order," strict child-rearing, a get-tough policy with Russia, and more lethal weaponry, I must be a tough cookie and a real stud. Of course a person might vote for one or the other of these for truly rational and intrinsic considerations, but the *pattern* of voting is a giveaway.

Such a pattern would most likely include also a preference for nuclear power, coal, and oil — the "hard" energy technology — over "soft" energy such as solar, wind, biomass, and geothermal. (See *Why "Soft" Technology Will not Be America's Energy Salvation*, by Petr Beckmann, distributed by the John Birch Society.)[2] "Hard" energy technology disrupts the environment more and endangers people more because it "rapes the earth" as in digging or drilling or heating the sea. It represents *man's* mastery over nature. "Soft" technology goes along more with nature, merely "harnessing" it, and is associated with environmental protection. It is felt as feminine. Coal, oil, and nuclear fission are concentrated energy sources, yielding more power per unit than solar, wind, and biomass, which are "dilute," weak. (It is hardly a digression to point out in passing that energy sources that are concentrated in this sense are also concentrated in the sense of centralized in the hands of large corporations, as Beckmann advocates, rather than "diluted" throughout the populace by means of, say photovoltaic panels on residential roofs. Since energy companies can't meter the sun, they prefer drawing from sources they can dole from, like coal, oil, and a few breeder reactors.)

We can predict that most people voting for gun freedom, capital punishment, and nuclear power or other "hard" energy will also oppose environmental regulation, which is regarded as softhearted and soft-headed, a concern only of giddy movie stars like Jane Fonda or of dowagers from the Sierra Club. Feeling tenderness for animals or for anything else is dotty and effeminate. Thus these issues are united not only by virtue of being traditional or normal, like the reproductive family, but also by the common thread of hardness or toughness that runs through them — false, to be sure, because it is all symbolic.

Getting tough on criminals by supporting capital punishment, harsher sentences, purchase of handguns to defend oneself, and reduction of civil rights for the accused brings out another aspect of this defense against weakness or softness in oneself. Researchers in authoritarianism called it "anti-intraception," the avoidance of turning inward and acknowledging feelings. Getting tough with others presupposes that one is different from them and does not deserve the hard treatment they do. Making punishment severer for criminals and reducing rights for the accused comes easier the less one acknowledges one's criminal impulses or the less one imagines ever being a defendant (which can happen very easily to the innocent once search-and-seizure protections are weakened and laws are then used against political opponents, a common way for a government to move toward fascism).

In other words, people most defending against unacknowledged impulses in themselves that they cannot control will come down hardest on criminals and take a general moralistic line, just as those most belligerent by personality will clamor most stridently to arm against belligerence in other individuals and nations. The weakness of inner controls, the default of self-regulation and self-responsibility, constitutes the main base of the authoritarian or fascist personality, which must rely on external authority because upbringing has forced one to look to others and distrust oneself. Fear of softness and fear of criminality in oneself go together precisely because the combination of strong negative impulses and weak inner controls is what engenders crime. In reality, of course, one masters negative impulses through self-knowledge, by getting tough with oneself.

It is a bitter truth that most convicts come from destitute environments, where authoritarian upbringing is the rule. (Of course, if laws were harsher for the so-called white-collar crimes of the corporate world, more well-to-do environments would be represented in prisons.) So getting tough on criminals partly represents better-off authoritarians rejecting worse-off authoritarians as a way of warding off a similar fate and partly represents just another form of removing minorities, the poor, and others one does not identify with. There is indeed a pressing practical problem of what to do with criminals, but we can solve it only in the measure that we can subtract from criminals the secret emotions with which we invest them.

In the soul-searching about the Vietnam war we can see again how this false toughness masks a resistance to self-knowledge. "Hawks" have claimed that America was blameless in Vietnam; the only problem was that a fainthearted public hamstrung the military and prevented it from using its full force. Today hawks still deplore the weakness of having examined ourselves and having concluded that we were implicated enough in the evil suffered by that country to warrant losing a war for the first time. Fighting enemies outside is strength; finding weaknesses inside is itself weakness. The role of this rule in anti-Communism was almost comically demonstrated by Reagan's second secretary of education, William Bennett, who complained in a speech he gave in Washington at the end of 1986 "that teachers in American schools focus too much on the perils of nuclear war and not enough on the perils of Communism. . . . 'It is not the business of American education to encourage unreasoning fear of any kind,' he said."[3] It is reasonable to fear what the other fellow is doing but not what we and he are doing in common. (If the perils of nuclear war are not reasonable grounds for fear, then why are all the governments of the world, including our own, so concerned about it?)

The spiritual approach to problems is to examine oneself along with the situation and to acknowledge any implication in the situation. It is not spiritual to claim the problem is a battle between good and evil and that God is on our side because we are good. This is surely the worst case of taking the Lord's name in vain, especially as it is used to excuse ourselves and rationalize interventions in other countries to support despotic governments that our founding fathers would have despised.

Behind the fear of self-examination is self-distrust, which ties together many symptoms in the syndrome of agnosis and which is a major if hidden issue in the banning of books. The power of literature to illuminate and to effect catharsis cannot act on me if I am too afraid of my feelings to admit that "there but for the grace of God go I." If I am just barely curbing impulses or staving off depression by sealing off feelings and perceptions beyond daily access, then of course I will react with great alarm to other people's expression of moods and deeds that strike me as violent or depressed, *without discriminating the form, tone, manner, and purpose with which these are presented.* Some primitive individuals, like the enraged spectator who stalks down the theater aisle to strangle the villain onstage, can't keep in mind a distinction between life and art because turbid emotions are set throbbing when they resonate with the depicted action.

But anyone, primitive or not, whose negative feelings begin to resonate too strongly with what he or she is seeing or reading will turn against the spectacle or book that arouses the feeling. How else is one to deal with such passions? Just as men sometimes are mean to women who, unwittingly or not, arouse desire that in the situation the men do not know what to do with, so the person unsure of moderating and balancing forces within himself will simply want to banish the object creating the problem for him. If we don't feel we have the grace of God then we merely feel "there go I," which is naturally a terrible feeling.

Self-distrust manifests strongly in reading, which is a form of role-playing. The reader "becomes" a character or at least "goes along" with the author's drift, willingly "suspends disbelief" for a while. Unless one can hold one's ego in abeyance and let another's mind hold sway, most reading is impossible. Laying aside the book, a reader may criticize and even reject the character or the author's ideas, but to enter another's point of view requires dropping guards.

Precisely because it is dangerous to do this with strangers in real life, lowering defenses in protected situations like reading and role-playing becomes important. Without safe situations permitting escape from the egoistic defensive stance to other points of view, how is one to learn something more than defense? Avis Hill made very plain in his interview that role-playing can pose the threat of losing one's identity. And there it is, the recurring bugaboo that you lose yourself if you try to enlarge yourself. The fear prevents expanding the identity beyond the pettiness that causes conflict, traps one in the conditioned ego, and forestalls the reunion of individual consciousness with the cosmic or God consciousness that is the goal of all religions. (The root meaning of "religion" is "retying.")

Psychologist Lawrence Kubie recognized the problem as it arises with creativity, which requires shuffling off these initial conditions and risking identity. Creative people, he says, have faith that they can lose themselves for a while *but always come back*. This way they get the advantage of the ego's stability but also slip its limitations. Hill was right that some movie stars become self-destructive because of identity problems but not, however, because they lose their identity from pretending for a while to be someone else but because they suffered from a weak identity in the first place and tried to fabricate a new one based on celebrityhood, which is subject to declining popularity or fading beauty and so brings on enormous anxiety. Like mature actors and creative artists, good readers *know* they will return to themselves.

If you have enough faith in yourself you know you can risk to know and not lose yourself. This gives courage in hard times. If you grew up within an environment that, by not resorting to fear and awe, implied you could trust yourself, you have some faith to resist agnosis when hard times do tempt everyone to seek the herd and pull on the blinders. Unblessed by such an upbringing, we can still liberate ourselves by coming to understand what limits thought, choice, and action.

18

Tales Out of School

By way of epitomizing the agnosis syndrome, let's try to find the common denominator between two of its apparently most unrelated advocacies — phonics and anti-Communism. As an educator specializing in language learning, I believe I understand the practical effects of emphasizing phonics in school, which helps in turn to figure out why people who exalt it to a religious status also interpret the Bible literally, build bigger weapons, segregate races, go "back to basics," and prefer to be "dead than Red."

Phonics is a method of teaching literacy by presenting the spelling of each phoneme of the language at the same time the phoneme is sounded. Alternative methods teach this paired association between the sounds and the spellings by employing larger language units — the whole word, the whole sentence, or some continuity of sentences — units, we note, that contain successively more meaning. Thus the child is shown a word while hearing it pronounced ("look-say") or follows with the eyes a simple text as someone reads it aloud ("read-along") or dictates something and watches as the other person writes the words down ("language experience"). For decades reading experts have quarreled acrimoniously over these methods, because the size of the *language* unit employed as the *learning* unit determines the amount of message, meaning, and hence motivation that a method can summon.

At its extreme, the controversy has raged between the phonics camp and the "reading for meaning" faction, a needless polarization fueled periodically by inflammatory polemics like Rudolph Flesch's *Why Johnny Can't Read* (because phonics is not taught) that never stop cursing the opposition long enough to reflect seriously on the host of sticky factors within and among individuals that alone can account for success and failure in literacy. Invariably, these polemics blame literacy failure on some *method*, whereas in fact a single method is rarely used to the exclusion of others and even when done so is not done so universally enough to account for a national result. Moreover, method alone would hardly ever make the difference between success and failure.

Blaming illiteracy on a method steers conveniently clear of parental and other social factors that play a large role in any language learning because of the basically social origin and function of language, which is first learned, after all, in the home. Consider habits of TV and video-games as well as the increase in single-parent families. Also, this criticism fits the familiar pattern of some parents defensively blaming schools for their children's behavior. Schools should of course take on as much re-sponsibility as possible for teaching literacy. I too have criticized schools for the way they go about it, but I believe they have erred in the direction of overdoing phonics under pressure not only from parents but from technocracy, which prefers the particle approach because it lends itself readily to mechanical programming and cheap testing.

In my textbooks and workshops for teachers I recommend interplay-ing these four main literacy methods according to individual children but to favor the whole-sentence and whole-text methods and to regard phonics as probably not necessary for reading, if the alternatives are fully employed, but as helpful for spelling and writing. Many children have learned to read and write spendidly without any phonics at all, but what makes the issue murky is that schools have seldom worked out the classroom management necessary to afford each child plenty of "read-along" and "language experience." Because these alternative methods to "look-say" and phonics seem more difficult to mount in a conventional classroom, they have been used less — which is my criticism of schooling — with the result that phonics and "look-say" have been used more and, though perceived by conservatives as rivals, have actually borne together most of the responsibility for poor literacy results, to the extent that methods do count.

When Elmer Fike rails against "look-say" as the culprit, according to conservative tradition, he speaks as a champion of phonics, whereas in fact the mainstay of schools for years has been the infamous "basal readers," which long ago perfected a blend of look-say and phonics by preteaching whole words for a story lesson and following this up with workbook drills on sound-letter relations. The problem here is that these two methods emphasize the smallest units of languages — syllables and isolated words — and this more technical and mechanistic approach makes it harder for children to associate reading with meaning and to tie into natural motivation to master literacy. Following a text while hearing it read, and dictating while watching the words being written down, engage more of the child's faculties and enlist more fully the will.

What I always found curious is that some laymen should not only take an interest in a particular teaching method — which is fine in itself — but should elevate it to a national cause. Whereas teachers who fight over these methods may champion phonics for purely professional reasons

not related to their other beliefs – they could be flaming liberals politically – almost invariably parents and others not having these professional reasons side with phonics because it suits a conservative cast of
mind.

"God believes in the beauty of phonics" means that those who see
themselves as God's spokespeople prefer phonics, precisely, I think,
because it shuts out content by focusing the child on particles of language
too small to have any meaning. In other words, what phonics really
amounts to for those who are sure they have a corner on God's mind but
are very unsure of being able to hold their children's minds is *another
way to censor books* (unconsciously, of course) *by nipping literacy itself
in the bud.*

An overemphasis on phonics, to the virtual exclusion of alternative
methods, which is what these proponents desire, especially when it is
part of a general back-to-basics approach replete with technocratic programming, is a fine formula for increasing functional illiteracy. Phonics
tests test phonics. They do not show if a person really can read and will
read later. But they are called "reading tests." The fixating of children's
attention on meaningless letters, inherent in phonics, combines only too
well with the lack of choice in school reading matter and the general arbi-
trariness and dullness of other content required in school to discourage
youth from reading. Teaching methods and school routines can and do
express the public's true attitude toward knowledge.

Literacy has from the beginning enabled individuals to liberate themselves by permitting them to bypass the oral culture, the local group, on
which they would otherwise have to depend for knowledge. Serfs can
bypass masters, merchants the government, Christians the priests, and
children their parents. Literacy is dangerous because books bring minds
together across the limits of time and space. Books build broader identities. They give access to that planetary perspective so feared by the part
of us clinging to lesser group identity. Once literacy supplants or com-
petes with oracy, we may "lose our children" to other ways of thinking.

Through school censorship one can control only some of the reading
matter students may encounter. How to limit what they may find to read
out of school? A good way is to cripple literacy at the outset, to make
reading so technical and meaningless that youngsters will, especially after
sampling the lifeless basal readers and other sanitized pablum often served
for them in school, simply not seek books any further or will find the act of
reading so painful that they virtually give it up. I accuse no one of doing
this deliberately, but I think the unconscious fear of letting youngsters
acquire knowledge, on their own – of putting this dangerous tool into their
hands – explains the true cause of the popularity of phonics, which is
increasing as our nation regresses deeper into apprehensions of disorder.

As it is for phonics in particular, so it is with "basic skills" more generally. Like "fundamentalist," "basic" makes a claim for precedence or priority, for some primacy owing to deeper truth or broader scope or higher
goal. But just as "fundamentalist" turns out to mean "literal," so "basic" as
applied to school skills turns out to mean "rote." Going "back to basics"
means emphasizing even more than in the past the three R's of reading,
writing, and arithmetic, to which we have to add the learning of an arbi-
trary miscellany of deeds and dates from history and odd facts from
nature. These are not hard and not the real issue.

What these "basics" share in fact, and what defines them, is memoriza-
tion. Reading is reduced to phonics; writing to spelling and punctuating
and (irrationally) labeling parts of speech; arithmetic to tables and set
steps. All of these can be memorized, are not difficult, and entail little
thought. Furthermore, if these little facts, along with those of history and
science, were taught embedded within the thinking processes they are intended to serve, they would be learned faster and better. Going "back to
basics" means stripping facts of context and purpose in order to drill on
them in isolation. By making them so dull and meaningless to learn that
they have to be retaught endlessly, it is possible to pretty well fill up the
curriculum so that students never get to use their higher minds or to learn
how to learn on their own.

This approach short-circuits higher thinking and higher aspects of consciousness. Thus as with phonics and reading, all while making a great
show of emphasizing the things that count most — the "basics" — one in
fact very effectively cripples the true basics — how to use the mind, com-
municate, acquire knowledge for oneself, and create.

This is surely a perversion of *anyone's* values, but it is happening daily
across this land because fear perverts. It seems like hypocrisy to claim to
feature literacy but in fact be sabotaging it, but again, this kind of pressure on schools from many parents, not just fundamentalists, represents
unconscious motives stemming from agnosis. In fact, for many people
education is not the real goal of schooling. They want school to continue
the indoctrination of home, a goal literacy may thwart. But then, unwitting self-contradiction characterizes the state of mind reflected in agnosis
and awaits a self-perception which is also part of what one doesn't want
to know.

Along with most other English educators I know, I have struggled for
years to supplant exercises in formal grammar with actual writing experience, but the grammar mystique operates so powerfully in the mind of
much of the public that teachers, specialists, and superintendents all go
along with it whether they believe in it or not because they don't dare to
buck a tradition so solidly lodged in the public psyche. This mystique
was forcefully invoked in the book objections, which complained that

literature was taking up room that should be allotted to grammar study. Literature is dangerous and grammar safe. Like other reading, literature has subject matter; like phonics, grammar does not.

During the nineteenth century, when a large immigrant population flooded American schools, for whom English was a second language, there may have been some sense to teaching grammatical analysis, but practical experience of the classroom and special research on the effects of grammar teaching both have for a long time shown clearly that such instruction does not improve a student's speaking, reading, or writing but, by displacing the practice itself of these activities, does actual harm. Among English educators, researchers, and linguists there is broad consensus about the futility of parsing and diagraming and labeling, whether the grammar be old-fashioned or newfangled. Nor is there any *logical* reason to think that these artificial exercises should be able to affect long-conditioned speech habits.

Nearly all grammatical "errors" are deviations made by a whole speech population, not personal mistakes, and the best way to learn standard dialect is to speak with native speakers of it, that is, to learn it the way anyone learns the basic grammar of a language as a child. Negative thinking decrees, however, that instead of children acquiring this way an additional dialect, they will all end up speaking a nonstandard dialect, fear of which animates segregationists as much as anything even though all the evidence shows that the nonstandard speaker adopts standard dialect when integrated. Thus segregation works against solving the very problem the agitation is supposedly about, "bad grammar."

The other main benefit that formal grammar study was alleged to confer was a greater facility with sentence construction for more effective oral and written expression, but the practical way to improve these is to discuss and write more, to read a lot, and to exercise the thinking processes. As it is, most "composition" in American schools is not authentic writing but fiddling with given material, doing dummy drills, or plagiarizing. A major reason American children write poorly is that they are seldom asked actually to author.

Again the pattern is plain. Many parents push hard for teaching methods that are vacuous and innocuous. Grammar teaching is a red herring. Its unconscious purpose is to fill time and thus to *prevent* practice in speaking and writing, thinking and growing — as do phonics and rote drills. Like reading, writing is dangerous if youngsters truly take it on as a personal tool. If content comes from the students, as it must in a successful writing program, adults lose control of it. So instead of inculcating planned subject matter, adults find themselves fostering independent investigation. Control of subject matter is the key. A very successful movement to teach real writing has been under way since the mid-seventies, but the more this promising trend takes hold the more signs of parental anxiety appear. I predict, in fact, that the next surge of censorship will concern student writing, which has rarely been criticized before only because it was mostly neglected or limited to some sort of writing about the reading. Controlling reading material effectively constrains the subject matter of writing, thus killing two birds with one stone. Students who really author outgrow just being somebody's children.

It is not mere cynicism on my part to say that perhaps the majority of the American public wants its children to spend school time doing false busywork. It is a way of putting children on hold, in suspended animation, so that they will remain as we made them, as if children *belong* to parents. It took me years of work in curriculum development to understand that schools are as negative as they are because they are doing just what much of the public thinks it wants (and what many teachers themselves do not believe in). I naïvely thought that improvement just waited on better ideas. My first perception that change was balked by politics and public relations came when I saw of what tough psychological stuff was made the irrational obstinacy behind formal grammar teaching. Then I began to see how other teaching "methods" likewise existed for noneducational reasons, for antieducational reasons, in fact.

Grammar in particular, moreover, is tied in with social distinctions. A shibboleth was originally, in the Bible, the test word that the Gileadites used to detect the escaping Ephraimites, who could not pronounce the initial *sh*. Like color and physical features, speech is a quick way to tell who is us or them. As a teacher I have noticed that the people most concerned about grammar teaching are those whose speech betrays nonstandard grammar and pronunciation, who have newly arrived or are living on a social margin. Stigma is trauma, but fear of being outcast or miscaste must not be allowed to dictate negative school practices. Ironically, it is mixing that overcomes the dialectical differences that call such painful attention to social discriminations. Behind the apparently academic issue of grammar stalks the omnipresent specter of identity.

Like "back to basics," the book objection called "invasion of privacy" masks its very opposite and appeals far beyond the book banners. The fact is that the kind of "traditional" school that many parents want truly does invade a youngster's privacy by the regimentation, the indoctrination of official views, the standardized curriculum, the manipulative methods, the infernal and incessant testing, and the imposition of silence, immobility, and passivity. All this violates normal human functioning, not to mention civil rights. (The only adults so treated are soldiers, criminals, and the insane.) To all this some parents would add a dress code, saluting the flag, and other niceties of submission and conformity.

Forced continually to do many things one does not want or need or see the value of, placed for years on end in the role of responder to others' planned stimuli, minted into a coin like other coins in a national technocracy — these constitute the real invasion of privacy, not the providing of means for youngsters to look inside and express themselves. Making someone read censored books merely increases that violation. Proponents of school prayer would invade privacy even more. School prayer is not forbidden in school, as people like Fike claim, since anyone can pray virtually any time, but rather it is forbidden for schools to *institute* a prayer because that will mean organizing a group activity and hence imposing a time, place, setting, leadership, and, very likely in some places, a particular religion.

Unlike mere biasing of reading selection toward some ideology, the very format and procedures of traditional schooling invade privacy virtually every moment and aspect of a student's school day. While focusing on controversial books, we take for granted classroom conditions that affect students more profoundly than what they read there. The direction of *this* bias is toward uniformity and mental arrestation as desired by that aspect of the human being that does *not* want to know.

"Invasion of privacy" expresses an opposition to self-examination, to allowing or inviting youngsters to look at what they think and feel and to express some of this. I object to self-examination and self-expression too if they are forced, but it is clear that people applying this term would never make room in the curriculum for activities enabling youngsters to discuss and write their own ideas at their own choice. As I've indicated, the real intent of the popular emphasis on the mechanics of language — phonics, spelling, punctuation, grammatical analysis and rote drills — is to make sure that language is not used for those purposes of finding out and speaking out for which it principally exists.

To channel and illuminate feeling, to sharpen and enrich thought, a learner must have opportunities to plan and carry out projects, engage in open discussions, read widely, write many different sorts of discourse, solve problems, build things, and generally be free to apply mind and speech to internal and external matters. When children are permitted to do these things, it becomes impossible still to control their thoughts.

In one of his novels called *Giles Goat-Boy* John Barth has a character say, "Self-knowledge is bad news," a humorous way of expressing why nearly anyone might want to avoid self-examination. "Invasion of privacy" reveals its true meaning only when considered along with what is perhaps the most common objection to books — the presence of what is called morbidity and depression, violence and cruelty, profanation and lust, all the main negative emotions. Parents who fear negative emotions within themselves sense that their children contain the same things and don't for a moment want anyone to know what is going on in there. To the extent that we feel we are sitting on the lid of a seething cauldron we oppose self-examination and self-expression. We may prefer stone boys and girls.

Self-distrust brings on this denial. If we feel our own potentiality for morbidity, violence, or lust lies close to the threshold of action, we may feel we have to deny it by refusing to look inside. But since these forces cannot really be ignored, we become vigilant — for signs of them *outside*, in others, in books. We project. Instead of taking the view that examining and expressing ourselves may be ways to defuse, manage, and transform negative potentialities, we assume, with a fatalistic lack of faith, that we cannot allow any turning inward, that we are incapable of dealing successfully with our emotions. One *expects* the insides to be wicked and dangerous — a superlative form of negative thinking that constitutes itself the real danger, because denial forces us to act out rather than work out dangerous feelings. Parents seriously inclined this way intuitively know that they have acted out negative emotion on their children and that, as a result, their children have bottled up a lot of explosive passion themselves. Child abusers are usually children of child abusers. Invasion of privacy indeed.

We who are brought up to regard ourselves as sinners falling short of the high moral standards constantly reiterated around us are often forced into denial as a defense against the awful and imminent possibility that we are terrible persons, no better in fact than beasts. (It becomes most important then to dissociate oneself from animals.) Having never succeeded in fulfilling the moral code, judging from beratings or beatings, we feel basically hopeless and hapless (morbid and depressed). If timely self-examination and appropriate self-expression never become available to us, we must spend half of the time denying and projecting our feelings — censoring these violent, depressing, lustful books will banish our violence, depression, and lust — and the other half acting out the feelings in defiance of all that collective coercion and in the spirit of "I'll bloody well be myself, whatever you others think." ("Rugged independence.")

If some teachers have probed children and tried to require them to look inward, I suggest they may sometimes have done so because it is very difficult to manage a classroom containing very many pent-up, acting-out children. They often become the "behavior problems" who don't learn and who hinder other children. Typically, children suppressed at home vent their rage in school. Overly strict parents vaunt their children's obedience but don't see the hell they raise away from home.

Truly spiritual upbringing has ever insisted on examining oneself. To be moralistic is not to be moral. Both Protestants and Catholics have promulgated ways of scrutinizing one's inner life, sometimes alone as in meditation and sometimes with a counselor or confessor and sometimes in frank group sessions. Similarly, in secular circles psychotherapy has continued these traditions through individual analysis and group interactions. Much ordinary peer talk such as the teenager's telephone soul talks and the housewife's coffee klatch accomplish needed introspection as participants exchange feelings and react to the others' feelings. It is a terrible inversion to use "invasion of privacy" to defeat "know thyself."

Working in tandem with this inversion is another — construing "Jesus saves" to mean that one does not need to work at knowing oneself and mastering oneself because Jesus takes care of everything for you. (Recall the misinterpreting of "Journey of the Magi.") Regardless of what one believes or professes, it is not possible to be moral without understanding oneself. To advance this understanding in school it is not at all necessary to question children about themselves; reading and writing and discussing will accomplish this quite appropriately if content is not dictated or censored and if these basic activities are not crowded out by meaningless busywork. After all, it is as much for self-understanding as for anything that books and talk and writing exist.

What do these ways of refusing to know have to do with the lack of faith that sees Communism and Darwinism as excessively threatening? This returns us to the hanging question about the connection between phonics and anti-Communism, which necessitated a tour of the classroom from our special viewpoint of agnosis and limited identity. Phonics can be used to decorticate reading by making it meaningless. This ultimate censorship prevents the individual from bypassing the oral knowledge and teachings of his or her group, with whom alone he or she is supposed to identify and from whom alone he or she is supposed to draw knowledge. The deification of phonics and the fulmination against Communism both serve to maintain in-group unity, the one by limiting knowledge and the other by limiting identity.

Precisely parallel to the fear that children may repudiate the parents' teachings if exposed to authors holding other values is the fear that citizens of our country will jettison national principles if made aware of other ideologies. What explains this lack of self-confidence, of faith in what one believes? Why trust in a free-enterprise marketplace of material goods but not in an open marketplace of ideas?

Communists espouse three ideas abhorred by their enemies — atheistic materialism, collectivism, and internationalism. These collide, respectively, with Christianity, the "rugged individualism" of free enterprise, and patriotism, three central identities for many Americans. As the phonics war is not what it seems, neither is the anti-Communist crusade. By making reading a technical matter instead of a means of knowing, phonics fanatics neutralize it below while prating of three R's above. By attacking materialism, collectivity, and internationalism in the Soviet world, anti-Communists give the impression that these three traits do not characterize our own society, whereas it is precisely because of similarities that Communism can serve as a handy psychological target for projection.

Leaving materialism to last, let's consider collectivism first. Any tendency toward agnosis and the group mind is collectivistic and will find expression in customs or institutions, whether these be of the official government or not. Defying federal regulation does not make one any less collectivistic if one behaves unthinkingly as a member of a group. Conformity to a subculture rather than to a larger society is still conformity. But, to deny that one depends tremendously on others and feels real only in the parent group, it may seem necessary to denounce some form of collectivism as it manifests in an outsider society.

Ironically, capitalism today has nearly become, through corporate conglomeration and collusion between government and industry, as collectivistic and monopolistic as Communism, which has moved toward capitalistic marketing and private ownership of business, not only in China and some Iron Curtain satellites but even, more recently, in Russia itself, where Mikhail Gorbachev's reforms in this direction were strongly ratified in June of 1987 by the Communist party's Central Committee. Collectivism takes many forms in different societies, sometimes in the public sector, often in the private, but nearly always expressing the same needs of the individual for the group. Mass media, vast technocracies, and drifts toward standardization characterize our whole society. It becomes academic to quibble over which part of the society the pressure to conform is coming from. But identity maintenance requires the exaggeration of differences between us and them.

Regarding internationalism, I have remarked earlier that rightists despise the United Nations, which extremists regard as a Communist instrument. (In an ABC film of 1987 much discussed as a sop thrown to conservatives, *Amerika,* the U.S.S.R. has taken over the U.S. after softening by liberals and an occupation by U.N. troops.) The very viability of independent nations is being tested today by international forces of all sorts, some beyond the law like international crime and terrorist organizations that have their own governments without a country, some within the law like multinational corporations and cartels and the intricate webs of global monetary and trade interactions, which run well beyond the control of any nation but affect all nations. America has been made up of course of immigrants from many nations since early days and is today even more of an international nation than ever within and more than ever extending influence around the world. The more that these and many other indicators of planetary integration increase, the more patriotism is reaffirmed by those who feel their identity threatened by them. The fact is that nations are on the way out even as some are still emerging. While it may be emotionally satisfying to place blame for this on the Soviets, it is these other forces that will compel the transcending of nations, not the U.N. and Communism.

Their insistence on differences blinds anti-Communists to the increasingly homogenizing effect that world developments are having on all countries, enemies or not. And the more enemies contend with each other the more they resemble each other. This is a paramount but overlooked law of war. Surely, Americans need to reflect on the fact that the facet of our psyche so opposed to Communism as to risk war to "contain" it most resembles the Communist in behavior. It restricts thought and speech, bullies outsiders, supports discrimination against minorities, enforces conformity, and, most significantly, bases ego strength on group identity defined by enemies.

Even the Communist's materialism is shared by anti-Communist fanatics, but this is a pervasive issue that requires a long-range orchestration of motifs to bring out. Certainly, taken at face value, fundamentalism takes a strong stand against materialism both as selfish, physical desires and as repudiation of soul, divinity, and a higher impalpable reality governing the tangible world. It's of no small significance that, as a modern movement, fundamentalism was born during the period when Darwin and Marx began setting the framework for the twentieth century, on which Freud and Einstein built.

Darwin said we evolved from lower animals. Marx said our history is about competition for money. Freud said instinct (mostly sexual) determines our behavior. All three philosophies place humankind at the mercy of material and mechanistic forces in our environment and in our nature and exclude reference to transcendent or spiritual dimensions to life. Then Einstein had to come along and cap it all, the absolutist feels, by making a whole blooming theory out of relativity. Others were following suit — the logical positivists saying no statement could mean anything, Heisenberg announcing his Uncertainty Principle, Dewey winning a generation of educators with his Humanism, and the Existentialists picking up Neitzsche's "God is dead" and preaching that humans must rely only on themselves and not on a Big Sky Father.

Indeed, to the extent we lack faith we could certainly take all this as the forces of materialism drawing on to a victory and feel some strenuous apocalyptic drum-beating is definitely in order. I do not myself accept Darwin, Marx, Freud, or any materialistic doctrine as more than a sort of truth limited by its very materialism, but I think materialism *is* coming to a head — for purposes of a spiritual evolution which it is serving. These four figures have played masterful roles in raising consciousness to higher levels than before. For one thing, they have helped people understand better just how, precisely, we are trammeled in the webs of matter, how automatically nature and society may program us to act, and how we chronically delude ourselves.

What is following on the heels of all these revelations are realizations that we do not have to let ourselves be biologically programmed or historically trapped or environmentally conditioned — materially mired. The concepts of Darwin, Marx, and Freud are being refined and elevated, fused with more recent knowledge to synthesize an understanding more likely to enable people to attain the ideals to which we have aspired but fell so short of as to acquire only more guilt.

The fundamentalists are not wrong to reject the materialism itself, but anyone is mistaken to scorn the knowledge such thinkers contribute, for their insights help to avoid moralizing against materialism while at the same time falling into its pitfalls. What affinity we have with animals, how much history is a mean struggle for money, how much we blindly act out instinctual drives — these are all up to us. These geniuses may have accurately described only the human past or the habits of the great majority, not the ultimate potentiality. Everything depends on being conscious enough to acknowledge our past enslavement. As the spiritual master Gurdjieff taught, liberation can come only after full acknowledgment of our automatism and our sleep.

As for Einstein, he was always metaphysically inclined and has helped enormously, like some other twentieth-century scientists, to make apparent that crucial aspects of our universe are not visible and tangible, even with the aid of sophisticated instruments, but can be apprehended only nonmaterially, through mathematics and other purely mental means. His formula converting matter to energy — $E = mc^2$ — broke open the way for us to understand the physical world as a condensation on our lower plane of reality of subtler, incorporeal forces on higher planes. Walk into any bookstore featuring John Birch or other very conservative or fundamentalist materials and you will find books specifically aimed at refuting Einstein's work. He has become the new Darwin.

The theory of relativity does not destroy universal truths. It is one itself. But because human understanding is imperfect in our present state, our formulation of laws has to be constantly revised as we evolve, as Darwin, Marx, Freud, and Einstein undoubtedly expected their theories to be. "For *now* we see through a glass, darkly; . . . *now* I know *in part.*" The "universal truths" just keep getting more comprehensive as we integrate our understanding of the world and evolve in consciousness. Most people will surely pass through Darwin, Marx, Freud, and Einstein on their way to higher truths because, mired in matter, we have to climb up through matter. Some rare souls may indeed bypass them and other worldly means, but you will not likely find such persons banning books, interpreting the Bible literally, calling us "back to basics," or arming against the Commies.

Darwin threatened identity with change, evolution epitomizing in fact, by the altering of even species themselves, the specter of nothing staying put so you can count on it. Marx threatened customary identity by placing transnational classhood over church, state, and family, three key bases of traditional membership. Freud threatened identity by showing that we are not who we seem to be, that under the conscious self and social figurehead there lives another person or persons with features and motives of which we usually remain unconscious. Einstein threatened identity by proclaiming that what is true depends on the vantage point of the observer, whose own being cannot of course be exempt from this general relativity. "Things are not what they seem — including you" seems to be the message of all four. This is actually a spiritual message, because it breaks the veneer of mundane matter, refuses to believe the world of appearances, points beyond local differences, and bespeaks a higher reality than the solid objects we cling to for stability. But to the extent we feel we must identify ourselves as concrete and fixed, the idea that things are not what they seem arouses a terror bordering on the preternatural.

The censor-bigot part of us sincerely attacks materialism and insists on universal truths. But it understands spirituality materialistically and universality parochially. It is not wrong. It parodies the evolved soul as the child parodies the adult. It has a right to its own level of expression of divinity, its own stage of the spiritual journey. We are all burlesquing the Supreme Being. But the fundamentalist in us must learn that what it believes is final is only provisional, because only so much can it grasp now. Darwin, Marx, and Freud — and Einstein too — *do* have to be outgrown sooner or later. Life no doubt *is* simple once you have attuned to the highest plane of it. Much knowledge *does* focus on negativity and distract us from the ultimate reality. We *shouldn't* clutter our minds with the infinite multiplicity of social information and physical facts. Laws of action and laws of knowledge *are* related, because living right is living in accord with cosmic laws. But these laws are surely not learned through limiting but by identifying most comprehensively — cosmically.

With this ultimate identification, we are told, the individual consciousness partakes of cosmic consciousness and so achieves that direct and full knowledge called gnosis. To their credit, the underlying concern of the book objectors was religious. But what stands in the way of gnosis, the goal of all religions, is agnosis, which is the blocking of consciousness, as anesthesia is the blocking of the senses and amnesia the blocking of memory. How far consciousness may expand depends very much on how widely the individual identifies across humanity and the rest of nature.

The ego is a social artifact based partly on cultural differences. Dissolve the distinctions on which it is constructed and you undermine it. Since all but the rarest souls identify the ego in turn with their body, people feel this assault on ego as physical dying. Understandably, then, to the extent our ego identity depends on sex, race, nation, religion, or ethos, we will fight to the death the erasing of those distinctions.

But defense is a losing game. Perpetual mobilization of an individual or a nation squanders resources. To defend against the Other is to ward off higher consciousness. It alone is equal to dealing with the world's conflicts, which stem, precisely, from our social need to limit knowing and identifying. How to save one's soul and how to save the world are the same. The spiritual way is the practical way. As we identify so we know. Only by identifying with the culture-free and cosmic nature of a Christ or Buddha does one learn what they tried to teach us and assume their power. This means molting lesser selves.

References
Notes
Index

References

Kanawha County Textbook Controversy

"Boycott Leader Says Demonstrators Got 'Out of Hand.'" *Sunday Oregonian*, Sept. 15, 1974.

"A Brief Chronology of the West Virginia Textbook Crisis." *Arizona English Bulletin*, Feb. 1975, 203–12.

Candor-Chandler, Catherine. *A History of the Kanawha County Textbook Controversy, April 1974–April 1975*. Ed.D. diss., 1976. Ann Arbor: Univ. Microfilms International, 1982.

Charleston Daily Mail, Apr. 1974 through Apr. 1975.

Charleston Gazette, Apr. 1974 through Apr. 1975.

Chriss, Nicholas C. "West Virginia Hills Echo with Anger over Textbooks." *Los Angeles Times*, Sept. 19, 1974.

Conley, Thelma R. "Scream Silently: One View of the Kanawha County Textbook Controversy." *Journal of Research and Development in Education* 9, No. 3, Spring 1976, 93–101.

Dawkins, John. "Is Minority Opinion Telling You What to Teach?" *Language Arts*, Mar. 1976, 250–53.

_____. "Textbook Author Comments on Hillocks." *School Review*, Nov. 1978, 124–26.

Egerton, John, "The Battle of the Books." *Progressive*, June 1975, 13–17.

Fike, Elmer. "Textbook Controversy in Perspective." *Charleston Gazette*, Nov. 14, 1974.

_____. *Textbook Controversy Essays*. Privately published collection of variously dated essays by Fike.

Franklin, Ben. "Textbook Dispute Has Many Causes." *New York Times*, Oct. 14, 1974.

Harper, James. "Textbook War: '3 Little Pigs' Among the Casualties in West Virginia." Knight Newspapers dispatch, *San Francisco Sunday Examiner and Chronicle*, Nov. 17, 1974, Sec. A, 4.

Hefley, James C. "The Truth about West Virginia." Ch. 11 in his *Textbooks on Trial*. Wheaton, Ill.: Victor Books, 1976, 157–76.

Hill, Avis, and Company. *Textbook War—Hills of West Virginia*. Audio disc privately recorded at Stage 4 Recording Studios, Charleston, W.Va., 1975. Stereo 31443.

Hillocks, George, Jr. "Books and Bombs: Ideological Conflict and the Schools —
A Case Study of the Kanawha County Textbook Controversy." *School Review*, Aug. 1978, 632–54.

Jenkinson, Edward B. "The Textbook War in Kanawha County." Ch. 2 in his
Censors in the Classroom: The Mind Benders. Carbondale: Southern Ill. Univ.
Press, 1979, 17–27.

Kaderabek, Ginger. "Controversial West Virginia Texts Used in Metro Without
Protest." *Nashville Banner*, Mar. 3, 1975.

Kanawha County School Board Minutes, Apr. 1974 through Apr. 1975.

Lewis, Rev. James. "Ugly Demons in West Virginia Textbook War." *Los Angeles
Times*, Nov. 4, 1974.

"Militant Ignorance." *Arizona Daily Star*, Sept. 26, 1974.

National Education Association. *Kanawha County, West Virginia: A Textbook
Study in Cultural Conflict*. Washington, D.C.: National Education Association, 1975.

Parker, Franklin. *The Battle of the Books: Kanawha County*. Bloomington, Ind.:
Phi Delta Kappa Educational Foundation, 1975.

"Schoolbooks That Stirred up a Storm." *U.S. News & World Report*, Nov. 4,
1974, 61–62.

Scott, Austin. "Textbooks Anger Parents." *Washington Post*, Sept. 13, 1974.

———. "West Virginia Schoolbook Protest Apparently Got Out of Hand."
Washington Post, Sept. 15, 1974.

Trillin, Calvin. "U.S. Journal: Kanawha County, West Virginia." *New Yorker*,
Sept. 30, 1974, 119–27.

"West Virginia Hills Echo with Anger over Textbooks." *Los Angeles Times*, Sept.
9, 1974.

"What Your Children Will Read . . ." Advertisement paid for by the Business and
Professional People's Alliance for Better Textbooks. *Charleston Gazette*, Nov.
14, 1974, and (revised) Apr. 1975.

General

Adorno, T. W., Else Frenkel-Brunswik, D. J. Levinson, and R. W. Sanford. *The
Authoritarian Personality*. New York: Harper, 1950.

Allen, Gary. "Get US Out: The U.N. Threatens the United States." *American
Opinion*, Jan. 1972, 1–22.

"The American Way." *San Francisco Chronicle*, Dec. 8, 1986, 10.

Arendt, Hannah. *The Origins of Totalitarianism*. New York: Harcourt, Brace &
World, 1966.

Arons, Stephen. "The Crusade to Ban Books." *Saturday Review*, June 1981, 17–
19.

Association for Supervision and Curriculum Development. "Censors at Work."
ASCD Update, Nov. 1981.

Beckmann, Petr, Why "Soft" Technology Will not Be America's Energy Salvation.
Different Drummer Booklet No. 6. Boulder, Colo.: Golem Press, 1979.

Bogdan, Deanne. "The Censorship of Literature Texts: A Case Study." In *Literature in the Classroom*, Ed. Ben F. Nelms. National Council of Teachers of English Yearbook for 1986. Urbana, Ill.: NCTE, forthcoming.

Bogdan, Deanne, and Stephen Yeomans. "School Censorship and Learning Values Through Literature." *Journal of Moral Education*, Oct. 1986, 197–211.

Botel, Morton, and John Dawkins. *Communicating, 1–6*. Lexington, Mass.: D. C. Heath & Co., 1973.

Cawthon, Raad. "Banned Book Issue Is Hard to Read." *Clarion-Ledger* (Jackson, Miss.), Sept. 12, 1982.

Corporation for Public Broadcasting. "Books Under Fire!" Transcription of a "Crisis to Crisis" program transmitted Sept. 10, 1982. Kent, Ohio: PTV Publications, 1982.

Farrell, Edmund, James Miller, et al. *America Reads*. Glenview, Ill.: Scott, Foresman & Co., 1973.

Fike, Elmer. *Elmer's Tune*. Private annual publication since 1968 of essays by Elmer Fike reprinted from various periodicals.

Fromm, Erich. *Escape from Freedom*. 1941. New York: Holt, Rinehart, & Winston, 1964.

Gallup, George, Jr. "Public Evenly Divided between Evolutionists, Creationists." Press release of the Gallup Poll, Aug. 29, 1982.

Glatthorn, Allan. *Dynamics of Language*. Lexington, Mass.: D. C. Heath & Co., 1971.

Goldstein, Kenneth M., and Sheldon Blackman. *Cognitive Style: Five Approaches and Relevant Research*. New York: John Wiley and Sons, 1978.

Hefley, James C. *Textbooks on Trial*. Wheaton, Ill.: Victor Books, 1976.

Heindel, Max. *The Rosicrucian Cosmo-Conception or Mystic Christianity*. Oceanside, Calif.: Rosicrucian Fellowship, 1909.

Hofstadter, Richard. "The Paranoid Style in American Politics." In his *The Paranoid Style in American Politics and Other Essays*. New York: Alfred A. Knopf, 1965.

Horswell, Cindy. "More Books Rejected as Censorship Effort Grows." *Houston Chronicle*, Dec. 21, 1986.

Houghton Mifflin Company. "Censorship." *Market News*, intracompany newsletter, Sept. 1980.

Jenkinson, Edward B. *Censors in the Classroom: The Mind Benders*. Carbondale: Southern Ill. Univ. Press, 1979.

Katz, Gregory. "School Censorship Rise Cited." *USA Today*, Aug. 15, 1985.

Kemerer, Frank R., and Stephanie Abraham Hirsh. "School Library Censorship Comes Before the Supreme Court." *Phi Delta Kappan*, Mar. 1982, 444–46.

Kristol, Irving. "Pornography, Obscenity, and the Case for Censorship." In his *On the Democratic Idea of America: A Collection of Essays*. New York: Harper & Row, 1972. Distributed by Elmer Fike in Kanawha County, W.Va.

Littell, Joseph. *Language of Man*. Chicago: McDougal, Littell & Co., 1971–73.

London, Harvey, and John E. Exner, Jr., eds. *Dimensions of Personality*. New York: John Wiley & Sons, 1978.

McClosky, Herbert, and Alida Brill. *Dimensions of Tolerance: What Americans Believe about Civil Liberties*. New York: Basic Books and the Russell Sage Foundation, 1983.

"Marching on the School Fronts." *San Francisco Examiner and Chronicle*, Dec. 1, 1974.

Michaels, Marguerite. "Public School Book Censors Try It Again." *Parade*, Nov. 25, 1979, 4–5.

National Council of Teachers of English. "NCTE Convention Sessions on Censorship, Academic Freedom." News release, Nov. 1, 1974.

Park, Charles. "The New Right: Threat to Democracy in Education." *Educational Leadership*, Nov. 1980, 146–53.

Piasecki, Frank Edward. *Norma and Mel Gabler: The Development and Causes of Their Involvement Concerning the Curricular Appropriateness of School Textbook Content.* Ph.D. diss., North Texas State Univ., 1982. Ann Arbor: Univ. Microfilms International, 1984.

Pooley, Robert, and Stephen Dunning. *Galaxy.* Glenview, Ill.: Scott, Foresman & Co., 1969–72.

"Preachers in Politics." *U.S. News & World Report*, Sept. 24, 1979, 37–41.

"The Pro-Family Movement." *Conservative Digest*, May/June 1980, 14–30.

Rensberger, Boyce. "Evolution Since Darwin." *Science*, Apr. 1982, 40–45.

"Right-wing Clan Still Wants Funding Cuts." CPS dispatch from Washington, D.C. In *Daily Aztec* (San Diego State Univ.), Dec. 11, 1984.

Roberts, John. *The Mythology of the Secret Societies.* Oxford: Oxford Univ. Press, 1972.

Rokeach, Milton, et al. *The Open and Closed Mind.* New York: Basic Books, 1960.

Smith, Vernon, and Violet Neuschultz. *Contemporary English.* Morristown, N.J.: Silver Burdett Company, 1973.

Steiner, Rudolf. *Cosmic Memories.* Spring Valley, N.Y.: Anthroposophic Press, 1959.

Textbook Advisory Committee of Kanawha County. Unpublished, untitled report to the Kanawha County School Board of objections to textbooks. 1974.

Webster, Nesta. *Secret Societies and Subversive Movements.* Christian Book Club of America, 1924.

Welch, Robert, *The Blue Book of the John Birch Society.* Belmont, Mass.: Western Islands, 1959.

Werner, Heinz. *Comparative Psychology of Mental Development.* New York: Science Editions, 1948.

Zweigler, Joy. *Man.* Chicago: McDougal, Littell & Co., 1971–72.

Interaction

Moffett, James (senior author/editor), et al. *Interaction: A Student-Centered Language Arts and Reading Program, K–12.* Boston: Houghton Mifflin Co., 1973. Comprising in addition to 800 activity cards, dozens of games, and 80 hours of recordings, 175 paperback volumes of diverse reading material. Individual volumes cited in the present work follow.

Adventure Stories 1. Level 1. Ed. Irving Wasserman, James Higgins, and James Moffett.

Autobiography 1. Level 3. Ed. Robert G. Pierce and James Moffett.

Ballads. Level 3. Ed. Bee Thorpe, Peter F. Neumeyer, Robert M. Helm, and James Moffett.

Eyewitness Reportage. Level 3. Ed. E. Graham Ward, Robert G. Pierce, and James Moffett.

Fables. Level 3. Ed. Herbert Kohl and James Moffett.

Fictional Diaries. Level 3. Ed. Betty Jane Wagner, Roberta Koch Suid, and James Moffett.

Fictional Memoir 2. Level 3. Ed. Roberta Koch Suid and James Moffett.

Folk Tales 1. Level 2. Ed. Ronald Goodman and James Moffett.

Humorous Stories. Level 3. Ed. James Higgins and James Moffett.

Informative Articles 2. Level 3. Ed. Betty Jane Wagner and James Moffett.

Letters 1. Level 4. Ed. E. Graham Ward and James Moffett.

Lyric Poetry. Level 3. Ed. Robert G. Pierce, Peter F. Neumeyer, and James Moffett.

Monologue and Dialogue 1. Level 4. Ed. Christopher Brooks, Floren Harper, E. Graham Ward, and James Moffett.

Myths. Level 2. Ed. Ronald Goodman, Robert G. Pierce, Betty Jane Wagner, and James Moffett.

Narrative Poetry. Level 3. Ed. Peter F. Neumeyer, Robert G. Pierce, and James Moffett.

Reportage and Research 1. Level 4. Ed. E. Graham Ward and James Moffett.

Scripts 2 and *3.* Level 3. Ed. Floren Harper and James Moffett.

Short Plays 1. Level 2. Ed. Roberta Koch Suid, James Higgins, Murray Suid, and James Moffett.

Transcripts 2. Level 3. Ed. E. Graham Ward and James Moffett.

Also by James Moffett

Points of View: An Anthology of Short Stories. Ed. with Kenneth R. McElheny. New York: New American Library, 1966.

Student-Centered Language Arts and Reading, K–13: A Handbook for Teachers. With Betty Jane Wagner. 3rd ed. Boston: Houghton Mifflin Co., 1983.

Notes

Prologue. West – By God – Virginia

1. Lorena A. Anderson, letter, May 25, 1973.

1. Storm in the Mountains

1. West Virginia State Board of Education Resolution, Dec. 11, 1973.
2. Memorandum of Dr. Daniel B. Taylor, state superintendent of schools, Aug. 16, 1973. Quoted in Candor-Chandler, *Kanawha County Textbook Controversy*, p. 43.
3. *Citizens for Parents' Action Newsletter*, vol. 1, undated, 1971. Quoted in Candor-Chandler, *Kanawha County Textbook Controversy*, p. 30.
4. National Education Association, *Kanawha County, West Virginia*, p. 58.
5. Fike, "Textbook Controversy in Perspective," part of a two-page advertisement by the Business and Professional People's Alliance for Better Textbooks in the *Charleston Gazette*, Nov. 14, 1974.
6. Candor-Chandler, *Kanawha County Textbook Controversy*, p. 51.
7. National Education Association, *Kanawha County, West Virginia*, p. 59.
8. Hefley, *Textbooks on Trial*, p. 160. In the introduction Hefley describes the publisher, Victor Books, as "a division of Scripture Press, a respectable, foundation-owned evangelical Sunday School publisher" and states that the editorial director of Victor Books commissioned him to write this biography of the Gablers.
9. Candor-Chandler, *Kanawha County Textbook Controversy*, p. 75.
10. Ibid., p. 61.
11. "Kanawha County PTA Board Opposes Certain Texts," *Charleston Daily Mail*, June 19, 1974.
12. West Virginia Human Rights Commission, press release, June 26, 1974.
13. Candor-Chandler, *Kanawha County Textbook Controversy*, p. 65; Hefley, *Textbooks on Trial*, p. 163.
14. Hefley, *Textbooks on Trial*, p. 163.
15. Joint statement of the ten ministers, June 24, 1974, quoted in Candor-Chandler, *Kanawha County Textbook Controversy*, p. 71.

246

16. "27 Ministers Join to Oppose Texts," *Charleston Gazette*, June 27, 1974.

17. "Dunbar Ministers Hit Books," *Charleston Gazette*, June 27, 1974.

18. Candor-Chandler, *Kanawha County Textbook Controversy*, p. 90.

19. "Text Protesters Reject Board Review's Offer," *Charleston Gazette*, Sept. 12, 1974.

20. Jenkinson, *Censors in the Classroom*, p. 22.

21. "Boycott Leader Says Demonstrators Got 'Out of Hand,' " *Sunday Oregonian*, Sept. 15, 1974.

22. "Moore, Melton Sniping Catches Public in Middle," *Charleston Daily Mail*, Sept. 29, 1974.

23. "West Virginia Hills Echo with Anger over Textbooks," *Los Angeles Times*, Sept. 9, 1974.

24. Conley, "Scream Silently," p. 95.

25. Ibid., p. 97.

26. "Boycott Leader Says Demonstrators Got 'Out of Hand,' " *Sunday Oregonian*, Sept. 15, 1974.

27. Fike, "Textbook Controversy in Perspective."

28. Hefley, *Textbooks on Trial*, p. 175.

29. Trillin, "Kanawha County, West Virginia," p. 121.

30. Candor-Chandler, *Kanawha County Textbook Controversy*, p. 164.

31. Hefley, *Textbooks on Trial*, p. 171.

32. Kanawha County School Board Minutes, Nov. 21, 1974.

33. National Education Association, *Kanawha County, West Virginia*, p. 244.

34. "Marching on the School Fronts," *San Francisco Examiner and Chronicle*, Dec. 1, 1974.

35. Memorandum Order, Jan. 30, 1975, K. K. Hall, United States district judge, quoted in Candor-Chandler, *Kanawha County Textbook Controversy*, p. 180.

36. Candor-Chandler, *Kanawha County Textbook Controversy*, p. 190.

2. The Reverberating Network

1. Hillocks, "Books and Bombs," p. 632.

2. Candor-Chandler, *Kanawha County Textbook Controversy*, pp. 198–99.

3. Hillocks, "Books and Bombs," p. 636.

4. Personal interview, June 1982. This person wished not to be named.

5. Dawkins, "Is Minority Opinion Telling You What to Teach?" p. 250.

6. Kemerer and Hirsh, "School Library Censorship," p. 444.

7. Bogdan and Yeomans, "School Censorship," p. 198.

8. Ibid., p. 200.

9. Personal correspondence from someone wishing not to be named.

10. Ibid.

11. Personal correspondence.

3. Kanawha County and Orange County

1. Candor-Chandler, *Kanawha County Textbook Controversy*, p. 128.
2. Ibid., p. 174.
3. Ibid., p. 171.
4. Hillocks, "Books and Bombs," p. 636.
5. Dr. Charles Bertram, "Voter Reaction to the Kanawha County, West Virginia, Textbook Protest," internal paper, Appalachian Educational Laboratory, Nov. 8, 1974, quoted in Candor-Chandler, *Kanawha County Textbook Controversy*, p. 150.
6. Interview, June 1982.
7. Ibid.
8. Hefley, *Textbooks on Trial*, p. 166.
9. Ibid., p. 167.
10. Ibid., p. 177.
11. Houghton Mifflin Company, "Censorship."
12. Michaels, "Public School Book Censors," p. 5.
13. Illinois Congressman Phillip M. Crane, form letter, Dec. 2, 1974.
14. Ibid.
15. Kaderabek, "Controversial West Virginia Texts Used in Metro Without Protest."
16. Candor-Chandler, *Kanawha County Textbook Controversy*, p. 166.
17. National Education Association press release, Feb. 6, 1975.
18. National Education Association, *Kanawha County, West Virginia*, p. 58.
19. Candor-Chandler, *Kanawha County Textbook Controversy*, p. 177.
20. National Education Association press release, Feb. 6, 1975.
21. Michaels, "Public School Book Censors," p. 4.
22. Gallup, "Public Evenly Divided."
23. McClosky and Brill, *Dimensions of Tolerance*. Other findings in this study show surprisingly weak support by Americans for civil liberties.

4. Father, Make Them One

1. Lewis, "Ugly Demons in West Virginia Textbook War," pt. 2, p. 7.

5. Free Enterprise

1. Fike, "The Textbook Dispute Updated," from a privately published collection by him, *Textbook Controversy Essays*. This article is separately dated Jan. 1976.

7. Race War, Holy War

1. National Education Association, *Kanawha County, West Virginia*, p. 29.
2. Conley, "Scream Silently," p. 97.
3. Ibid., p. 98.
4. Ibid.
5. Ibid., p. 99.

8. Commies and Sex

1. National Education Association, *Kanawha County, West Virginia*, p. 51.
2. Candor-Chandler, *Kanawha County Textbook Controversy*, p. 69.
3. Dawkins, "Textbook Author Comments on Hillocks," p. 124.
4. Hillocks, "Books and Bombs," p. 652.
5. National Education Association, *Kanawha County, West Virginia*, p. 48.
6. Personal interview, June 1982.
7. "What Your Children Will Read . . . ," *Charleston Gazette.*
8. Ibid.
9. James Leo Herlihy and William Noble, "Blue Denim," in *Scripts 3*, pp. 108–9.
10. Ibid., pp. 130–31.
11. "What Your Children Will Read . . . ," *Charleston Gazette.*
12. Ibid.
13. National Education Association, *Kanawha County, West Virginia*, p. 47.

9. McGuffey Rides Again

1. In such a document the more reliable way to locate quotations is by publisher's program and book title, since these provide the organization of the objections.
2. Hillocks, "Books and Bombs," p. 643.
3. Botel and Dawkins, *Communicating*, 1–6.
4. Literary texts are quoted throughout this book as quoted in the book of objections when the objections are attached to them.
5. Littell, *Language of Man.*

10. Anyone for the Classics?

1. Farrell, Miller, et al., *America Reads.*
2. Zweigler, *Man.*

11. The Innocence Is the Crime

1. Althea Gibson, "I Always Wanted to Be Somebody," in *Autobiography 1*, p. 14.
2. Dick Gregory, "Not Poor, Just Broke," in *Autobiography 1*, pp. 27–38.
3. John Steptoe, "Train Ride," in *Adventure Stories 1*, p. 20.
4. Al Young, "A Dance for Ma Rainey," in *Lyric Poetry*, p. 108.
5. Norman Jordan, "Black Warrior," in *Lyric Poetry*, p. 51.
6. James Baldwin, "My Dungeon Shook: Letter to My Nephew," in *Letters 1*, pp. 34–37.
7. Bill Moyers, "Mathis, Texas," in *Reportage and Research 1*, p. 61.

12. Man's Head, Beast Body

1. Indra Devi, "Yoga for Americans," in *Informative Articles 2*, pp. 36–37.
2. Ibid., p. 38.
3. Ibid., p. 61.
4. See, for example, Heindel, *The Rosicrucian Cosmo-Conception*, or Steiner, *Cosmic Memories*.
5. Rensberger, "Evolution Since Darwin."
6. Theodore Roethke, "Snake," in *Lyric Poetry*, p. 40.
7. In 553 A.D. the Fifth Ecumenical Council ratified Justinian's anathemas of the great third-century Christian theologian Origen, who had in such works as *On First Principles* and *Commentaries on John* argued for a cosmology including reincarnation, which was commonly believed in also by Gnostics and other early Christians. Origen was the first of many to argue that some passages in the Bible make no sense unless reincarnation is assumed.
8. Charles Darwin, "Tierra del Fuego," in *Eyewitness Reportage*, p. 26.
9. Arendt, *Origins of Totalitarianism*, pp. 178–79.

13. Reading Comprehension

1. "The Calley Trial," in *Transcripts 2*, p. 100.
2. Lenny Jenkins, "Birds, Beasts, and Bat," in *Fables*, pp. 15–16.
3. Ewan MacColl, "The Ballad of the Carpenter," in *Narrative Poetry*, p. 61.
4. T. S. Eliot, "Journey of the Magi," in *Monologue and Dialogue 1*, p. 57.
5. "The Cherry Tree Carol," in *Ballads*, p. 71.
6. Arthur Hoppe, "The True Christian," in *Fables*, pp. 12–13.
7. Humbert Wolfe, "The Gray Squirrel," in *Lyric Poetry*, p. 98.
8. Ring Lardner, "I Can't Breathe," in *Fictional Diaries*, p. 45.
9. Sondra Spratt, "Hoods I Have Known," in *Fictional Memoir 2*, p. 41.

14. Petrified

1. Wayne Figueroa, "Little Black Riding Hood," in *Humorous Stories*, p. 8.
2. Howard Chace, "Ladle Rat Rotten Hut," in *Humorous Stories*, p. 30.
3. Carl Sandburg, "How They Broke Away to Go to the Rootabaga Country," in *Folk Tales 1*, p. 25.
4. Rod Conybeare, "A Spider Spectacular," in *Short Plays 1*, p. 105.
5. William I. Kaufman, "The Giant Caterpillar," in *Myths*, p. 43.
6. Gina Berriault, "The Stone Boy," in *Points of View*, p. 342.
7. Ibid., p. 348.
8. Ibid., p. 351.
9. Ibid., p. 353.

15. Ideology and Bed-Wetting

1. Jenkinson, *Censors in the Classroom*, p. 29.
2. Arons, "The Crusade to Ban Books," p. 17.
3. Katz, "School Censorship Rise Cited."
4. Horswell, "More Books Rejected as Censorship Effort Grows."
5. "Preachers in Politics," *U.S. News & World Report*, Sept. 24, 1979.
6. Memorandum of the White House Private Sector Task Force of Aug. 18, 1986.
7. Paul Weyrich, interview in *Conservative Digest*, May/June 1980, p. 15.
8. Welch, *Blue Book of the John Birch Society*, p. 180.
9. "Right-wing Clan Still Wants Funding Cuts," *Daily Aztec*, Dec. 11, 1984.
10. Goldstein and Blackman, *Cognitive Style*, p. 19.
11. Werner, *Comparative Psychology of Mental Development*.
12. In Hofstadter, *Paranoid Style in American Politics*. For a more thorough study of conspiracy theory see Roberts, *Mythology of the Secret Societies*. For a presentation of conspiracy by a rightist believer see Webster, *Secret Societies and Subversive Movements*, obtainable in American Opinion Bookstores run by the John Birch Society.
13. Howard Ehrlich, "Dogmatism," in London and Exner, *Dimensions of Personality*.
14. Ibid., p. 153.
15. Rokeach et al., *Open and Closed Mind*, p. 365.
16. Ibid., p. 75.
17. Loyal Jones, *Appalachian Values* (Berea, Ky.: Berea College Appalachian Center, 1973), pp. 110–11. Quoted in National Education Association, *Kanawha County, West Virginia*, p. 9.
18. Donald Goodenough, "Field Dependence," in London and Exner, *Dimensions of Personality*, p. 165.
19. Ibid., p. 166.
20. Ibid.
21. Ibid., p. 167.

22. Ibid.
23. Goldstein and Blackman, *Cognitive Style*, p. 36.
24. Ibid., p. 18.
25. Ibid., p. 24.
26. Ronald Dillehay, "Authoritarianism," in London and Exner, *Dimensions of Personality*, pp. 123–24.
27. Ibid., p. 112.
28. Ibid., p. 113.
29. Ibid., p. 114.

16. Group Rule

1. Moffett and Wagner, *Student-Centered Language Arts and Reading*, p. 2.
2. Terrel Bell, "Schools, Parents, and Textbooks," speech delivered to the School Division, Association of American Publishers, in Cherry Hill, N.J., Dec. 2, 1974.
3. Ibid.
4. Ibid.
5. Harper, "Textbook War."
6. National Education Association, *Kanawha County, West Virginia*, p. 34.

17. Playing with I.D. Cards

1. See, for example, Allen, "Get US Out."
2. Beckmann, *Why "Soft" Technology Will not Be America's Energy Salvation* (Boulder, Colo.: Golem Press, 1979). The choice of Golem for the name of this press is curious: in the Jewish mysticism known as Cabalism a golem is a man-made clay creature who may overwhelm his master, a kind of evil animated zombie. Thus many Jews called Hitler Golem.
3. "The American Way," *San Francisco Chronicle*, Dec. 8, 1986.

Index

John Birch Society, 13, 38, 42, 43, 44, 108, 191, 215
"Johnny Crow's Garden," 130
Jordan, Norman, 140–41
Journal of Research and Development in Education, 19, 99
"Journey of the Magi" (Eliot), 132, 162, 163–64, 232
Joyce, James, 131

Kanawha County, West Virginia: behavior of mayors in, 36; character of, 6, 8; industrial district in, 6–7; population of, 6. *See also names of individual cities and towns*
Kanawha County Association of Classroom Teachers, 21, 42
Kanawha County Coalition for Quality Education, 20, 23
Kanawha County School Board of Education: adoption of language arts books by, 13, 16, 53; advisory bodies of, 12; building dynamited, 22; burning of Bibles by, 56; citizen consultation to, 12, 16, 24; members arrested, 23, 36; 1970 elections, 13; 1974 elections, 14; picketing of, 17, 18; replacement of Curriculum Advisory Council, 12; reprimanded by supporters, 21, 42; resignations from, 20–21; resolution on textbook selection, 23, 28; and sex education, 12–13; threatened, 19; and truancy, 23; withdrawal of textbooks by, 18, 95. *See also* Curriculum Advisory Council; English Language Arts Textbook Committee; Textbook Review Committee
Kanawha County School District: alternative school offered, 24, 42; boycott of (1974), 18–20, 23, 36; consolidation of schools in, 12; creationism textbook program in, 27; effects of textbook controversy in, 27; extent of, 9; morale in, 27; religious club in, 76; school closing in, 19;

textbook selection for, 11, 24
Kanawha County School Health Education Study (SHES), 12–13
"Kanawha County Surprise" (Hoye), 91
Kean, John, 188
Keats, John, 132, 133
Keyes, Daniel, 29
Khomeini, Ayatollah, 190, 191
Kinsolving, Matthew, 14
Kipling, Rudyard, 128, 130
Kittle, Robert, 24
Knievel, Evel, 82
Kramer, Jane, 113
Krug, Judith, 188
Kubie, Lawrence, 223
Ku Klux Klan (KKK): in antibook protest, 42, 43, 54; Fike's opinion of, 37; Graley's opinion of, 68; increased membership in, 197; protesters as members of, 22

"Ladle Rat Rotten Hut" (Chace), 175–76
Lamb, Charles, 129
Lang, Andrew, 130
Language of Man series (McDougal, Littell), 13, 126, 156, 179
Lanier, Sidney, 129
Lardner, Ring, 150, 169–70
Lardner, Ring, Jr., 150, 169
La Rouche, Lyndon, 189
Laurence, Margaret, 29
Lay My Burden Down (Botkin), 138
Leach, Maria, 130
Legends, 148–49
Leonardo da Vinci, 129
Let's Improve Today's Education, 41
Letters (Ward and Moffett), 142
Lewis, Rev. James, 53–54, 56, 87–88, 90
Lewis, Oscar, 171–72
Lincoln, Abraham, 129
Listening to America (Moyers), 143
"Little Black Riding Hood" (Figueroa), 175
Little Black Sambo, 79
Locke, Elsie, 130

James Moffett, national consultant in English education to schools and universities and author in education, is the author of *Student-Centered Language Arts and Reading, K–13: A Handbook for Teachers* (with Betty Jane Wagner); *Teaching the Universe of Discourse; Active Voice: A Writing Program across the Curriculum;* and *Coming on Center: Essays in English Education*. His school materials include, as senior author/editor, *Interaction: A Student-Centered Language Arts and Reading Program, K–12*, and, as senior editor with others, *Active Voices, I–IV*. Moffett's anthologies include *Points of View: An Anthology of Short Stories*, edited with Kenneth R. McElheny, and *Points of Departure: An Anthology of Nonfiction*.